ROADMAP™ A2

STUDENT'S BOOK and eBook

Lindsay Warwick and Damian Williams

Contents

3

Contents

EXTENDED ROUTE

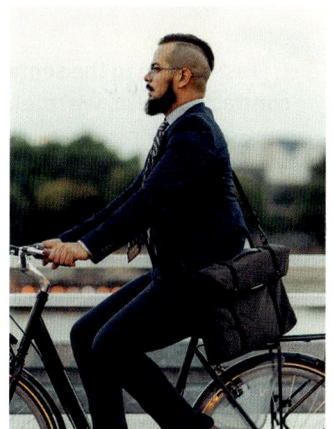

1A People and places

> **Goal:** introduce yourself
> **Grammar:** verb *be* – positive and negative
> **Vocabulary:** countries and nationalities

Listening

1 Look at the photos. Where are the people?

> a meeting   a party   university

2 a 🔊 **1.1** Listen to three conversations. Match them with the places in photos A–C.

b Listen again and choose the correct alternatives.
1 I'm from a small town in *Scotland/Wales*.
2 I'm from the *Melbourne/Sydney* office.
3 Ah, but you aren't *British/Australian*, right?
4 We're from the *Los Angeles/New York* office.
5 **A:** Where are you from, Daniel?
  B: I'm from *Argentina/Mexico*. And you?

c Work in pairs. Look at the names of the people from conversations 1–3. Where are the people from?

> Alex   Claire   Daniel   Gabriel and Angela
> Lewis   Maya   Rachel

Grammar

3 Read the grammar box and complete the table with the correct contractions. Use Exercise 2b to help you.

Verb *be* – positive and negative

+		
I	¹ **I'm** /am	Anna.
He/she/it	's/is	from Australia.
We/you/they	² **you've** /are	Mexican.

-		
I	'm not/am not	from Scotland.
He/she/it	isn't/is not	Argentinian.
We/you/they	³ **we aren't** /are not	American.

4 a 🔊 **1.2** Listen to the sentences and notice how the contractions (*I'm, we're,* etc) are pronounced.
1 I'm British.
2 We're from New York.
3 It's cold in here.
4 They aren't American.
5 It isn't my first time here.
6 I'm not a student.

b Listen again and repeat.

5 a Complete the conversation with the correct form of *be*.
A: Hello, I ¹ **I'm** Lena.
B: Hi, Lena. My name ² **'s** Nick. Nice to meet you.
A: And you.
B: This ³ **'s** Melanie.
A: Hi, Melanie. Where ⁴ **'re** you from?
C: We ⁵ **'re** from Brent. It ⁶ **'s** far from here, only one kilometre. What about you?
A: I ⁷ **'m** from Witney. It ⁸ **'s** a town near Oxford.

b 🔊 **1.3** Listen and check your answers.

6 a Work in groups of three. Practise the conversation in Exercise 5a.

b Repeat the conversation. Change the information so it's true for you.

📱 Go to page 116 or your app for more information and practice.

Vocabulary

7 **a** Work in pairs. Match the countries in the box with photos a–h. Can you think of any other people, things, food, etc. from these countries?

> Australia China Egypt Greece Japan
> Mexico Russia Spain

b 🔊 1.4 Listen and check your answers.

Greece *Australia*

a — *china*

b

c

d

e — *mexico*

f

g — *Russia*

h

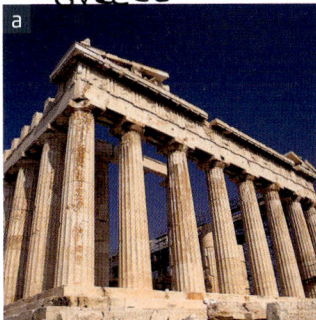

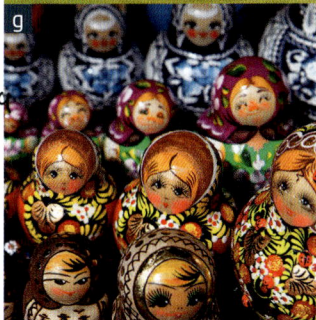

8 **a** Complete the table with the correct countries and nationalities.

Country	Nationality
	-n/-an/-ian
Australia	1_____
Brazil	Brazilian
Egypt	Egyptian
Mexico	2_____
3_____	Russian
the US	American
	-ish
Poland	Polish
4_____	Spanish
5_____	Turkish
the UK	British
	-ese
China	Chinese
Japan	6_____
	Irregular
Greece	Greek

b 🔊 1.5 Listen and check your answers.

9 **a** Listen again and underline the stressed syllables in the nationalities in Exercise 8a.

  Austra̲lian

b Listen again and repeat.

10 Work in pairs. Where are these people and things from? Say the nationality.

> **A:** *I think Benedict Cumberbatch is British.*
> **B:** *Yes, that's right. / I'm not sure. / No, he's American.*

Japan

> Benedict Cumberbatch   Donald Trump   kung fu
> pizza   samba dancing   sushi

📱 Go to page 136 or your app for more vocabulary and practice.

Speaking

PREPARE

11 You're going to introduce yourself at a conference. Think of a new name, a new nationality and the town or city you are from. Make notes.

Egypt

SPEAK

12 **a** Introduce yourself to people at the conference.

> **A:** *What's your name?*
> **B:** *I'm Isabel and this is Rafael.*
> **A:** *Nice to meet you. Where are you from?*
> **B:** *We're from Spain. What about you?*

b Work in pairs. Share information about the other people at the conference.

Spain

> **Develop your writing**
> page 86

All about me

Pocket Calendar

> **Goal:** ask and answer questions
> **Grammar:** questions with *be*
> **Vocabulary:** question words

Listening and vocabulary

1 a Work in pairs. How many words do you know for each topic? Use the photos to help you.
- colours *red; blue*
- months *January; December*
- hobbies *football; dancing*
- feelings (adjectives) *happy; tired*
- jobs *teacher; doctor*

b Work in groups of four and compare your answers. Are any the same?

2 Complete Larissa's social media profile with the words in the box.

good   November   pink   walking

Friendly Face

Larissa Norte
Feeling ¹ good

From: Rio, Brazil
Birthday: 25th ² November
Hobbies: 😊 tennis, ³ walking
Favourite colour: ⁴ pink
Favourite actor: Jennifer Lawrence
Favourite food: Italian

3 a Match questions 1–7 with answers a–g. Use the words in bold to help you.
1 **What's** your favourite **colour**? g
2 **Where** are you **from**? e
3 **Who's** your favourite **actor**? c
4 **When's** your **birthday**? f
5 **What's** your favourite **food**? b
6 **How** are you **today**? a
7 **Are** you **interested** in reading? d

a I'm OK.
b Chinese food. No, maybe it's Indian. No, it's Chinese.
c I think Simon Pegg is really good.
d Yes, I love it!
e I'm from Napoli, in Italy.
f It's in September.
g It's blue.

b 🔊 1.6 **Listen and check your answers.**

4 a Complete the questions with the correct question words or form of the verb *be*.
1 When is your birthday?
2 Where is your friend from?
3 What's your favourite food?
4 Who your favourite actor Jude Law?
5 Where is your teacher from?
6 How are you today? Are you OK?
7 Who's your best friend?
8 Are you interested in art?
9 When is your next English class? Is it today?
10 Is it Friday today?

b Work in pairs. Ask and answer the questions.

📱 Go to your app for more vocabulary and practice.

Grammar

5 Complete the grammar box with the correct form of *be*. Use Exercises 3 and 4 to help you.

Questions with *be*

Yes/No questions

Am/Is/Are	Subject	Other information	Short answers
¹ Am	I	late?	Yes, I am. No, I'm not.
² Is	he/she/it	Greek?	Yes, he/she/it is. No, he/she/it isn't.
³ Are	we/you/they	interested in art?	Yes, we/you/they are. No, we/you/they aren't.

Wh- questions

Question word	am/is/are	subject
Where	⁴ is / are	your teacher from?
What	⁵ are	your favourite films?

6 a 🔊 1.7 **Listen to the sentences. Does the speaker's voice go up or down at the end?**

1 Are you from Argentina?
2 What's your favourite food?
3 Are you OK today?
4 Where is he from?

b Listen again and repeat.

7 a **Put the words in the correct order to make sentences.**

1 who / your / favourite singer / is ?
   Who is your favourite singer?
2 are / your parents / the US / from ?
3 photography / are / you / interested in ?
4 is / your / birthday / when ?
5 today / are / you / how ?
6 why / are / in this class / you ?
7 your / what's / favourite / month ?
8 are / tired / today / you ?
9 your / is / teacher / Spain / from ?
10 second name / your / is / what ?

b **Work in pairs. Student A give an answer to one of the questions in Exercise 7a. Student B say the correct question. Swap roles.**
   A: *December.*
   B: *What's your favourite month?*

📱 Go to page 116 or your app for more information and practice.

Speaking

PREPARE

8 **You're going to make a social media profile about your partner. First, write some questions to ask your partner. Use the ideas below to help you.**
   • name
   • nationality/country
   • hobbies/interests
   • favourite (actor/singer/food, etc)

SPEAK

9 a **Work in pairs. Ask and answer your questions. Use the Useful phrases to help you. Make notes of your partner's answers.**

> **Useful phrases**
> OK, first question …
> Next question …
> That's interesting!
> Why is Iggy Pop your favourite singer?

b Make a social media profile for your partner.

c Look at your social media profile. Is all the information correct?

> **Develop your listening**
> page 87

1c For sale

Vocabulary

1 Look at the picture and answer the questions.

1 Is it a shop, market or supermarket?

2 Are the objects new or old?

2 a Match the words in the box with photos A–N.

> bike   board games   books   camera   clock
> lamp   laptop   pictures   rings   skateboard
> suitcase   sunglasses   tennis racket   umbrella

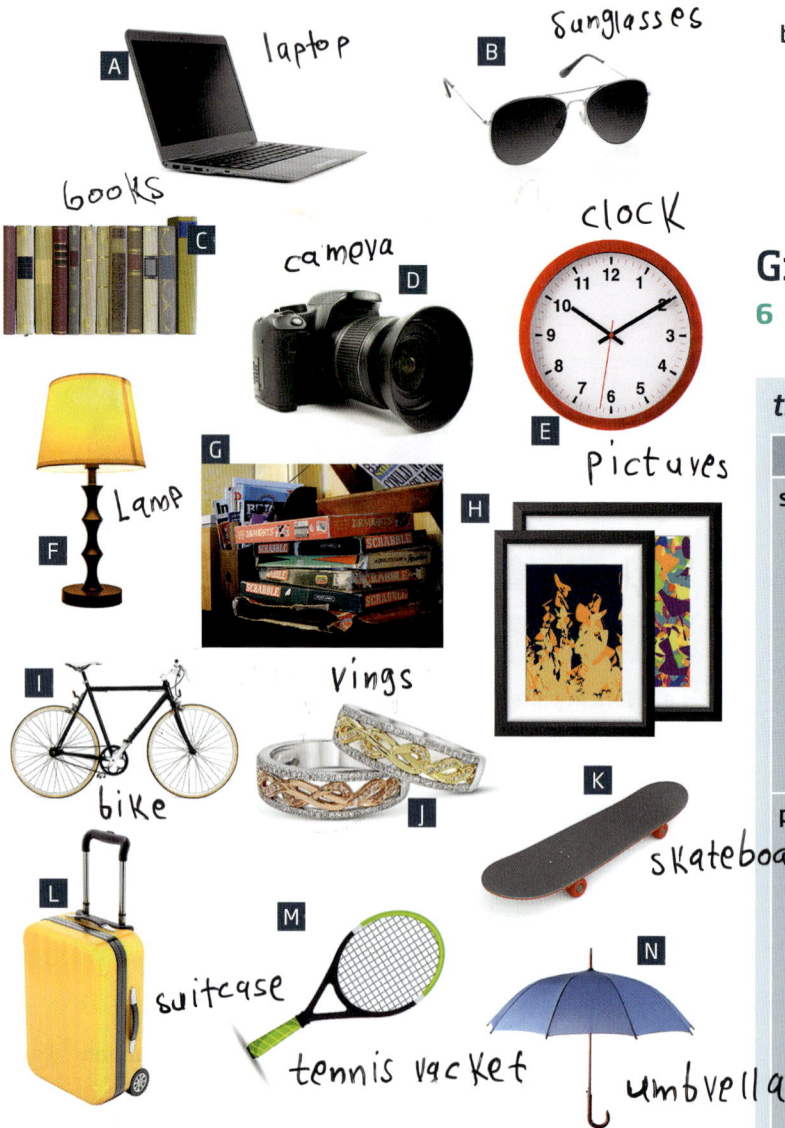

A laptop

B sunglasses

C books

D camera

E clock

F lamp

G board games

H pictures

I bike

J rings

K skateboard

L suitcase

M tennis racket

N umbrella

b 🔊 1.14 Listen and repeat the words.

3 Work in pairs. Close your books. How many objects in the photos in Exercise 2a can you remember?

📱 Go to your app for more practice.

Listening

4 🔊 1.15 Listen to Jake and Chris shopping at a market. What does Chris want to buy?

5 a 🔊 1.16 Listen to Jake and Chris talking to the seller. What do they buy?

b Listen again and complete the sentences with the correct information.

1 The bikes are about _____ years old.

2 The sunglasses cost £ _____ .

3 The lamp costs £ _____ .

4 Jake pays £ _____ .

Grammar

6 Read the grammar box and choose the correct alternatives. Then complete the examples.

this, that, these and *those*

	near	far
singular	¹*this / these* _____ *lamp is nice.*	*that* **That's** *a nice bike.*
plural	²*this / these* *Are* _____ *sunglasses only a pound?*	*those* *Look at* **those** *bikes.*

9 Put the words in the correct order to make sentences.

1 are / those / How much / shoes?

2 lamp / That / really / is / nice

3 is / How old / that / bike?

4 shoes new? / Are / these

5 That / ring / very pretty / is

6 Is / £5? / book / this

7 love / I / guitar / that

8 is / Where / clock / that / from?

📱 Go to page 116 or your app for more information and practice.

Speaking

PREPARE

10 Work in pairs. You are at a market. Student A is selling things at the market, and Student B is buying things. Student A: Turn to page 151. Student B: Turn to page 154. Read the instructions.

SPEAK

11 a Work in pairs. Student A: Ask the seller questions about the things for sale. Decide what you want to buy. Student B: Answer the customer's questions. Use the Useful phrases to help you.

> **Useful phrases**
> That's a nice book. How much is it?
> That book is five pounds.
> How old is that picture?
> It's about 30 years old.
> OK, I'll take it!

b Swap roles and repeat.

c Report back to the class. What objects do you have?

7 a 🔊 1.17 **Listen to the pronunciation of** *this* **and** *these.* **Which sound is short and which is long? Underline the phrase you hear.**

1 *this book / these books*

2 *this laptop / these laptops*

3 *this lamp / these lamps*

4 *this printer / these printers*

5 *this bike / these bikes*

b Listen again and repeat.

8 a Choose the correct alternatives to complete the sentences about the pictures.

1 *That / This* clock is very big!

2 Are *these / those* rings for men or women?

3 *This / That* lamp's really nice.

4 *These / Those* laptops are all new.

b Work in pairs. Point to objects in the pictures in Exercises 6 and 8a for your partner to say what it is/ they are.

A: What's this?

B: It's a lamp. What are these?

A: They're rings.

Develop your reading
page 88

Goal: tell the time

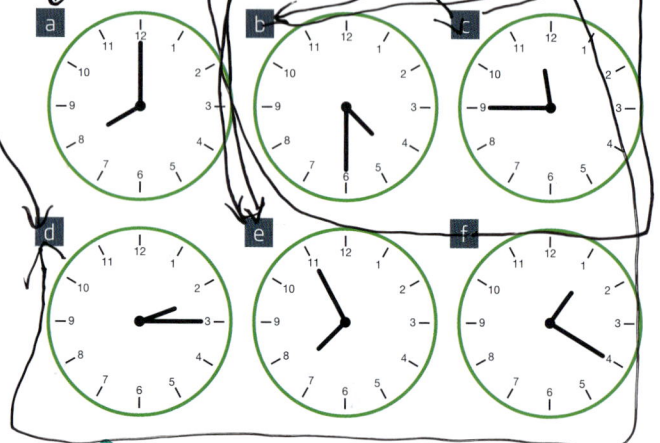

A — Aditya, London
B — Akari, Tokyo
C — Sergei, Moscow
D — Leandro, Buenos Aires
E — Jennifer, Dallas

1 Look at the photos. What countries are the people from? What are their nationalities?

A: She's from Japan.
B: Yes, she's Japanese.

2 a 🔊 1.18 **Listen to a conference call. What's the time in each location? Choose the correct alternatives.**

1 It's 6.15 a.m./6.50 a.m. in Dallas.
2 It's 10.15 p.m./2.15 p.m. in Moscow.
3 It's 12.15 p.m./12.45 p.m. in London.
4 It's 5.15 a.m./9.15 a.m. in Buenos Aires.
5 It's 9.15 a.m./9.15 p.m. in Tokyo.

b Listen again. Tick the phrases in the Useful phrases box that you hear.

Useful phrases

Asking for the time
What's the time (in Buenos Aires)? ✓
What time is it (there)?

Telling the time
It's six fifteen in the morning. [6.15] ✓
It's four twenty p.m. [16.20]
It's half past two in the afternoon. [14.30]
It's three o'clock in the morning. [03.00]
It's a quarter to six in the evening. [17.45]

3 a Match the times in the box with clocks a–f. Sometimes more than one answer is possible.

> a quarter past two   a quarter to twelve
> eight o'clock   eleven forty-five   twenty past one
> five to eight   half past four   four thirty
> one twenty   seven fifty-five   two fifteen

b 🔊 1.19 **Listen and check. Then listen and repeat.**

4 Choose the correct alternatives.

1 **A:** What's the/a time?
   B: It's a quarter two/to six.
2 **A:** What's the time at/in Nairobi?
   B: It's four thirty/half p.m.
3 **A:** What time it is/is it there?
   B: It's a half/half past ten in the morning.
4 **A:** What's the time there/here?
   B: It's seven twenty-five a.m./in a.m.

5 Work in pairs. Ask for and tell the time with the clocks in Exercise 3a. Tell the time in different ways.

A: What's the time on clock a?
B: It's eight o'clock. What time is it on clock e?
A: It's seven fifty-five.

6 You are going to have a conference call. First, think about:
- your name
- your location
- your nationality
- the time where you are now

7 a Work in groups. Have a conference call. Introduce yourself. Write down the names, locations, nationalities and times of the other people in your group.

b Work in pairs. Tell your partner about the other people in your group in Exercise 7a.

Go online for the Roadmap video.

Check and reflect

1 Choose the correct alternatives.

1 My name *are/'s* Carla. I *'m/'s* American.
2 My mother *aren't/isn't* Italian. She *'m/'s* Spanish.
3 Kate and Graham *are/is* from a small town in Australia.
4 We *'s/'re* Spanish but our father *is/are* from Poland.
5 They *isn't/aren't* students.
6 My teacher *isn't/is* Japanese. He*'s/are* from China.
7 I'm from the US but my boyfriend *isn't/is*. He*'s/are* Italian.
8 This is Maria. She *'s/are* from Brazil.

2 Complete each sentence with a country or nationality.

1 He's from the UK. He's _____ .
2 They're from _____ . They're Greek.
3 I'm from Poland. I'm _____ .
4 She's from _____ . She's Turkish.
5 We're from China. We're _____ .
6 They're from _____ . They're Mexican.
7 I'm from Australia. I'm _____ .
8 You're from _____ . You're Egyptian.

3 a Think of five famous people from different countries and write their names. Make sure you know which country they're from.

b Work in pairs. Say the names of the famous people. Guess where your partner's people are from.

A: Kate Winslet.
B: She's American.
A: No, she's from the UK.

4 a Match questions 1–6 with endings a–f.

1 What's
2 Where are
3 Are you
4 Who's your
5 How old
6 Where are your

a a doctor?
b parents now?
c favourite singer?
d your job?
e you from?
f are your brothers and sisters?

b Work in pairs. Ask and answer the questions.

5 Choose the correct alternatives.

1 **A:** *Is/Are* her name Catherine?
  B: Yes, it *is/are*.
2 **A:** Where *is/are* you from?
  B: I *'m/'s* from Russia.
3 **A:** *Are/Am* they from Türkiye?
  B: No, they *isn't/aren't*. They're from Spain.
4 **A:** What *are/'s* your email address?
  B: It *'s/'re* jaime21@email.uk.
5 **A:** *Are/Is* you a nurse?
  B: No, I *'s/'m* not. I'm a doctor.

6 Choose the correct alternatives.

1 Don't go by car. Take your *bike/lamp*.
2 I want to play tennis but I don't have a *racket/sunglasses*.
3 It's raining – take your *umbrella/rings*.
4 I work on my *laptop/skateboard* in a café.
5 My son plays on his *umbrella/skateboard* every day.
6 My family sometimes play *board games/printer*.
7 On holiday, I sometimes read *suitcases/books*.
8 Take a photo with your *pictures/camera*.
9 The *camera/pictures* of your holiday are nice.
10 That *lamp/printer* is beautiful.

b Work in pairs. Which of the objects in Exercise 6a do you have in your home?

I have a camera, board games …

7 Choose the correct alternatives.

1 **A:** What's *this/these*?
  B: It's my pen. Do you like it?
2 **A:** I like *that/those* sunglasses.
  B: Thank you. They're from Italy.
3 **A:** Are *this/these* your keys?
  B: No, *that/those* are my keys over there.
4 **A:** What's *that/those* over there?
  B: It's my bag.
5 **A:** Hi Karen. *This/That* is Phil.
  B: Hi Phil. Nice to meet you.

8 Work in pairs. Take some objects out of your bag and put them on your desk. Ask and answer questions about them.

A: This is my pencil, that's my mobile phone. What are those?
B: These are my keys.

9 Write the times.

1 08.15   3 6.45   5 09.00
2 03.00   4 3.30   6 11.20

It's a quarter past eight in the evening.

Reflect

How confident do you feel about the statements below? Write 1–5 (1 = not very confident, 5 = very confident).

- I can introduce myself.
- I can ask and answer questions.
- I can talk about things for sale.
- I can tell the time.

Want more practice?
Go to your Workbook or app.

2A Families

> **Goal:** describe your family
> **Grammar:** possessive adjectives and possessive 's
> **Vocabulary:** family members

Vocabulary and listening

1 a Match quotes 1–4 with photos A–D.

1. *We're just a small family – me, my wife and our daughter.* **B**

2. *There aren't any children in our family, but we still have lots of fun!* **C**

3. *I have a very big family: lots of brothers and sisters, uncles and aunts!* **A**

4. *My grandson and granddaughter live with me. My grandchildren are my world!* **D**

b Work in pairs and discuss the questions.
1. Are you from a big or small family?
2. Where is your family from?
3. Who is your favourite person in your family?

2 a 🔊 2.1 Listen to Dominic talk about his family with his girlfriend Anna. Answer the questions.
1. Whose family do they talk about? *Dominic hes famiy*
2. Do you think it is a big or small family? *big family*

b Listen again and complete the family tree with the names in the box.

Arthur   Charlotte   Jack   Kerry   Lily   Sally

3 Match family members 1–8 with a–h.

1 mother *c*		a grandma	
2 father *d*		b parents	
3 mother + father *b*		c mum	
4 son + daughter *f*		d dad	
5 grandfather *h*		e grandparents	
6 grandmother *a*		f children	
7 grandfather + grandmother *e*		g grandchildren	
8 grandson + granddaughter *g*		h grandad	

📱 Go to your app for more practice.

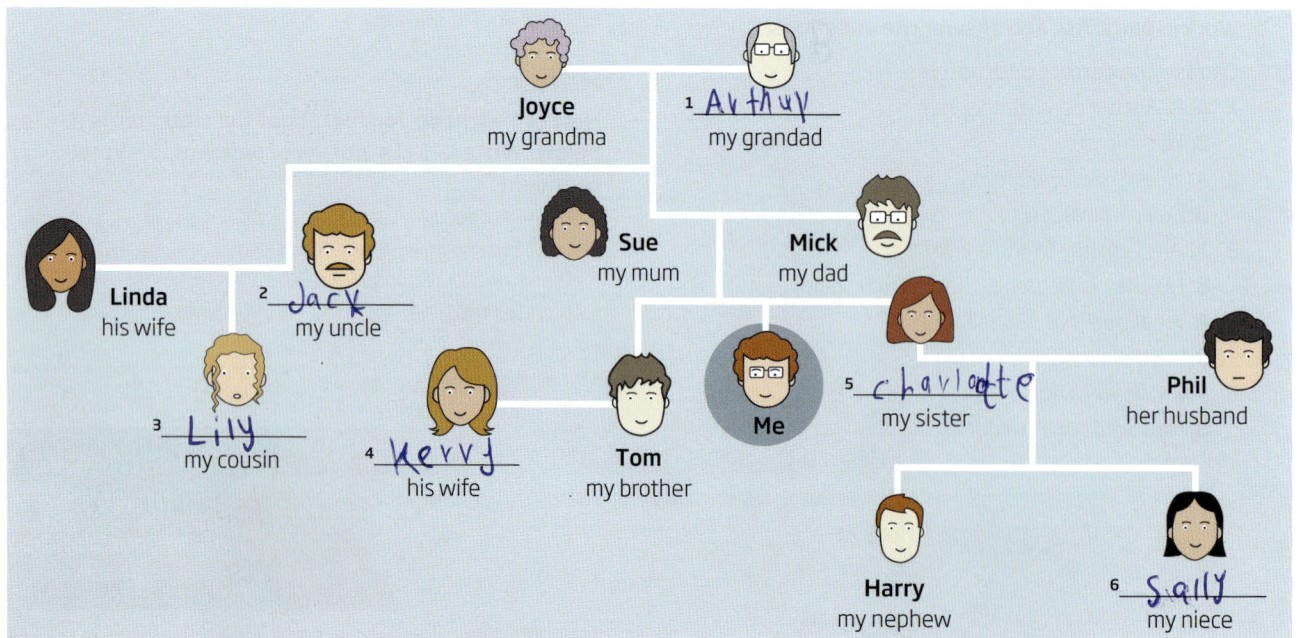

Joyce my grandma   1 *Arthur* my grandad

Linda his wife   2 *Jack* my uncle

Sue my mum   **Mick** my dad

3 *Lily* my cousin

4 *Kerry* his wife   **Tom** my brother   **Me**   5 *Charlotte* my sister   **Phil** her husband

Harry my nephew   6 *Sally* my niece

Grammar

4 a Read the grammar box and choose the correct alternatives in sentences 1–5.

possessive adjectives and possessive 's

possessive adjectives

subject pronouns	possessive adjectives
I	my
you	your
he	his
she	her
it	its
we	our
you	your
they	their

1 That's Tom, right? He's *you/your* brother.
2 And that's *his/her* wife, Kerry?
3 That's *my/I* sister Charlotte and *his/her* husband, Phil.
4 Are those *they/their* children?
5 They're *our/we* grandparents.

possessive 's

Jack's wife
NOT ~~the wife of Jack~~
My mother's brother
NOT ~~the brother of my mother~~

b 🔊 2.2 **Listen and check.**

5 a 🔊 2.3 **Listen to the sentences and notice the pronunciation of 's.**
1 This is Ana's husband.
2 Is that Nick's mum?
3 Georgia is Charlotte's cousin.
4 Who is Maria's brother?

b Listen again and repeat.

6 Choose the correct alternatives.
1 **A:** Is that *Carl/Carl's* wife?
  B: No, it isn't. It's *his/her* sister!
2 **A:** What's your *grandma's/grandma* name?
  B: *Her/His* name's Phillippa.
3 **A:** That's Melissa, *John is/John's* new girlfriend.
  B: Yes, I know. She's *their/our* manager at work.
4 **A:** Is that *your/you* uncle?
  B: Yes, it is. And that's *her/his* wife and *they're/their* son, Kevin.

7 Complete the sentences with the correct possessive adjective.
1 My brother lives in Boston with _____ wife.
2 I live here with _____ sister.
3 We like _____ teacher.
4 My cousins live with _____ parents.
5 She lives with _____ husband in Manchester.

📱 Go to page 118 or your app for more information and practice.

Speaking

PREPARE

8 a Your new friend is meeting your family or friends for the first time. First, write the names of eight family members or friends.

b Make notes about each person. Think about:
• who they are in your family (e.g. *my brother's wife*)
• their age
• where they're from
• any other information about them

SPEAK

9 a Work in pairs. Describe your family or friends to your partner. Use the Useful phrases to help you and ask questions to find out more information.

Useful phrases
Who's (Heni)?
She's my brother's wife.
They're my aunt and uncle.
Svetlana is their daughter.

b Tell the class something interesting about your partner's family or friends.

Develop your listening page 89

15

After the party

> **Goal:** say who things belong to
> **Grammar:** *whose* and possessive pronouns
> **Vocabulary:** everyday objects 2

Vocabulary

1 a Think of three objects you always take to each of these places.
- work/school
- a birthday party
- on holiday
- everywhere (in your bag)

b Work in pairs and compare your objects.

2 Match the objects in the box with photos A–N.

cap	driving licence	earrings	gloves	hairbrush
handbag	make-up	necklace	notebook	
phone charger	purse	scarf	sweater	wallet

3 a 🔊 2.10 Listen to the words in the box in Exercise 2. How many syllables does each word have?
cap - 1, driving licence - 4

b Listen again and repeat.

4 Work in pairs. Which of the objects in Exercise 2 …
- can you see in the picture above?
- do you have in your bag?
- do you have at home?

📱 Go to page 137 or your app for more vocabulary and practice.

Listening

5 a 🔊 2.11 Listen to Dominic and Anna talking at the end of the party. Which objects in Exercise 2 do they mention?

b Listen again. Which objects belong to each of these people?
1 Dominic's grandma
   earrings, gloves
2 Charlotte
3 Jack and Linda
4 Harry
5 Anna

Grammar

6 🔊 2.12 Listen to the extracts from Dominic and Anna's conversation and choose the correct alternatives.
1 *Whose/Who* earrings are these?
2 That scarf's *her/hers*, too.
3 Whose notebook *are/is* this?
4 Is it *theirs/their*?
5 That cap is *his/he*, too.
6 Is it *yours/you*?
7 Yes, it's *mine/my*.

9 Complete the conversations with the correct possessive pronoun.

1 **A:** Is this Karen's handbag?
 B: Yes, it's _hers_. (she)

2 **A:** That's my sweater.
 B: No, it isn't. It's _mine_ (I)

3 **A:** _Whose_ gloves are these? (who)
 B: They're _yours_ (you)

4 **A:** That's Anna and Sue's make-up.
 B: Yes, and that hairbrush is _theirs_ too. (they)

5 **A:** Whose earrings are these?
 B: They're _ours_. (we)

6 **A:** _Whose_ driving licence is this? (who)
 B: It's _his_. (he)

10 a Work in groups. Choose three objects in your bag and put them on the table in the middle of your group.

b Ask and answer questions about the objects.
 A: *Whose pen is that?*
 B: *It's hers. Whose hairbrush is this?*
 C: *It's mine.*

Go to page 118 or your app for more information and practice.

Speaking

PREPARE

11 Work in pairs. You're going to talk about who things belong to. Student A: Turn to page 152 and follow the instructions. Student B: Turn to page 154 and follow the instructions.

SPEAK

12 a Ask and answer questions about who the objects in your box belong to. Use the Useful phrases to help you.

Useful phrases
Whose cap is this?
Is this your hairbrush?
Are those Harry's gloves?
No, they're mine.

b Show each other your boxes and check.

Develop your reading
page 90

7 Read the grammar box and choose the correct alternatives.

Whose and possessive pronouns

Ask about possession with *whose*.
Whose cap is this? It's John's.
Whose headphones are these? They're Fiona's.
Use possessive pronouns to talk about who things belong to.
It's Catherine's handbag. = It's **hers.**
It's my parents' car. = It's **theirs.**

Subject pronoun	Possessive adjective	Possessive pronoun
I	my	¹my/mine
you	your	yours
he	his	his
she	her	²her/hers
it	its	its
we	our	³our/ours
you	your	yours
they	their	⁴their/theirs

Use possessive 's with people's names.
They're Jack's.
If there are two or more people, only add possessive 's to the last person.
It's Harry and Sally's.

8 a 2.13 Listen to the sentences and notice the sound of the letter *s*.

1 It's her**s**.
2 Those gloves are their**s**.
3 Are these earrings your**s**?
4 This is hi**s**.
5 That charger's our**s**.

b Listen again and repeat.

2c Special things

> **Goal:** describe objects
> **Grammar:** *have got*
> **Vocabulary:** adjectives describing objects

Reading and vocabulary

1 Work in pairs. What objects do you have with you today?

a phone, a book and a bag

2 a Look at the adjectives in the box. Which of your objects in Exercise 1 do they describe?

beautiful – my phone

> beautiful broken brown comfortable gold
> heavy large light modern old round
> soft special square useful

b 🔊 2.14 Listen and underline the stressed syllable in each word.

beautiful

c Listen again and repeat.

3 Read about objects that are special to four people. Match photos A–D with each person. Why is their object special?

4 Work in pairs. Take turns to describe your objects in Exercise 1. Your partner will guess what you are describing.

> **A:** *It's large and gold.*
> **B:** *Your phone?*

Go to page 137 or your app for more vocabulary and practice.

Go to page 137 or your app for more vocabulary and practice.

What things are IMPORTANT to you?

We've all got a lot of things these days – clothes, shoes, jewellery, books, mobile phones, etc. Most of these things are useful for our everyday lives but some objects are also special to us for other reasons. Four of our readers tell us what objects are special to them.

Megan, 35 D
'I've got lots of photos of my husband, but there's one special photo I love. We're on holiday in Spain, he's got his favourite cap on, and he looks so happy. It's a beautiful photo.'

Aisha, 25 B
'I've got a teddy bear called Bob. I'm 25 years old and he's the same age as me so he's an old friend. He's large, brown and soft and he's got big ears and big round eyes. I love him a lot. He's really important to me.'

Nick, 44 C
'I'm a writer, so my laptop's very important. All my books are on there. It's small, light and modern and it's always with me. It's useful for my work and everything else, too.'

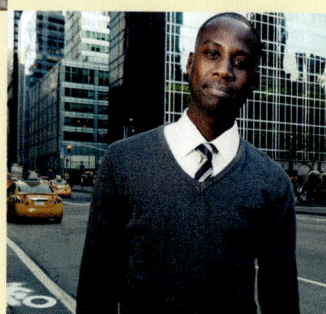

Darius, 21 A
'I've got my grandad's old watch. I haven't got it with me today because it's broken, but I love it. It's heavy and not very comfortable, but it's different. It's gold and square.'

D

Grammar

5 Read the grammar box then find other examples of *have/has got* in the article.

have got

	+	-	?
I/You/We/They	have got/'ve got	haven't got	Have ... got?
	I've got a nice photo.	*You haven't got* any pets.	*Have you got* a watch?
	We have got a laptop at home.	*They haven't got* a car.	*Have they got* a laptop?
	They've got a big car.	*I haven't got* a teddy bear.	*Have we got* any money?
He/She/It	has got/'s got	hasn't got	Has ... got?
	He's got a large house.	*She hasn't got* big ears!	*Has he got* a sister?
	She has got five sisters.	*He hasn't got* blue eyes.	*Has she got* a laptop?

6 a Complete the questions and answers with *has* or *have*.
1. **A:** *Has* Evan got any sisters?
   B: Yes, he *has*. He's got one.
2. **A:** *Have* you got a laptop?
   B: Yes, I *have*. I've got an old one.
3. **A:** *Has* Maisie got any children?
   B: Yes, she *has*. She's got two daughters.
4. **A:** *Have* they got a car?
   B: Yes, they *have*. They've got an old Ford.

b 🔊 2.15 Listen and check your answers.

c Listen again and repeat.

7 a Make sentences using the prompts so they are true for you.
1. I / a coffee maker.
   I haven't got a coffee maker.
2. My family / three cars. *has got three cars*
3. I / a good camera on my phone.
4. One of my good friends / a busy job.
5. My brother or sister / tablet.
6. My parents / a house in the countryside.
7. I / reading glasses.
8. My grandparents / a mobile phone.

b Work in pairs and compare your answers.
I haven't got a coffee maker. I don't like coffee.

8 Work in pairs. Ask and answer questions using *have got* and the things or people in the box.

> a bike   brothers and sisters   a cousin   a large car
> a musical instrument   a new phone
> an old teddy bear   a pet

> **A:** *Have you got a bike?*
> **B:** *Yes, but it's not very good. It's so old.*

📱 Go to page 118 or your app for more information and practice.

Speaking

PREPARE

9 a You're going to find out what objects are special to people in your class. First, think of three special objects you've got and write them down.

b Write two or more adjectives to describe each object. Think about why these three things are special to you.
Watch - old, round, silver

SPEAK

10 a Talk to at least three people in the class. Tell them about your special objects. Use the Useful phrases to help you.

> **Useful phrases**
> I've got (an old camera).
> It's (large) and (heavy).
> It isn't (modern) or (light).
> It's around (ten) years old.
> It's special because (it's my dad's/it's useful/it's important for my job).

b Report back to the class. What objects are special to your classmates? Why?

Develop your writing
page 91

19

> **Goal:** buy things in a shop

1 **Discuss the questions.**

1 What kinds of shops do you go to every week?
2 Who do you go with?
3 What things do you buy?

2 a 🔊 2.16 **Listen to four conversations in shops. Which conversation matches with the photo?**

b **Listen again and choose the correct alternatives.**

1 Sorry, where are the *cakes/drinks*?
2 That's £1.25, *please/thanks*.
3 That's £8.75 *change/money*.
4 Have you got *any/some* medicine for a cold?
5 How *many/much* bottles would you like?
6 Can I *have/take* a cheese sandwich, please?
7 How much is *everything/that*?
8 Would you *like/want* a bag?
9 How *many/much* is this book?
10 *What/Where's* the café?

c **Listen again. Tick the phrases in the Useful phrases box that you hear.**

Useful phrases

Asking questions: assistant
How many (bottles) would you like? ✓
Would you like a bag? ✓
Anything else? ✓
Here you are.

Asking questions: customer
Have you got any (medicine for a cold)? ✓
Can I have (a cheese sandwich), please? ✓

Saying where things are: assistant
The (drinks) are over there/on the third floor. ✓

Asking where things are: customer
Where's the (café)? ✓

Paying for things: assistant
That's (£1.25), please. ✓
That's (£8.75) change. ✓
Cash or card?

Paying for things: customer
Where do I pay?
How much is (this book)? ✓
How much are (these pens)?
How much is that? ✓
Can I pay by card? ✓

3 a 🔊 2.17 **Listen to five phrases in the Useful phrases box. Who is more polite each time, Speaker 1 or Speaker 2? How do you know?**

b 🔊 2.18 **Listen and repeat. Try to sound polite.**

4 a **Make conversations using the prompts.**

1 **A:** you / sell / stamps?   *Do you sell stamps?*
   B: yes / how many?   *yes, how many stamps*
   A: two   *Two, Please.*   *Would you like?*
   B: here. / else?   *Here you are. Anything else?*
   A: no. / how much?   *No, thank you. How much is that?*
   B: £1.38

2 **A:** Where / the shoes?
   B: over there
   A: how much / these?
   B: £28
   A: where / I / pay?
   B: here. / £28
   A: here
   B: £2 / change. bag?
   A: No. / got one

b **Work in pairs. Practise the conversations in Exercise 4a. Try to sound polite**

5 **You're going to buy something in a shop. Work in pairs. Student A: Turn to page 151. Student B: Turn to page 154. Follow the instructions.**

6 a **Work in pairs and practise the conversation in Part 1.**

b **Now practise the conversation in Part 2.**

Go online for the Roadmap video.

Check and reflect

1 a Rearrange the letters to make family members. The first letter is in bold.

1 tesir**s** _sister_
2 daer**g**natfrh _grandfather_
3 nsr**p**eat _parents_
4 n**c**eei _niece_
5 oiu**s**nc _cousin_
6 **w**henep _nephew_
7 **e**brohrt _brother_
8 **e**clnu _uncle_
9 t**m**eroh _mother_
10 **d**hirecln _children_

b When possible, write the name of a person in your family next to each family member in Exercise 1a.

sister – Maria

2 a Complete the sentences with a possessive adjective or possessive 's.

1 Dan and Lisa are married. Dan is Lisa _Lisa's_ husband.
2 Richard is married to my mother. He's _her_ father. _my_
3 Alicia is married to Roberto. She's _his_ wife.
4 Agata is Pawel _Pawel's_ daughter.
5 David and Tomas are brothers. Leonardo is _their_ father.
6 Emma and I are married. _Our_ children are Oliver and Abby.
7 Guilia and Luigi are Sara _Sara's_ grandparents.

b Work in pairs. Talk about three people in your family in Exercise 1b.

Maria's my sister. She's a nurse.

3 Choose the correct alternatives.

1 **A:** _Whose_/ Who's glasses are these?
  B: They're my / _mine_.
2 **A:** Is that _your_/ yours jacket?
  B: No, it isn't. Andy has a blue jacket. Maybe it's his / theirs.
3 **A:** Are those Sally's gloves?
  B: No, her /_hers_ are red not black.
4 **A:** _Who's_/ Whose that man over there?
  B: It's _my_/ mine brother.

4 a Complete the sentences with the correct pronoun.

1 This bag isn't _mine_. It's Karen's. My bag's brown.
2 Antonio's coat is big. This one's small. I don't think this is _his_.
3 We've got Tim and Mara's address but they haven't got _ours_.
4 Ana's car is silver. Maybe this one is _hers_.
5 Sorry, Jon, that's my pen. This one is _yours_.
6 Where's Fran and Greg's house? Is that one _theirs_?

b Work in pairs. Ask and answer questions about objects in the classroom.

**A:** Whose book is that over there?
**B:** I think it's Dennis's book.

5 Which everyday object is the odd one out?

1 purse	wallet	hairbrush	handbag
2 cap	phone	gloves	scarf
3 earrings	handbag	ring	necklace
4 laptop	printer	tablet	phone charger
5 sweater	glasses	make up	cap

6 Make positive or negative sentences with _have got_.

1 Ben _has got_ a smartwatch. (+)
2 We _haven't got_ any coffee. (−)
3 Emily _hasn't got_ a brother. (−)
4 Filip and Lidia _have got_ two children. (+)
5 I _haven't got_ any money. (−)
6 You _have got_ some food on your jacket. (+)
7 Max _hasn't got_ a job. (−)

7 a Complete the conversations with _has/have (got)_.

1 **A:** _Have_ you _got_ an umbrella? It's wet outside.
  B: Yes, I _have_ Here it is.
2 **A:** I _have got_ my wallet with me. It's at home.
  B: That's OK. I _have got_ some money.
3 **A:** _Has_ Sofia _got_ a boyfriend?
  B: No, she _hasn't_. Why?
4 **A:** _Have_ you _got_ any orange juice?
  B: I'm sorry, we _haven't_. We _have got_ apple juice.
5 **A:** _Has_ Marc _got_ a new job?
  B: Yes, he _has got_. He works at the hospital now.

b Work in pairs. Ask and answer three questions with _Have you got …?_

**A:** Have you got a printer?
**B:** No, I haven't.

8 a Complete the sentences with an adjective. Use the first letter(s) to help you.

1 My new car isn't l _big_. It's small.
2 What's the time? My watch is b _s___.
3 I've got a lot of things in my bag. It's h _eavy_.
4 My scarf is a nice br _own_ colour.
5 My bathroom mirror is a s _square_ shape. It isn't round.
6 My teddy bear feels lovely. He's very s _oft_.
7 My flat is old, not m _odern_, but it's OK for me.
8 I love my sofa. It's very c _omfortable_.

b Work in pairs. Take turns to describe an object and guess what it is.

It's small and modern. It's got a screen. It's very useful.

Reflect

How confident do you feel about the statements below? Write 1–5 (1 = not very confident, 5 = very confident).

- I can describe my family.
- I can say who things belong to.
- I can describe objects.
- I can buy things in a shop.

Want more practice?
Go to your Workbook or app.

21

3A Free time

> **Goal:** talk about free-time activities

> **Grammar:** present simple with *I, you, we* and *they*; adverbs of frequency and time expressions

> **Vocabulary:** free-time activities 1

Reading

1 **Discuss the questions.**

1 What do you do in your free time?

2 What things do other people in your country do in their free time?

2 a **Read the introduction to the article. Answer the questions.**

1 Do we have more or less free time these days?

2 Is it a good thing or a bad thing?

b **Read the comments. Match each person with photos A–E. Do they have hobbies? Are their lives 'all work and no play'?**

All **work** and no **play**?

I think our lives are all work and no play these days. It's sad, because our free time is really important! We asked some of our readers what they do in their free time. Are their lives all work and no play?

I work a lot. I've got two jobs and I study so I rarely have free time. I go for a bike ride once or twice a month. In the evenings I go online and talk to my friends. I sometimes paint. I go out and paint interesting places. I draw pictures of people, too. – **Joe, 28** E

I don't usually go out on weekdays because I'm busy with work. I meet my friends every Saturday and we go for a walk or for a coffee. Sometimes, we go to a concert or go to a club. I love music! – **Annie, 31** D

I have three children so my evenings and weekends are all about them. When I have free time, I watch sport on TV, especially football. I don't do sport, I just watch it! – **Alfie, 34** C

I'm quite lucky. I have my own business so I never work at the weekend. I love Sunday mornings. I read the newspaper for a few hours. Later, I often visit a museum or something. – **Tilly, 30** A

Free time? We've got two children. We don't have free time! We cook food three times a day, we clean the house and we play with our children. They love games. Then we sleep for a few hours. That's our day! – **Karen, 27** B

Vocabulary

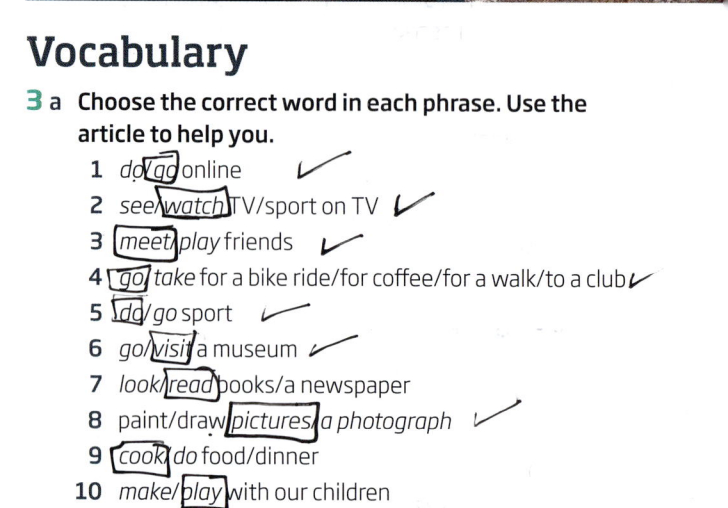

3 a **Choose the correct word in each phrase. Use the article to help you.**

1 *do/go* online ✓

2 *see/watch* TV/sport on TV ✓

3 *meet/play* friends ✓

4 *go/take* for a bike ride/for coffee/for a walk/to a club ✓

5 *do/go* sport ✓

6 *go/visit* a museum ✓

7 *look/read* books/a newspaper ✓

8 paint/draw *pictures/a photograph* ✓

9 *cook/do* food/dinner ✓

10 *make/play* with our children

b **Which activities in Exercise 3a can you see in photos A–E?**

4 a **Tick the activities in Exercise 3a that you do.**

b **Work in pairs. Tell each other about the activities in Exercise 3a you do. Which activities do you both do?**

> **A:** *I go online and I read a newspaper.*
> **B:** *Me too.*

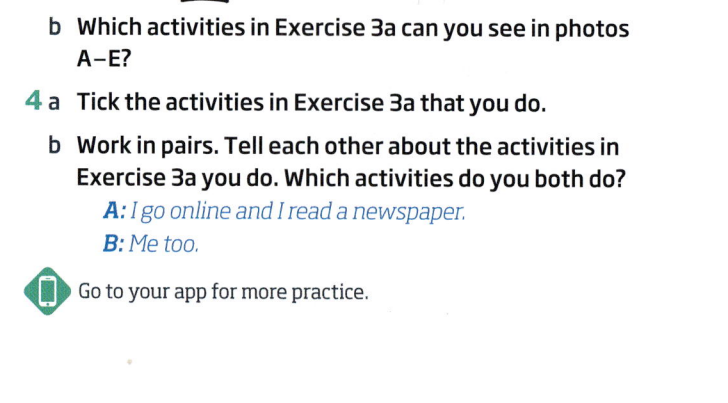

Go to your app for more practice.

Grammar

5 Read the grammar box and choose the correct alternatives.

Present simple with I, you, we and they; adverbs of frequency and time expressions

Use the present simple to talk about things that are true [1]~~now~~/~~in the future~~.

Use [2]~~aren't~~/~~don't~~ + infinitive to make negative sentences.

+	I/You/We/They	go	online. for a coffee.
-	I/You/We/They	don't (do not) go	out with friends. to a restaurant.

Use time expressions to say when or how often something happens, e.g. *at the weekend, three times a week*.

*I read the newspaper **on Sunday mornings**.*

*I go for a bike ride **once or twice a month**.*

Use adverbs of frequency to say how often something happens. These come before the main verb but after *don't* and after the verb *be*.

*I **don't usually go out** on weekdays.*

*I'm **always** busy.*

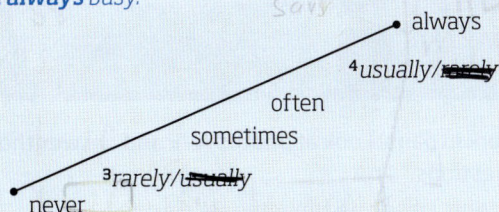

always
[4] usually/~~rarely~~
often
sometimes
[3] rarely/~~usually~~
never

6 a 🔊 3.1 Listen to the sentences and notice the pronunciation of the adverbs of frequency. Which syllable is stressed?

1 I rarely go out with friends.
2 I always work at the weekend.
3 I'm sometimes free in the evenings.
4 I usually play football after school.
5 We never cook on Fridays.
6 I often get up late on Sundays.

b Listen again and repeat.

7 Make the positive sentences negative and make the negative sentences positive.

1 I watch a lot of sport on TV.
  I don't watch a lot of sport on TV.
2 I don't play tennis in the summer.
3 We don't have a lot of free time at the weekend.
4 Our children like video games.
5 They often make pasta for dinner.
6 We always have pizza on Friday evenings.
7 The children don't usually go online in the evenings.
8 I always paint every day.

8 a Put the words in the correct order to make sentences.

1 I / ride at the weekend / go / for a bike / always
  I always go for a bike ride at the weekend.
2 I / sometimes / sport / on TV / watch
3 usually / together in the / evenings / My family and I / have dinner
4 cook dinner at home / a week / I usually / twice
5 I / watch / funny videos online / often
6 I / my friends / at the weekend / sometimes meet / for coffee
7 I / often / in the mornings / go for a run
8 sleep late / I / on Saturday mornings / rarely

b Change the sentences in Exercise 8a so they are true for you.
  I never go for a bike ride at the weekend.

c Work in pairs. Tell each other your sentences in Exercise 8b. Give more information.
  I never go for a bike ride at the weekend because I don't have a bike!

📱 Go to page 120 or your app for more information and practice.

Speaking

PREPARE

9 🔊 3.2 You're going to talk about free-time activities. First, listen to three classmates talk about free-time activities. Are the sentences true (T) or false (F)?

1 All the students in the group do sport every day.
2 Only one of the students always meets friends at the weekend.
3 They find one thing that everyone does.

10 Think about your free-time activities. What do you do and how often do you do it? Make notes.
  go for a walk - in the evenings
  visit a museum - twice a month

SPEAK

11 a Work in groups. Tell your group about your free-time activities. Try to find three things that you all do.

Useful phrases
Me too!
Oh, I don't usually …
Well, I often …
And you?

b Report back to the class. Did you find three things that you all do?

Develop your writing
page 92

A night's work

> **Goal:** describe daily routines
> **Grammar:** present simple with *he, she* and *it*
> **Vocabulary:** everyday activities

Vocabulary and reading

1 a Match phrases 1–12 with pictures a–l.

1 do exercise	7 go to bed
2 do my hair	8 go to work
3 get dressed	9 have a shower
4 get ready	10 have breakfast/lunch/dinner
5 go to the gym	11 leave home
6 get up	12 start work/school

b Work in pairs and discuss the questions.
1 Which activities do you do every day?
2 When do you do these activities?
I get up at 7 a.m., then I have a shower and get dressed.

📱 Go to page 138 or your app for more vocabulary and practice.

2 a Work in pairs. Look at photos A–E and answer the questions.
1 What jobs do you think the people do?
2 When do you think they go to work?

b Read the texts and match Keira and Liam with two of the photos.

Keira gets up at 2 a.m. She has a shower then gets dressed. She leaves home at 3 a.m. and gets to work at 3.30. She has a quick breakfast at work, then she gets ready for the breakfast TV programme. She reads the plan for the morning. The programme starts at 5 a.m. when most people are asleep.

Liam loves his job but it's hard work. He gets up at 3 p.m. and spends time with his family. He leaves for work at 8.30 p.m. because he worries about the traffic. He starts work at 10 p.m. He works in the hospital and helps the patients and doctors. He doesn't have lunch but he has coffee and a snack. He finishes work at 6 a.m. and has dinner. He gets home at 7 a.m. and goes straight to bed because he's very tired!

c Read the texts again. Complete the sentences with *Keira* or *Liam*.
1 _____ sees his/her family in the afternoon.
2 _____ leaves home an hour after he/she gets up.
3 _____ goes to bed when he/she gets home.
4 _____ has breakfast at work.
5 _____ gets up in the afternoon.
6 _____ starts work when most people go to bed.

3 Work in pairs. Do you think it's good to start work early? Why/Why not?

Grammar

4 a Read the grammar box and choose the correct alternatives.

Present simple with *he, she* and *it*

Use the present simple to talk about daily routines.
Keira **gets up** at 2 a.m.
Liam **starts** work at 10 p.m.

+	He/She/It	starts (work)	at 10 p.m.
-	He/She/It	doesn't start (work)	

To form the present simple with *he, she* or *it*, add
1 -*s*/ -*e* to the verb.
It **starts** at 11 p.m.
She **loves** her job.
When the verb ends with -*s*, -*z*, -*x*, -*sh*, -*ch* or -*o*, add
2 -*ies*/ -*es*.
He **finishes** work at 7 a.m.
He **goes** straight to bed.
When the verb ends with a consonant + -*y*, delete the -*y*
and add **3** -*ies*/ -*es*.
He **worries** about the traffic.
He **carries** a big bag around with him all day.
For negative sentences, use **4** *don't*/*doesn't* + infinitive.
She **doesn't like** her job.
He **doesn't have** lunch.

b Find more examples of the present simple with *he/she/it* in the texts in Exercise 2.

5 a 🔊 3.3 Listen to the sentences. Are the sounds in bold /s/ or /z/?

1 He get**s** home at 7 a.m.
2 She doe**s**n't go to bed late.
3 She start**s** work at 9.30.
4 He leave**s** work early.
5 She work**s** at home.
6 He ha**s** lunch at 1 p.m.

b Listen again and repeat.

6 Complete the text about Craig's day with the correct form of the verbs in brackets.

Craig's a security guard at an office building. He **1**_____ (get up) at 8 p.m. and **2**_____ (have) a shower. He has a big breakfast and **3**_____ (read) the news online. Then he **4**_____ (get) ready for work. He **5**_____ (put on) his uniform and **6**_____ (leave) home at 9.30 p.m. He gets to work at 10 p.m. and **7**_____ (meet) the other security guard. They check the building. He **8**_____ (walk) around the building for 30 minutes every hour, then he **9**_____ (watch) TV or reads a magazine for thirty minutes. He **10**_____ (not have) lunch, but when he **11**_____ (finish) work he has a big dinner. In the morning, he **12**_____ (not do) anything. He **13**_____ (go) to bed at around 12.30.

7 a Make notes on activities you do every day. Use the phrases in Exercise 1a to help you.

I get up at 11 a.m.
I don't have lunch.

b Work in pairs. Talk about your daily routines. Is anything the same?

c Work with a different partner. Compare your daily routines.

I get up early but Maria gets up late.
He goes to work before me.

📱 Go to page 120 or your app for more information and practice.

Speaking

PREPARE

8 You're going to talk about a friend who has a different routine from you. Make notes about the differences between you.

Me - I get up early - Laura - gets up late
Me - work in an office - Laura - no job

SPEAK

9 Work in pairs. Tell your partner about you and your friend. Whose friend has the more different routine?

Develop your reading
page 93

3c Going out

> **Goal:** ask about free-time activities

> **Grammar:** present simple questions

> **Vocabulary:** free-time activities 2

Reading

1 Discuss the questions.

  1 Do you go out every week, e.g. to a restaurant with friends, to the cinema, etc.?

  2 Where do you usually go?

  3 Who do you usually go with?

2 a Look at pictures A–D in the quiz. What activities do they show?

  b Do the quiz.

  c Work in pairs. Compare your answers and give more information.

  A: I sometimes go out on a Friday night but not every week. Sometimes I stay at home and watch a film.

  B: So, your answer is b?

  A: Yes.

  d Turn to page 153 and read your results. Do you agree?

Grammar

3 Read the grammar box and choose the correct alternatives. Use the quiz to help you.

Present simple questions

Yes/No questions

Question			Short answer
¹*Do/Does*	I/you/ we/ they	ever buy clothes online?	Yes, I/you/we/they ²*do/does.* No, I/you/we/they ³*don't/doesn't.*
Does	he/ she/it	work?	Yes, he/she/it does. No, he/she/it doesn't.

Use *ever* with *yes/no* questions to mean *at any time*. It comes ⁴*before/after* the subject.
*Do you **ever** cook at home?*

Wh- questions

How often	⁵*do/does*	I/you/ we/they	go out on a Friday night?
What	⁶*do/does*	he/she/it	do?

Do you prefer the quiet life?

Find out with our quiz.

1 How often do you go out on a Friday night?

  a I always go out somewhere with my friends.

  b I sometimes go out, but when I'm tired I stay in.

  c I hardly ever go out. I usually stay at home with a book or a film.

2 What do you usually do on your birthday?

  a I have a big party at a restaurant and invite everyone I know!

  b I go out for a meal with some of my friends and family.

  c I invite some friends and family to my home.

3 It's Saturday evening. What do you say to your best friend?

  a 'Where do you want to go tonight?'

  b 'Do you want to stay in or go out tonight?'

  c 'Do you want to come to my house tonight?'

4 You're at home alone at the weekend. How do you feel?

  a I hate it! It's really boring.

  b OK. I sometimes go out but I often stay in.

  c I love it. I often spend time by myself.

5 Do you ever buy clothes online?

  a No, I don't. I love clothes shops.

  b Not usually. I go to the shops near my house.

  c Yes, I do. I buy almost all my clothes online.

6 What kind of sport do you usually do?

  a I go to the gym or a sports club.

  b I usually run near my home.

  c I do exercise at home.

4 a 🔊 **3.4 Listen and complete the questions with** *do* **or** *does.* **Are** *do / does* **stressed or unstressed?**

1 **A:** _____ you ever go to the cinema?
   B: No, I don't.

2 **A:** _____ she do any sport?
   B: Yes, she does.

3 **A:** Do you ever have parties?
   B: No, I _____.

4 **A:** Does he ever go to the gym?
   B: Yes, he _____.

b Listen again and repeat.

5 a Put the words in the correct order to make questions. Add *do* **or** *does.*

1 you / video games / play / ever ?
   Do you ever play video games?

2 music / where / listen to / you ?

3 the piano / play / you ?

4 TV / you / how often / watch ?

5 watch / where / films / you ?

6 on your own / go / you / to the cinema / ever ?

7 listen to / when / you / music ?

8 the cinema / how many times a year / you / go to ?

b Work in pairs. Take turns to ask and answer the questions in Exercise 5a. Do you do similar things?

📱 Go to page 120 or your app for more information and practice.

Vocabulary

6 a Complete the phrases with the words in the box.

> to a concert   a football match   games online
> the piano/guitar   the radio   a song
> to the theatre   a video online

1 play   video games / _____ / _____
2 listen to music / _____ / _____
3 watch   TV/a TV programme
            a film / _____ / _____
4 go   to the cinema / _____ / _____

b Look at the activities in Exercise 6a. Which activities do people usually ...

1 do at home?
2 do outside the home?
3 do inside and outside the home?

7 Work in pairs. Take turns to ask five questions with *Do you (ever) ...?* **and the activities in Exercise 6a. Ask questions to get more information.**

A: Do you ever go to the theatre?
B: Yes, I do. I go about once a year.
A: Where do you go?
B: I go to a theatre in my town.

📱 Go to your app for more practice.

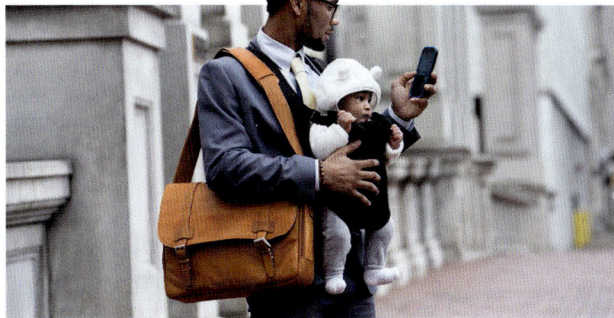

Speaking

PREPARE

8 a 🔊 **3.5 You're going to write a quiz about free-time activities. First, listen to Jordan and Martina doing a quiz and answer the questions.**

1 What's the name of the quiz?
2 What is Martina's result?
3 Does she think the result is correct?

b Listen again. Match questions 1–6 with answers a–f.

1 How many times a week do you go out?
2 What do you do when you go out?
3 How many different activities do you do on a Sunday?
4 Do you often go to concerts or to the theatre or cinema?
5 How often do you go dancing or to a party?
6 Do you often stay at home and read books, watch films or play games online?

a I meet friends.
b No, not really.
c Once or twice.
d Yes, I do. Most evenings.
e I don't know. Four or five.
f Not often. A few times a year, that's all.

9 Work in pairs. Write five questions to ask other students about free-time activities.

SPEAK

10 a Ask your questions to a few different people in the class. Do you think they prefer a busy life or a quiet life? Use the Useful phrases to help you.

> **Useful phrases**
> OK, this is my first question.
> So, I think that you prefer a busy/quiet life.
> That's correct. / That's not correct!

b Report back to the class. Who prefers a busy life, and who prefers a quiet life?

Florence and Marc have a busy life, but Fleur, Louis and Corentin prefer a quiet life.

> **Develop your listening**
> page 94

> **Goal:** buy tickets

1   Match photos A–D with the places in the box.

| cinema   concert   football stadium   theatre |

2 a 🔊 3.10 Listen and match conversations 1 and 2 with two of photos A–D.

b Listen to the conversations again and tick the phrases in the Useful phrases box that you hear.

Useful phrases

Assistant
How can I help you?
The (six thirty) film is sold out.
There are still some available.
Where do you want to sit?
Do you want to sit together?
I'm sorry, there aren't any seats together.
Here you are.
No problem./Certainly./Yes, of course.
That's (sixty pounds).

Customer
How much is a ticket?
I'd like two tickets for the (game), please.
Near the front/back, please.

3 a 🔊 3.11 Listen to the Useful phrases and underline the stressed words.

  How can I help you?

b Listen again and repeat.

4 a 🔊 3.12 Listen to two more conversations. What's the problem in each one?

b Listen again and complete the conversations.

1
A: How ¹_____ is a ticket for *Mamma Mia*?
B: Do you want to go to the 4 p.m. or the 7 p.m. show?
A: 7 p.m.
B: They're forty ²_____ each.
A: Oh, that's expensive. How much is a ticket for the 4 p.m. show?
B: Twenty pounds each.
A: OK. I'd like two ³_____ for the 4 p.m. show, please.
B: No problem. ⁴_____ forty pounds.

2
A: How ⁵_____ I help you?
B: Hi, I'd ⁶_____ four tickets for the Gary Priestley concert tonight, please.
A: I'm sorry, tonight's show is ⁷_____ out.
B: Oh, really? What about tomorrow?
A: Let me see … oh yes, there are still some ⁸_____.
B: Great, I'll have them!

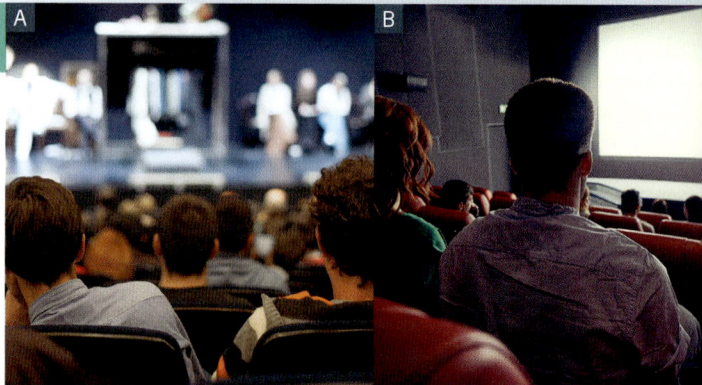

5   You're going to practise buying tickets for the events below. First, think of questions the assistant and customer can ask and how they can answer in each situation.
- a concert
- a film at the cinema
- a musical
- a sports game

6 a Work in pairs. Student A: You are the assistant. Student B: You are the customer. Practise buying tickets in each situation in Exercise 5.

b Swap roles and repeat.

7   Work with a new partner. Practise the conversations again with new information.

🎥 **Go online for the Roadmap video.**

Check and reflect

1 Correct the mistakes in five of the sentences.

1 My parents doesn't watch TV much.
2 I go for a walk with my friend at weekend.
3 We do sport three times a week at school.
4 You do read magazines.
5 I don't likes museums.
6 We lives in a big house.

2 a Complete the sentences with the verbs in the box so they are true for you. Use positives and negatives.

do   go   like   play   read   visit   watch

1 I _____ .
2 My family _____ .
3 My friends and I _____ .
4 My parents _____ .
5 The people in my class _____ .

b Work in pairs and compare your sentences. How many things do you have in common?

3 a Match verbs 1–6 with a–f.

1	do	a	museums
2	go	b	dinner
3	cook	c	for a coffee
4	paint	d	pictures
5	visit	e	TV
6	watch	f	sport

b Complete the sentences with the verbs and nouns in Exercise 3a.

1 Would you like to _____ for a _____ with me tomorrow morning?
2 I never _____ _____ at the weekend. I prefer to go to a restaurant or café.
3 In summer, I often sit outside and _____ _____ of the flowers and birds.
4 Do you _____ _____ in the evening? What are your favourite programmes?
5 I _____ _____ every weekend – sometimes football, sometimes tennis.

4 a Complete the sentences with the verbs in brackets.

1 My sister _____ (not like) her job.
2 My mum _____ (start) work at 10 a.m.
3 Jack _____ (not have) breakfast in the morning.
4 Our teacher _____ (speak) Japanese.
5 My friend _____ (work) in a big company.
6 Sally _____ (go) to school on Saturday mornings.
7 My brother _____ (not have) lunch at work.
8 Chris _____ (not see) his family in the morning.

b Change sentences in Exercise 4a so they are true for you. Work in pairs and compare your sentences.
I don't start work at 10 a.m. I start work at 8 a.m.

c Work with another partner. Tell them about your partner in Exercise 4b.
Claudia starts work at 8 a.m.

5 Complete the questions with *do* or *does*.

1 _____ she like films?
2 _____ you ever go to the cinema?
3 What time _____ you get up in the morning?
4 _____ they have breakfast together?
5 What books _____ you like?
6 When _____ Mark get home?
7 _____ your brother work hard?

6 a Write five sentences about people in your class that you think are true.
Maria doesn't like films.

b Find the people you wrote about in Exercise 6a and ask them questions. How many of your sentences are correct?
A: Maria, do you like films?
B: No, I don't.

7 a Choose the correct alternatives.

1 Do you *listen to/watch* music in your car?
2 Does your brother *watch/go to* the cinema at the weekend?
3 Do you *play/watch* the guitar?
4 Do you *watch/listen to* TV in the evening?
5 Does your friend *go to/play* games online?
6 Do you *watch/listen to* the radio at work?
7 Does your family *go to/watch* the theatre together?

b Work in pairs. Ask and answer the questions in Exercise 7a.

8 a Choose the correct alternatives.

I ¹*get/go* up early, usually about 6 o'clock, because I want to ²*go to/have* the gym. After the gym, I ³*start/have* a shower, ⁴*get/go* dressed, ⁵*get/do* my hair and ⁶*leave/go* to work. I ⁷*go/start* work at 8, and I ⁸*have/go* lunch at 12.

b Work in pairs. Tell your partner about your morning routine.

Reflect

How confident do you feel about the statements below? Write 1–5 (1 = not very confident, 5 = very confident).

- I can talk about free-time activities.
- I can describe daily routines.
- I can ask about habits and routines.
- I can buy tickets.

Want more practice?
Go to your Workbook or app.

> **Goal:** talk about your city
> **Grammar:** *there is/are*
> **Vocabulary:** places in a city

A

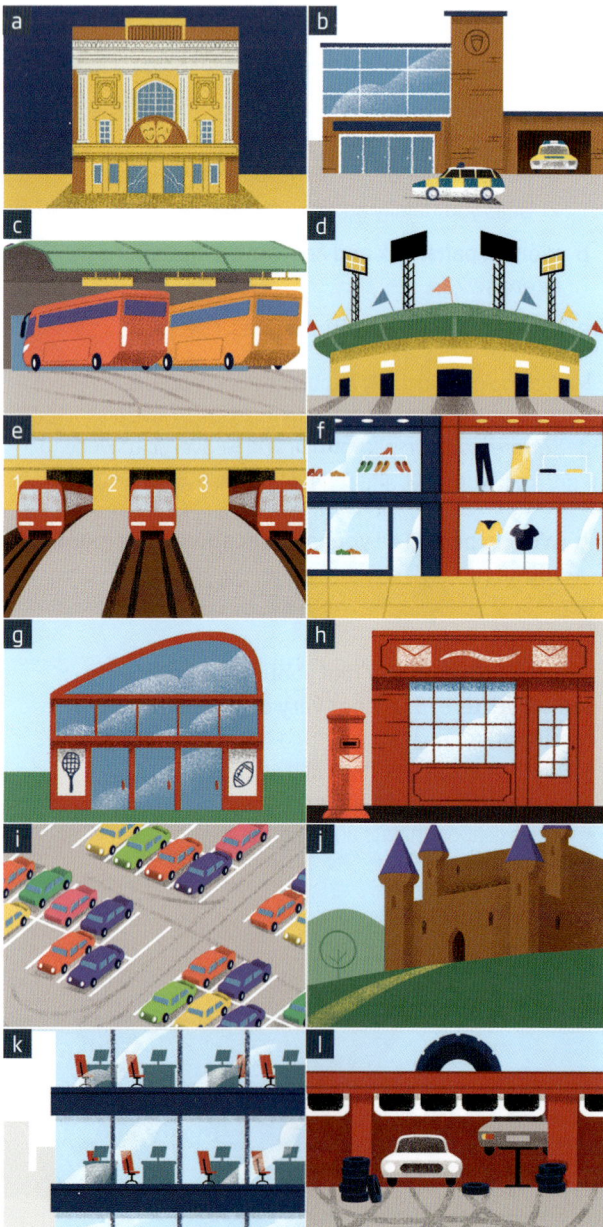
B

Vocabulary and listening

1 Look at photos A–D and discuss the questions.

   1 What can you see in the photos?

   2 Do you live in a small or a big place?

   3 Do you like your home town? Why/Why not?

2 Match the places in the box with pictures a–l.

> bus station   car park   castle   garage   offices
> police station   post office   shops   sports centre
> stadium   theatre   train station

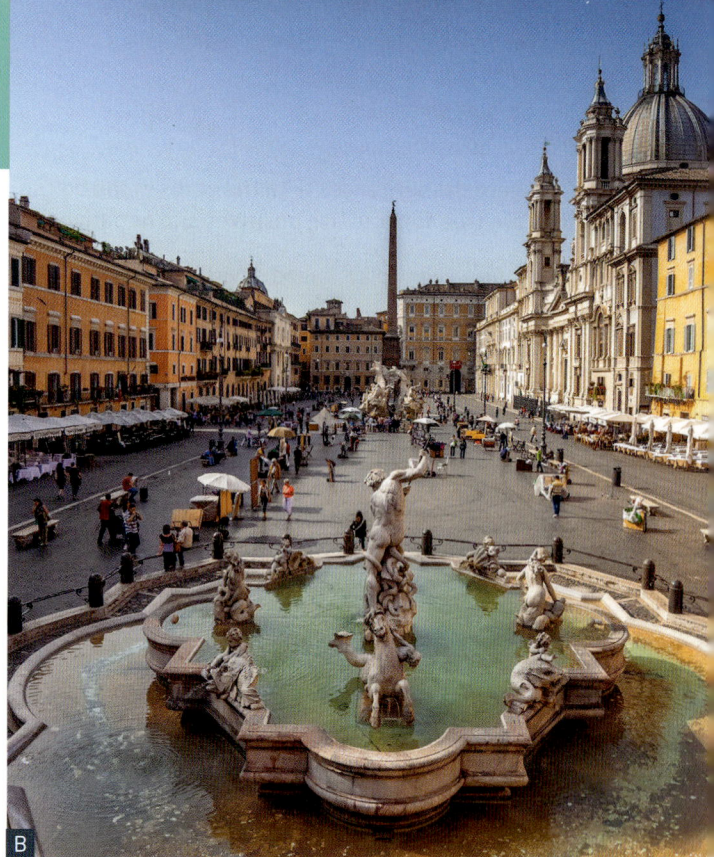

3 a 🔊 4.1 Listen to the words in Exercise 2 and underline the stressed syllables.

   bus station

  b Listen again and repeat.

4 a Read the descriptions and match them with the places in Exercise 2. Sometimes more than one answer is possible.

   1 You play or watch sport there.

   2 You buy things there.

   3 You send letters from there.

   4 You travel somewhere from there.

   5 You take your car there when it has a problem.

  b Choose three other places in Exercise 2. Write a sentence for each one describing what you do there.

  c Work in pairs. Read your sentences for your partner to guess the place.

5 a 🔊 4.2 Listen to someone talking about their city. Which places in Exercise 2 do they talk about?

  b Listen again and choose the correct alternatives.

   1 There are *a lot of/some* shops.

   2 There isn't *a/some* bus station.

   3 There aren't *any/a* train stations in other parts of town.

   4 There are *any/a lot of* visitors to the castle.

   5 There's *some/any* green space near the centre.

📱 Go to page 139 or your app for more vocabulary and practice.

C

D

Grammar

6 Read the grammar box and choose the correct alternatives.

There is/are

Use *There is(n't)/are(n't)* to introduce places and things. Use:

a *There is(n't) a/an +* ¹*singular/plural* noun

There's *a cinema in my area.*

There isn't *a train station in my town.*

b *There are some +* ²*singular/plural* noun

There are some *big parks in my city.*

c Change *some* to *a lot of +* plural noun to describe a ³*small/big* quantity.

There are **a lot of** *little shops.*

d *There aren't any +* ⁴*singular/plural* noun

There aren't any *offices in this part of the city.*

e *There is some/a lot of +* ⁵*countable/uncountable* noun

There's some *empty space in the centre.*

7 a 🔊 4.3 Listen and notice how the words link together.

1 There's a train station.

2 There aren't any offices.

b 🔊 4.4 **Mark the linking in these sentences. Then listen and check.**

1 There are some cafés.

2 There isn't a hospital.

3 There are a lot of parks.

4 There aren't any garages.

c Listen again and repeat.

8 Choose the correct alternatives.

I love my city. There ¹*is/are* a lot of places for young people. In the centre, there are ²*any/some* cafés and there's ³*a/an* big cinema. There aren't ⁴*a/any* shops in my area, but in the centre ⁵*there are/there's* a big shopping centre where you can spend time with friends. There ⁶*isn't/aren't* a train station but there are ⁷*a lot of/any* buses so it's easy to get around. Come and visit!

9 a Complete the sentences with *a, an, some, any* and *lot.*

1 There's _____ hospital.

2 There isn't _____ train station.

3 There are a _____ of garages.

4 There are _____ cinemas.

5 There aren't _____ shops.

6 There isn't _____ police station.

7 There are a _____ of museums.

b Work in pairs. Which of the sentences in Exercise 9a are true where you live?

There's a hospital but there isn't a police station.

📱 Go to page 122 or your app for more information and practice.

Speaking

PREPARE

10 Work in pairs. You're moving house and you want to decide which place to move to. Student A: Turn to page 155. Student B: Turn to page 152. Follow the instructions.

SPEAK

11 a Work in pairs. Talk about Towns A and B. Make notes about your partner's town.

b Work in pairs. Decide which of the places you'd like to move to. Use the Useful phrases to help you.

Useful phrases

Town A is good because there are lots of …

What do you think?

I don't like Town B. There isn't …

OK, so Town B?

Develop your writing
page 95

〉 **Goal:** describe your home

〉 **Grammar:** articles

〉 **Vocabulary:** things in a home

Vocabulary

1 **Discuss the questions.**

   1 Do you live in a flat or house?

   2 How many rooms in a house can you name?

    kitchen, bedroom…

2 a **Match the words in the box with pictures A–J.**

> bath   cupboard   curtains   downstairs
> fridge   furniture   garage   garden
> shower   upstairs   wardrobe

  b **Complete the sentences with the words in the box in Exercise 2a.**

    1 The glasses are in the _____ next to the fridge.

    2 We need some new _____ . Maybe a new table and chairs.

    3 Close the _____ . It's dark outside.

    4 The _____ isn't working. This milk isn't cold!

    5 I don't need a _____ , I always take a shower.

    6 Put your clothes in the _____ , not on the bed!

    7 The weather is nice today – let's sit in the _____ .

  c **Look at the photos. Which of the things in Exercise 2a can you see?**

   📱 Go to page 140 or your app for more vocabulary and practice.

Reading

3 a **Read the advertisement. Who would need a house like this?**

    a a single person

> **To buy: A three-bedroom house, in Walkley, Kent**
>
> An excellent home in a quiet area near good schools.
>
> The furniture in every room is new and the bathroom has a new shower and a bath. Two bedrooms are large and one is small, but great for a young child. All the bedrooms have wardrobes and beds. The kitchen has a big fridge and lots of cupboard space. There are also two garages and a big garden. The garden is perfect for parties in summer.

    b a family with children

  b **Read the description again and answer the questions.**

    1 Which things in the house are new?

    2 How many bedrooms does the house have?

    3 Which rooms in the house are big?

    4 What is in the kitchen?

    5 What is outside the house?

  c **Work in pairs and answer the questions.**

    1 What are the good things about the house?

    2 Are there any bad things?

    3 Is it a good place to live?

Grammar

4 a Read the grammar box and complete 1–3 with *the, a/an* or *no article*.

Articles

a Use **¹**_____ with a singular noun when we first talk about it. It means 'one'.

*This is **an** interesting house.*
*There's **a** big wardrobe in the bedroom.*

b Use **²**_____ when there is only one of something and in some phrases, e.g. *at the weekend, in the evening, all the time, the first, the second.*

***The** kitchen is big.*
*It's very dark in here in **the** morning.*
***The** first bedroom is nice, but the second one is small.*

c To mention something for the first time, use *a/an*. To mention it for the second time, use *the*.

*There's **a** big garden. **The** garden is great for summer parties.*

d Use **³**_____ with plural countable nouns, uncountable nouns and some phrases, e.g. *at/to school, at/to work, at night.*

*There are **curtains** in every room.*
*You can work at **home**.*

b Match sentences 1–5 with rules a–d in the grammar box. Use the underlined words to help you. You can use one rule more than once.

1 There are flowers in <u>the garden</u>.
2 It's cold <u>in the evening</u>.
3 There's <u>a really comfortable sofa</u> in <u>the living room</u>.
4 There are curtains in every room. <u>The curtains</u> are new.
5 It's nice to be <u>at work</u>.

5 a 🔊 4.5 Listen to the sentences. When is *the* a short sound? When is it a longer sound?

1 The bedroom's really big.
2 All the furniture in the house is very modern.
3 What's the address of the flat?
4 The apartment's very comfortable.

b Listen again and repeat.

6 Complete the sentences with *a/an, the* or *no article (–)*.

1 The bedroom has _____ big window.
2 We have our breakfast outside at _____ weekend.
3 There's _____ lovely tree in our garden.
4 I like my flat, but _____ friends say it's small.
5 There's _____ shower and bath in the bathroom. _____ shower's really good.
6 We sit outside at _____ night in _____ garden.
7 I go to _____ work by bus in _____ mornings.
8 I do my work in _____ dining room in _____ evening.

7 a Complete the sentences so they are true about your home. Write *a/an/the* if necessary and a noun.

1 There's ___*a big sofa*___ in the living room.
2 _____ is my favourite room.
3 Outside, there's _____.
4 I spend a lot of time in _____.
5 I don't like _____ in my home.

b Describe your home to your partner. Use your sentences in Exercise 7a to help you.

There are eight rooms in my house - four downstairs and four upstairs. There's a big sofa in the living room and a large TV. I love it. It's my favourite room.

📱 Go to page 122 or your app for more information and practice.

Speaking

PREPARE

8 a 🔊 4.6 You're going to describe a home. First, listen to Mark call an estate agent about a flat. Tick the things in the box he asks about.

> the area nearby   the cost of the flat   the furniture
> the garden   the neighbours   the number of rooms
> parking   what's in the bathroom

b Listen again and answer the questions.

1 How many rooms are there?
2 What furniture is in the living room?
3 What's in the bathroom?
4 Has the flat got a garden?
5 How far is the supermarket?
6 How much is the flat per month?

9 Work in pairs. Student A: Turn to page 156. Student B: Turn to page 158. Read your information. Plan what to say.

SPEAK

10 a Work in pairs. Student B: Ask Student A for information about the flat. Student A: Answer Student B's questions. Use the Useful phrases to help you.

Useful phrases

Hello, (Cathy) speaking.
I'm interested in the flat on (West Street).
I'd like to ask some questions.
Would you like to see the flat?
Yes, please./No, that's fine, thank you.

b Student B: Report back to the class. Do you want to rent the flat or not? Why/Why not?

Develop your reading page 96

4C Be prepared

A

> **Goal:** discuss what to take on a trip
> **Grammar:** *need* + noun, *need* + infinitive with *to*
> **Vocabulary:** equipment

Vocabulary and listening

1 a Match photos A–C with places 1–3.

1 the Atacama desert
2 the Arctic
3 the Amazon rainforest

b Work in pairs. Discuss the questions.

1 Would you like to visit the places in Exercise 1a?
2 Are there any similar places in your country?

2 a Match the things in the box with pictures a–n.

> backpack   batteries   blanket   boots   bowl
> can   gloves   hat   knife   map   mirror
> sunglasses   warm clothes   water bottle

B

a
b
c
d
e
f
g
h
i
j
k
l
m
n

b 🔊 4.7 Listen and check your answers.

c Listen again and repeat.

3 Work in pairs. Discuss which things in Exercise 2a are useful in the places in Exercise 1a.

I think the warm clothes are good for the Arctic.
A knife is useful for all three situations.

4 a 🔊 4.8 Listen to an interview with an expert about what to do in one of the places in Exercise 1a and answer the questions.

1 Which place does he talk about?
2 Which things in Exercise 2a does he mention?

b Listen again and complete the sentences with one word.

1 First, you need warm _____.
2 You need to _____ warm.
3 You need to _____ at night.
4 You need a _____ so you can cover your head.
5 You need to _____ help.
6 Your body needs _____ to take food in.

c Work in pairs. Do you agree with the expert's advice? Why/Why not?

📱 Go to your app for more practice.

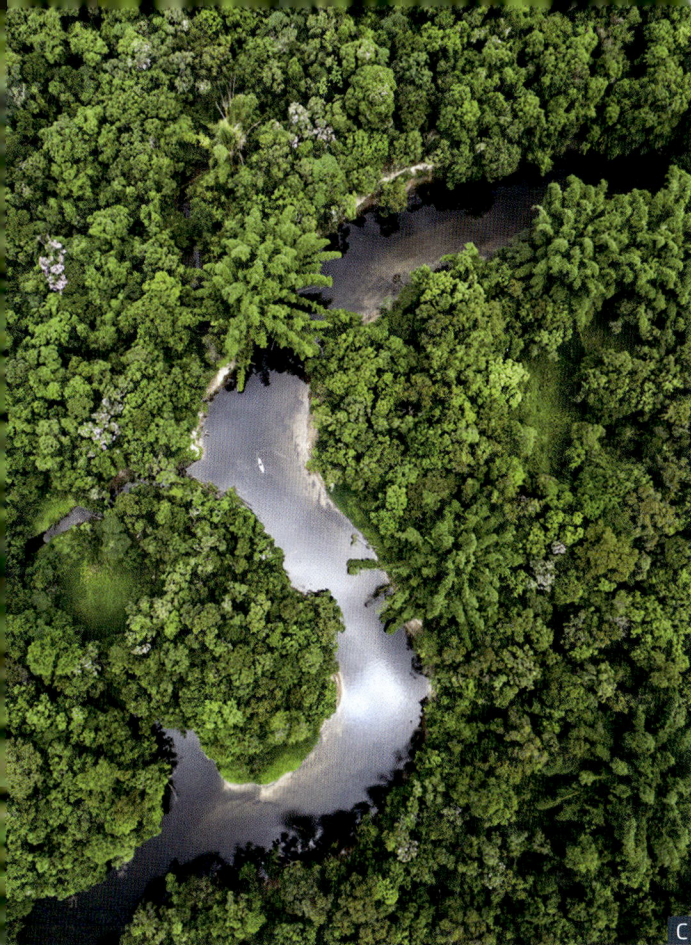

7 Complete the sentences with *need* and the words in brackets.

1 You _____ (walk) slowly in the day.
You need to walk slowly in the day.

2 I _____ (bowl).

3 She _____ (gloves) because it's cold.

4 We _____ (stay) dry.

5 You _____ (find) food.

6 They _____ (water bottle) when it's hot.

7 I don't _____ (take) a mirror.

8 They don't _____ (hats or gloves).

8 a Write two sentences for each situation, one with *need* + noun, one with *need* + infinitive, to say what you need.

1 in a city you don't know
I need a map.
I need to use public transport.

2 somewhere very hot

3 somewhere very cold

4 on an English course

5 at a job interview

6 cooking a meal for friends

b Work in pairs and compare your sentences in Exercise 8a. Are your ideas the same?

Go to page 122 or your app for more information and practice.

Grammar

5 a Read the grammar box and choose the correct alternatives.

> ### *need* + noun, *need* + infinitive with *to*
>
> Use *need* + **1***noun/infinitive* to say what objects are necessary in a situation.
> You **need gloves**. *It's cold outside.*
> We **need a knife** *in the forest.*
> Adjectives go **2***between/before* 'need' and the noun.
> I **need warm clothes** *in the desert at night.*
> You **need a big blanket** *in the desert at night.*
> Use *need* + **3***noun/infinitive with to* to say what it is necessary to do in a situation.
> You **need to stay** *out of the sun.*
> We **need to move** *at night.*
> Use *don't/doesn't need* to say what isn't necessary.
> We **don't need warm clothes**. *It's very hot there.*
> She **doesn't need to make** *a fire in the day.*

b Look at the sentences in Exercise 4b again. Is *need* followed by a noun or infinitive with *to* in each one?

6 a 4.9 Listen to the sentences. Are *to* and *a* stressed or unstressed?

1 We need to leave early.

2 I need a water bottle.

3 He needs to wear a hat in the sun.

4 You need a big knife.

5 They need to walk at night.

6 I need a blanket.

b Listen again and repeat.

Speaking

PREPARE

9 a 4.10 You're going to decide what things you need in a difficult situation. First, listen to Gavin and Kirsten deciding what they need. Which place in Exercise 1a are they talking about?

b Listen again. Which four things do they decide to take?

10 You're lost on an island. Choose five of the objects in Exercise 2a that you need and decide why. Make notes.

SPEAK

11 a Work in pairs. Say which five objects you think you need and why. Agree on five things you need together. Use the Useful phrases to help you.

> ### Useful phrases
> First, we need to (find a place to sleep). So we need …
> We can also use it to (cook with).
> How many things is that?

b Work with another pair. Decide on the five things you need.

Develop your listening
page 97

> **Goal:** ask for information

ROCK'S GYM

From £39.99 a month. Join now and get one month for free.
Sign up now!

Brightside CINEMA

What's on

Master of All

Friday 2nd	11.30	13.45	15.55	20.10
Saturday 3rd	12.15	15.30	20.10	
Sunday 4th	12.15	15.50	20.10	

THE WEYLAND HISTORY MUSEUM

Special Exhibition
MAPS OF THE WORLD

Come and learn about the history of the world with our amazing collection of maps!

Dates: 1–30 June
Open: 10–4 Tuesday to Sunday
Cost: Free

1 Look at the adverts and answer the questions.
1 What adverts can you see?
2 How much is the gym?
3 What time does the film start each evening?
4 What can you see at the museum in June?

2 a 🔊 4.16 Listen to three conversations. Match them with the adverts. What information does each person want?

b Listen again and complete the sentences.
1 Excuse me, is the museum _____ ?
2 _____ I take photos in there?
3 Is _____ a gift shop?
4 It's _____ the exit.
5 What time does the next film _____ ?
6 How much is a _____ ?
7 Where do I _____ ?
8 What time does the gym _____ tonight?
9 Are there _____ towels in the changing rooms?
10 _____ are the changing rooms?

c Look at the Useful phrases and check your answers.

Useful phrases

Asking if something is near
Is there (a gift shop) (near here)?
Are there (any towels) in (the changing rooms)?

Asking/saying where things are
Where are (the changing rooms)?
The (gift shop) is near the exit.

Asking about times
What time does the next film start?
What time does (the gym) open/close (tonight/on Sundays)?

Asking about price
Is (the museum) free?
How much is a ticket?
Where do I pay?

Asking for permission
Can I take photos in (there/the museum)?

3 a 🔊 4.17 Listen to the Useful phrases. Underline the stressed words.
Is there a <u>gift shop</u> near <u>here</u>?

b Listen again and repeat.

4 a Write the question for each answer.
1 The next train arrives in six minutes.
When does the next train arrive?
2 The ticket office is over there next to the café.
3 A ticket to London is £30.
4 Yes, there is a gym near here. It's on Wallis Street.
5 You pay at the ticket machines over there.
6 No, there aren't any cinemas in the town.
7 No, the concert isn't free. It costs £15.
8 No, you can't take food into the theatre.

b Make questions using the prompts.
1 What time / shops / open ?
2 How much / a taxi / to the airport ?
3 a swimming pool / near here ?
4 where / I / pay for / a train ticket ?
5 what time / the last bus ?
6 any parks / near here ?
7 where / the bus station ?
8 the city museum / free ?

c Work in pairs. Take turns to ask and answer the questions in Exercise 4b.

5 You're going to practise asking for information. Work in pairs. Student A: Turn to page 156. Student B: Turn to page 153. Read the information and make notes about what to say.

6 a Practise your conversations.

b Work with a different partner. Swap roles and practise the conversations again.

Go online for the Roadmap video.

Check and reflect

1 Complete the sentences with places. You have the first letter to help you.

1 At lunchtime, I sit outside in the **p**_____ and have my lunch.
2 I need some stamps from the **p**_____ **o**_____.
3 Let's go and watch a play at the **t**_____.
4 I go to the gym at the **s**_____ **c**_____ three or four times a week.
5 The next bus leaves at ten from the **b**_____ **s**_____.
6 Is the football match at the **s**_____ on Saturday?
7 There's a **p**_____ **s**_____ on the next street. The police officers there are very helpful.

2 a Complete the sentences with *is, isn't, are* or *aren't*.

1 There _____ any cinemas in my town.
2 There _____ a big park.
3 There _____ a stadium because it's only a small town.
4 There _____ some lovely clothes shops.
5 There _____ any expensive cafés.
6 There _____ some interesting museums.
7 There _____ any mobile phone shops.
8 There _____ a big post office.

b Work in pairs. Change the sentences in Exercise 2a so they are true for your town or city.

There are two cinemas in my town.
There isn't a big park but there are three small ones.

3 a Complete the sentences with one word.

1 There _____ a cinema here but there's one in the next town.
2 There _____ two big supermarkets near my house.
3 The park here is lovely. _____ are a lot of beautiful trees and flowers.
4 There aren't _____ good restaurants in this area.
5 There _____ a library here but there's a book shop.
6 It's a small town but there are _____ interesting buildings.

b Work in pairs. Talk about things in your town/city.

4 a Complete the text with *a/an, the* or no article (–).

My bedroom is my favourite room in my house. It's
¹_____ big room. On one side, there's ²_____ double bed.
On the other side, there's ³_____ sofa and
⁴_____ big TV. I sit there and watch a film on ⁵_____ TV in
⁶_____ evenings. The view from ⁷_____ window is pretty.
There's ⁸_____ park and a lot of trees. In ⁹_____ winter,
I sit at ¹⁰_____ home and look out of ¹¹_____ window. I
watch ¹²_____ people play football in the park. In ¹³_____
summer, I go to the park and sit in ¹⁴_____ sun.

b Work in pairs. Describe your favourite room in your house.

My favourite room is my bedroom. There's a small double bed.

5 Complete the sentences with the correct words.

1 We don't have a g_____e, so it's difficult to park the car sometimes.
2 The bathroom has a s_____r, but it doesn't have a b_____h.
3 I have a few big w_____s, because I have so many clothes.
4 The c_____s in my kitchen are all full.
5 The f_____e in my house is so old. I need a new sofa and a new table.
6 The c_____s in my bedroom are a horrible colour.
7 My f_____e is not cold enough. Sometimes the food goes bad quickly.

6 a Complete the sentences with the words in the box.

batteries   blanket   can   gloves   knife
sunglasses

1 Where are my _____? My hands are cold.
2 My radio is broken. Maybe it needs some new _____.
3 The sun's bright outside. You need to wear your _____.
4 I can't open this _____ of soup. Can you help me?
5 Have you got a _____? I need to cut this meat.
6 It's cold tonight. Do you want an extra _____ for your bed?

b Work in pairs. Which objects in Exercise 6a are useful for very cold places? Why?

7 Complete the sentences and questions with one word.

1 What _____ we need to buy for dinner tonight?
2 You _____ need a coat. It's warm outside.
3 I _____ some water. I'm really thirsty.
4 Rob needs _____ buy some milk at the shop.
5 Sara's car is really old. She _____ a new one.
6 Ellie _____ need a new coat. Her old one is fine.

Reflect

How confident do you feel about the statements below? Write 1–5 (1 = not very confident, 5 = very confident).

- I can talk about my city.
- I can describe my home.
- I can discuss what to take on a trip
- I can ask for information.

Want more practice?
Go to your Workbook or app.

What does he look like?

> **Goal:** describe people's appearance
> **Grammar:** position of adjectives
> **Vocabulary:** appearance

Listening and vocabulary

1 Look at the photos. What parts of the body and face can you see?

hair, ears, ...

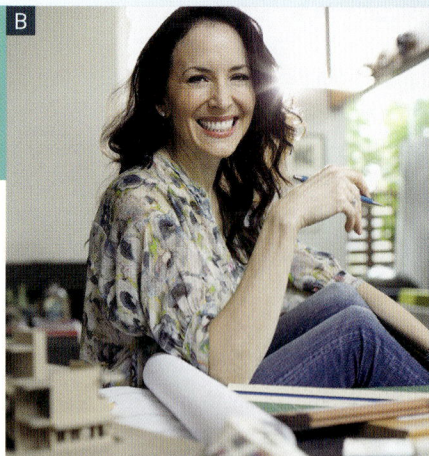

2 a Read about a podcast episode on remembering faces. How many faces does Person A need to remember?

Remembering faces

This is a famous experiment. Person A looks at photos of three people for thirty seconds. Person A then describes the people to Person B, who looks at the photos and says which people they are.

b 🔊 **5.1** Listen to Neil describing the faces below to Tina. What parts of the body does he mention?

c Listen again and complete the sentences with the parts of the body in Exercise 2b.

1 She's got long, dark _____ .
2 She's got brown _____ .
3 She's also got a thin _____ .

d Listen again and put faces A–C in the order you hear them.

3 a Look at the words in the box. Which ones can be used to describe ...

1 someone's body? *tall*
2 someone's eyes? *blue, brown*
3 someone's hair? *brown, blonde*
4 **someone's age?** *old*

black	blonde	blue	brown	dark	grey
large	long	old	short	small	tall	thin
young					

b Choose the correct alternatives.

1 She's not old, she's quite *tall/young*.
2 Her eyes aren't small, they're very *dark/big*.
3 He's not tall, he's *short/thin*.
4 She's got grey eyes and *small/long* hair.
5 His hair is blonde and his eyes are *long/blue*.
6 My hair is black but my brother's is *young/blonde*.
7 He's not *old/thin*. I think he's about 20 years old.
8 I can't remember. Are his eyes blue or *big/grey*?

c Work in pairs. Think about someone you know. Which adjectives in Exercise 3a can you use to describe them?

My brother – tall, thin, black hair ...

📱 Go to your app for more practice.

5 a 🔊 **5.2 Listen to the sentences. Are the adjectives stressed?**

1 He's got blue eyes.
2 My brother's very tall.
3 She's got long hair.
4 Sally's quite young.
5 Kevin's got blonde hair.

b Listen again and repeat.

6 Put the words in the correct order to make sentences.

1 young / looks / He
He looks young.
2 is / Your / tall / dad
3 hair / Shannon / short / has / got
4 short / He's / boy / a
5 got / dark / She's / hair
6 He's / a / short / got / nose
7 eyes / got / Clara's / brown / big
8 mum / has / hair / blonde / got / My / long

7 a Look at photos A–K. Which adjectives can you use to describe them? Make notes.

b Work in pairs. Choose one of the people in the photos but don't tell your partner who it is. Take turns to describe their appearance and guess who your partner is describing.

A: She's young. She's got long, dark hair.
B: Is it photo I?

📱 Go to page 124 or your app for more information and practice.

Speaking

PREPARE

8 You're going to try the experiment describing faces. Work in pairs and turn to page 155. Look at the people's faces for thirty seconds. Try to remember what they look like. Make notes if you want to.

SPEAK

9 a Student A: Close your book. Describe the people in your photos to your partner. Use the Useful phrases to help you. Student B: Look at your partner's photos and write the order they describe them.

> **Useful phrases**
> What does he/she look like?
> The first photo is a man/woman.
> Maybe she's quite young.
> He looks about thirty years old.

b Swap roles and repeat.

c Look at the photos together. Did you get the order right?

Grammar

4 Read the grammar box and choose the correct alternatives. Use the sentences in Exercises 2c and 3b to help you.

> ### Position of adjectives
>
> Use adjectives [1]*before/after* a noun.
> *He's a **young** man.*
> *She's got **long** hair.*
> Use adjectives [2]*before/after* the verbs *be* or *look*.
> *He's tall and thin.*
> *She **looks** young.*
> Use the words *quite* and *very* before the adjective to make the adjectives weak or strong.
> *She's **quite** young.*
> *He's **very** tall.*
> To ask about someone's appearance, use [3]*be like/look like*.
> *A: What does your brother **look like**?*
> *B: He's tall. He has grey hair and blue eyes.*

Develop your writing
page 98

5B How was it?

> **Goal:** describe an experience
> **Grammar:** was/were
> **Vocabulary:** adjectives to describe experiences

Vocabulary

1 a Match the activities in the box with photos A–D.

> go to the cinema   go on holiday   go to a party
> go to a restaurant

b Work in pairs and answer the questions.
   1 Do you often do these things in your free time?
   2 What other places do you go to in your free time?

2 Match the groups of words with the activities in Exercise 1a.
   1 actors/film/story *go to the cinema*
   2 music/people/location
   3 food/staff/menu
   4 hotel/beach/food

3 a 5.3 Listen to four conversations about experiences. For each one, answer the questions.
   1 Which place/experience are they talking about?
   2 Which words in Exercise 2 do they use?
   3 Which things do they like and dislike about their experience?

b Listen to the conversations again. Tick the adjectives in the box that you hear.

> amazing   awful   boring   brilliant   cool
> excellent   exciting   great   horrible   interesting
> lovely   nice   OK   perfect   terrible

c Work in pairs. Decide which of the words are positive and which are negative. Which word is not positive or negative?

d 5.4 Listen to the words and repeat.

4 Choose the correct alternatives.
   1 The hotel is *lovely/terrible*, and the sea is perfect.
   2 It's a *terrible/great* film. Don't watch it!
   3 The staff in the hotel are *excellent/horrible*. They always help me when I need something.
   4 The actors are great, but the story is *boring/exciting*.
   5 People say that restaurant is bad but I think it's *OK/boring*.
   6 This party is amazing! There are lots of *cool/terrible* people here.
   7 The staff are really nice there and the food is *perfect/awful*.
   8 The film isn't great. It's not very *exciting/awful*.

5 Complete the sentences with your own ideas.
   1 _____ is a brilliant film.
   2 I think _____ food is amazing.
   3 _____ is a terrible film.
   4 _____ is a nice country to visit for a holiday.
   5 In my favourite restaurant, the _____ is/are lovely.
   6 _____ is a really cool person.
   7 I never eat _____ . It's horrible.
   8 I love hotels with excellent _____ .

Go to page 140 or your app for more vocabulary and practice.

Listening

6 a 🔊 **5.5** Work in pairs. Listen to someone describing an experience and answer the questions.

1 What type of experience is it? (going to a restaurant, going to the cinema, etc.)
2 Is it a positive or negative experience?
3 How do you know?

b Listen again and tick the sentences you hear.

1 How was the party? ✓
2 How is the party?
3 It was great.
4 It was terrible.
5 How many people are there?
6 How many people were there?
7 It was a really good night.
8 It was a fantastic night.

Grammar

7 Read the grammar box and choose the correct alternatives.

was/were

The past simple of *be* is *was/were*.
The party **was** *great*.
The people **were** *lovely*.
Use ¹*was/were* (+) and ²*wasn't/weren't* (-) with *I/he/she/it*.
It **was** *a fantastic night*.
He **wasn't** *nice*.
Use ³*was/were* (+) and ⁴*wasn't/weren't* (-) with *you/we/they*.
I liked the actors. They **were** *excellent*.
The restaurants near the hotel **weren't** *very good*.
In questions the verb comes before the subject.
Was the food *good?*
Were the staff *nice?*
Use *was/were* to give short answers.
Was it good?
Yes, it was./No, it wasn't.
Were they interesting?
Yes, they were./No, they weren't.
Put *was/were* after a *Wh-* question word.
Why was *it terrible?*
How many *people* **were** *there?*

8 a 🔊 **5.6** Listen to the sentences. Are *was* and *were* usually stressed?

1 The food was nice and the people were great.
2 How was the beach?
3 The food wasn't great.
4 Were the people nice?

b Listen again and repeat.

9 Complete the sentences with *was(n't)* or *were(n't)*.

1 The party _____ awful. It was really boring.
2 The food _____ good but the music was nice.
3 The beaches _____ fantastic. They _____ so clean.
4 I wasn't happy because the music _____ awful.
5 The actors _____ great but the story was excellent.
6 The film was great, and the cinema _____ lovely.
7 _____ the restaurants good?
8 How many people _____ at the party?

10 a Think about the last time you went to a hotel and complete the sentences below.

1 The food _____ .
2 The people _____ .
3 The location _____ .
4 The pool _____ .
5 The room _____ .

b Work in pairs. Talk about your last hotel experience. Were they both good experiences?

📱 Go to page 124 or your app for more information and practice.

Speaking

PREPARE

11 a You're going to talk about a good or bad experience. Choose one of the topics below.

- going on holiday
- seeing a film at the cinema
- going to a party
- going to a restaurant

b Make notes about the experience. What was good or bad about it?

Food – amazing
Music – awful

SPEAK

12 a Work in pairs. Talk about your experience, and ask your partner about his/her experience. Use the Useful phrases to help you.

A: How was the food?
B: It was great. The salad was lovely!

Useful phrases

So, I was at (The Roxy Cinema/The Plaza Hotel) last week.
(The weather) was really nice but (the food) was awful.
Oh no!
That's great!

b Report back to the class. Was anyone's experience really good? Was anyone's experience really bad?

Develop your listening
page 99

5c ▷ You can do it!

▷ **Goal:** describe your skills
▷ **Grammar:** *can/can't* for ability
▷ **Vocabulary:** skills

Reading

1 Work in pairs. Tell your partner what you're good at/ not good at. Use the photos and the words in the box to help you.

> cooking   driving   playing the guitar   singing
> swimming   tennis

> *I'm good at tennis.*
> *I'm not good at singing.*

2 a Read about people's special skills. Who talks about …
   1 making something?
   2 doing something with their body?
   3 language?

> I can't really cook but I can bake very well. What can I bake? Lovely chocolate cakes. I always make one for my parents on their birthdays. – **Emi**

> I can draw people. I'm not a fantastic artist but I love drawing. My pictures aren't bad. – **Josh**

> I can spell the word 'Mediterranean'. I think that's special. My friends can't do it! Can you do it? – **Alice**

> I can keep a ball in the air with my feet for an hour but I don't do it often. It's boring after ten minutes! – **Robert**

> I can't do anything special. Oh! I can walk on my hands. Is that special? I don't think it is. Can other people do it? – **Rosie**

> I can speak two languages: English and Hindi but I can't write in Hindi. I can only speak it. My brother can do both but I can't. – **Ravi**

b Read the comments again. Are the sentences true (T) or false (F)?
   1 Emi makes cakes for people in her family.
   2 Josh thinks his pictures are very good.
   3 Alice's friends know the spelling of 'Mediterranean'.
   4 Robert often practises his skill.
   5 Rosie doesn't think her skill is important.
   6 Ravi speaks only one language.

c Work in pairs and discuss the question. Which skills in the article would you like to do?
> *I'd like to walk on my hands!*

Grammar

3 Read the grammar box and choose the correct alternatives.

can/can't for ability

Use [1]*can/can't* + infinitive to talk about skills you have.
*I **can speak** two languages.*
*My brother **can write** in English and Hindi.*
Use [2]*can/can't* + infinitive to talk about skills you don't have.
*I **can't write** in Hindi.*
*My friends **can't do** that.*
Use *can* + infinitive + *(really/very) well* to talk about [3]*strong/weak* skills.
*My brother **can speak** Italian **really well**.*
Use *can't* + infinitive + *(very) well* to talk about [4]*strong/weak* skills.
*I **can't cook very well**.*
Can and the [5]*subject/object* change position to make a question.
***Can** you **spell** 'Mediterranean'? (Yes, I **can**./No, I **can't**.)*
*What **can** I **bake**? (Lovely chocolate cakes.)*

4 a 🔊 5.12 Listen to the sentences. Is *can* stressed? Is *can't* stressed?
   1 I can ride a motorbike but I can't drive a car.
   2 Alex can play the piano very well but he can't sing.

b 🔊 5.13 Listen and choose the correct alternatives.
   1 I *can/can't* speak three languages.
   2 Matt *can/can't* play the guitar.
   3 She *can/can't* run very fast.
   4 *Can/Can't* you make chocolate cake?
   5 They *can/can't* swim very well.

c Listen again and repeat.

8 a Choose one skill in Exercise 7a. Find out how many students in the class have that skill. Ask for more information. Write down the answers.

> *A:* Can you play a musical instrument?
> *B:* Yes, I can.
> *A:* What instrument can you play?

b Report back to the class.

Go to your app for more practice.

Speaking

PREPARE

9 a You're going to talk about your skills for World Skills Day. First, read the local newspaper advertisement below. What does the newspaper want you to do?

WORLD SKILLS DAY COMPETITION

It's World Skills Day next week!
What things can you do? They can be special, different, funny or everyday skills. Write and tell us. There's £100 for the best ones!

b 5.15 Listen to Maria, Richie and Lizzie talking about their skills. What skills do they have? Which two skills do they want to tell the newspaper about?

10 Choose three to five skills you have. What can you say about them? Make notes.

SPEAK

11 a Work in groups. Tell each other about your skills. What are the best skills to tell the newspaper about? Choose three from your group.

> **Useful phrases**
> What can you do?
> I can (play chess) well.
> I can do that, too.
> Wow! I can't do that.

b Tell the class which three skills you chose. Decide which skill in the class is the best and why.

Develop your reading page 100

5 Make sentences using the prompts. Add *can* or *can't*.

1 I / run / very fast (-)
I can't run very fast.
2 Leon / make / wonderful pizzas (+)
3 They / sing / really well (+)
4 you / play tennis (?)
5 Billy / play / the violin (?)
6 we / speak Spanish / very well (-)

6 a Complete the sentences with *can* or *can't* so they are true for you.

1 I _____ play the guitar.
2 I _____ drive a car.
3 I _____ sing.
4 I _____ run fast.
5 I _____ paint.
6 I _____ speak another language well.

b Work in pairs and compare your sentences in Exercise 6a. Do you have the same skills?

Go to page 124 or your app for more information and practice.

Vocabulary

7 a Complete skills 1–12 with a verb in the box.

> bake   climb   cook   count   drive   fix   make
> play (x2)   run   speak   spell

1 _____ a car
2 _____ a tree
3 _____ a cake
4 _____ to 50 in French
5 _____ the word 'Mediterranean'
6 _____ a meal
7 _____ a computer
8 _____ a musical instrument
9 _____ five kilometres
10 _____ pizza
11 _____ chess
12 _____ another language

b 5.14 Listen and check. Then listen and repeat.

c Work in pairs. Ask and answer questions about the skills in Exercise 7a with *Can you ...?*

> *A:* Can you drive a car?
> *B:* No, I can't.

> **Goal:** make and respond to requests

1 Look at the picture and discuss what you think the people are saying.

2 a 🔊 5.16 Listen to conversations 1–4. Which conversation matches the picture?

b Listen again and answer the questions for each conversation.
1 What does each person ask for?
2 Does the other person say yes or no?
3 Tick the phrases you hear in the Useful phrases box.

3 a 🔊 5.17 Listen to the Useful phrases. Underline the stressed words.

Useful phrases

Making requests
Can/Could you help me with (the washing up), please?
Can/Could I borrow (your charger)?
Can/Could you lend me (a pen)?
Can/Could you (move your bag)?

Accepting requests
Sure, no problem.
Of course you/I can.

Rejecting requests
I can't, (I'm) sorry.
I'm sorry, I need it.
I'm afraid not.

b Listen again and repeat.

4 a Complete the conversations.
1 **A:** Excuse me, can you open that window?
   B: Sure, _____ problem.
2 **A:** Can I _____ five pounds, please?
   B: I'm afraid _____ . I don't have any money with me.
3 **A:** Could you _____ me your phone?
   B: I'm sorry, I _____ it. I'm waiting for a call.
4 **A:** Excuse me, can _____ open that door for me?
   B: _____ , no problem. Here you are.
5 **A:** Can you _____ me with something?
   B: What's that?
   A: Can you help me move this cupboard? It's so heavy.
   B: Of _____ I can. Just give me a minute.

b 🔊 5.18 Listen and check.

c Work in pairs and practise the conversations.

5 a Work in pairs. Read the information on your card below and think about what to say. Make notes. Use the Useful phrases to help you.

Student A
1 Your neighbour is having a party and it's late. Ask them to be quiet.
2 Your friend wants help with the washing up. Say no.
3 You want to borrow your friend's phone because you don't have yours. Ask them if you can.
4 Your friend wants to borrow some money. Accept.

Student B
1 You're having a party when your neighbour asks you to be quiet. Accept.
2 You want your friend to help you with the washing up.
3 Your friend asks to borrow your phone. Accept.
4 You need to borrow some money until next week. Ask your friend.

b Practise your conversations.

c Swap roles and repeat.

Go online for the Roadmap video.

Check and reflect

1 a Choose the correct alternatives.

1 My grandmother's an old woman but she looks *young/short*.
2 My brother's got a *long/tall*, thin face.
3 I have *short/tall*, dark hair.
4 My sister is very *short/long*.
5 My boyfriend thinks he's *long/tall* but I think he's average-height.
6 What does your sister *look/look like*?

b Work in pairs. Which of the sentences in Exercise 1a are true for you? Change the others so they're true.

2 Complete the sentences with *was(n't)* or *were(n't)*.

1 I _____ happy yesterday, but today I am.
2 We _____ in Mexico for our holiday last summer, it was great.
3 _____ you at home last night?
4 They _____ at the office yesterday because they _____ at a conference.
5 The teacher _____ here yesterday because she _____ on holiday.

3 a Make questions using the prompts. Add *was* or *were*.

1 Where / you / born?
2 you / always happy / when you / a child?
3 What / your favourite subject / school?
4 What / your favourite food / when you / a child?
5 your teachers / polite / school?
6 your dad / good cook / when you / a child?

b Work in pairs. Ask and answer the questions.

4 Complete the text with the adjectives in the box.

boring   clever   friendly   funny   kind   lazy
quiet

I have a big family, and everyone's very different. My dad thinks he's very **1**_____, but only he laughs. Really his jokes are old and **2**_____ – nobody laughs! My mum's very **3**_____. She loves talking to new people and has lots of friends. My older sister Diyah is at university doing a PhD. She's very **4**_____ and always was. My other sister Lia is the opposite. She never does any work and often just sits around. She's very **5**_____. What about me? I'm **6**_____ because I don't say much but I try to be **7**_____ and help other people when they need it.

5 Correct the mistakes in six of the sentences.

1 She can't to drive a car.
2 He cans play piano.
3 They can speak three languages.
4 Do you can bake a cake?
5 I can't playing chess.
6 You can fix a flat tyre?
7 Can you count to ten in Indonesian?
8 We can all to climb a tree.

6 a Think of three members of your family. Choose an adjective to describe each one and write a sentence to say why they're like this.
My brother. Lazy. He always sits on the sofa.

b Work in pairs. Tell your partner your sentences. Guess the adjective.
A: *My brother always sits on the sofa.*
B: *Lazy?*
A: *Yes!*

7 a Complete the questions with the verbs in the box.

bake   cook   drive   fix   play (x2)   speak   spell

1 Can you _____ a flat tyre?
2 Do you _____ another language?
3 How often do you _____ a cake?
4 What words can't you _____ in English?
5 Do you know how to _____ chess?
6 Can you _____ a car?
7 How often do you _____ a meal for someone else?
8 Can you _____ a musical instrument?

b Work in pairs. Ask and answer the questions in Exercise 7a.

8 a Write sentences about yourself using *can* or *can't* and the words and phrases in the box.

cook a meal   draw   drive a car
play a musical instrument   play chess   run 1 km
sing   speak another language   swim

I can cook.
I can't drive a car.

b Work in pairs and compare your sentences. Ask questions to find out more information.
A: *I can cook.*
B: *What's your favourite dish?*
A: *I like sushi. I love Japanese food.*

Reflect

How confident do you feel about the statements below? Write 1–5 (1 = not very confident, 5 = very confident).

- I can describe people's appearance.
- I can describe an experience.
- I can describe my skills.
- I can make and respond to requests.

Want more practice?
Go to your Workbook or app.

6A Events

> **Goal:** describe an event
> **Grammar:** past simple (regular verbs)
> **Vocabulary:** prepositions

Vocabulary

1 **Look at the leaflet and discuss the questions.**

　1 What can you see in the photos?

　2 Would you like to go to an event like this? Why/Why not?

2 a **Read some information about the festival and match sentences 1–4 with photos A–D.**

　1 The camping area is near the main festival stage, so it's easy to find at night. *C*

　2 The children's play area is next to the camping area. In this area, there are lots of activities for kids.

　3 Inside the food tent, you can find food from all over the world. We also have cooking classes all weekend! You can find the timetable for these classes on the noticeboard outside the tent.

　4 On Saturday, there will be music from pop group 'The Dream' at 5 p.m. and singer Mano Chu at 8 p.m. On Sunday, local pop group 'Dead Fingers' and hip-hop group 'Raspberry' will play in the afternoon.

b **Read the sentences in Exercise 2a again and correct the mistakes in the sentences.**

　1 The camping area is near the food tent.
　　The camping area is near the main festival stage.

　2 The camping area is easy to find in the morning.

　3 The children's play area is next to the main festival stage.

　4 You can find the timetable for cooking classes inside the food tent.

　5 On Saturday, there will be music from pop group 'Dead Fingers'.

　6 'Raspberry' will play in the morning.

c **Complete the phrases with the prepositions in the box.**

| at | in (x2) | inside | near | next to | on | outside |

　1 *inside / outside / in* the tent / the building / the shopping centre

　2 _____ the evening / June / the food tent / the afternoon / London / 2019

　3 _____ 10 p.m. / night / my friend's house / the weekend / the cinema / the entrance

　4 _____ / _____ my house / me / the city centre / the train station / where I work

　5 _____ Saturday / the floor / the music stage / the first day / Thursday evening

Come to this year's …

Summer Festival

Friday 10th — Sunday 12th June

A three-day festival for all the family!
See some amazing artists on our Live music stage.
Bring the kids to the Children's Magic Castle and 'Fun Zone' children's play area!
Stay the night in our beautiful camping area.
Visit the art area and get creative!
Try food from all over the world in our food tent.

3 a **Complete the sentences with your own ideas.**

　1 I like to meet my friends at *the cinema / a coffee shop*.

　2 I like to study in/at _____ (morning, night etc).

　3 I don't work on _____ (day of the week).

　4 I live near _____ (place).

　5 I wake up at _____ (time).

　6 My school/office is next to _____ (place).

b **Work in pairs and compare your sentences. Are your sentences the same?**

📱 Go to your app for more practice.

Listening

4 a 🔊 **6.1** Listen to Steve talking about the festival. Which places in the festival did he and his family go to?

b Listen again and choose the correct alternatives.
1 It *started/finished* on Friday night.
2 We *arrived/played* on Saturday morning.
3 We *stayed/studied* in a big tent together.
4 Someone *watched/painted* our faces.
5 Then we *tried/played* something different.
6 Our boy Ryan *liked/didn't like* it. He *laughed/cried* the whole time!

Grammar

5 Read the grammar box and choose the correct alternatives.

Past simple (regular verbs)

Use the past simple to talk about [1]*finished/unfinished* actions in the past.
*We **stayed** in a big tent.*
*Someone **painted** our faces.*
Form the past simple of regular verbs with [2]*-ed/-id* or *-d*.
*It **started** on Friday night.*
*We all **danced** – even me!*
For regular verbs that end in consonant + *y*, delete the *y* and add [3]*-id/-ied*.
*We **tried** something different.*
*He **cried** the whole time!*
Form the negative with *didn't +* [4]*infinitive/past simple*.
*I **didn't want** to do it.*
*Ryan **didn't like** it.*

6 a 🔊 **6.2** Listen to the past simple verbs and write the number of syllables you hear.

1 danced *One*   5 ended
2 arrived *Two*   6 watched
3 played   7 listened
4 studied   8 started

b Listen again and repeat.

7 Complete the sentences with the verbs in the box in the past simple.

cry   not arrive   not laugh   play   start   stay watch

1 I _____ a good film on TV last night.
2 James _____ football all weekend. He's tired today!
3 The comedy was really boring. I _____ at all.
4 The festival _____ on Saturday but we _____ until Sunday.
5 Anna _____ when she heard the bad news.
6 He _____ at his friend's house when he was in Edinburgh.

8 a Complete the sentences so they are true for you. Use the verbs from the lesson.
1 Last summer I _____.
2 When I was a child I didn't _____.
3 Last week I _____.
4 Last night I didn't _____.
5 A few years ago I _____.
6 Last weekend I didn't _____.

b Work in pairs and compare your sentences. Are any the same?

📱 Go to page 126 or your app for more information and practice.

Speaking

PREPARE

9 a You're going to describe an event you went to in the past. First, choose the type of event. Use the ideas in the box to help you.

a concert   a conference   a festival   a party a sports event

b Plan what you're going to say about it. Make notes about:
- where it was
- when it was
- who you were with
- what you did there
- what activities there were to do
- what you liked/disliked about it

SPEAK

10 a Work in pairs and describe your event to your partner using your notes in Exercise 9. Then, choose the most interesting event.

b Report back to the class. Describe the event you chose in Exercise 10a. Who in the class went to the most interesting event?

Develop your reading
page 101

6B A good weekend

> **Goal:** describe a good weekend
> **Grammar:** past simple (irregular verbs)
> **Vocabulary:** irregular verbs

Listening and vocabulary

1 Work in pairs. Look at the photos of people enjoying a good weekend and answer the questions.

1 Where are they?
2 What are they doing?
3 Would you like a weekend like this?

2 a 🔊 6.3 Listen to three people describing their weekends. Match the speakers with the descriptions in A–C.

A
On the morning of my birthday, my husband just **1**_____ for work and didn't say anything. But then he **2**_____ my suitcase to work at the end of the day and surprised me with a trip to Paris! We walked around the city and he **3**_____ me a beautiful scarf.

B
My wife and I **4**_____ really early and **5**_____ to Monterey Bay to go to the beach. We **6**_____ on the beach and then we **7**_____ some whales! We watched them for an hour.

C
Last summer my girlfriend finished our relationship. I **8**_____ really sad. My friends **9**_____ me to a music festival to make me feel better. We **10**_____ to a show one night where the band was amazing. At the end the singer **11**_____ her sunglasses into the audience and I **12**_____ them!

b Listen again and complete the summaries with the verbs in the box.

bought	brought	caught	drove	felt	left
sat	saw	threw	took	went	woke up

3 a Match verbs 1–12 with their irregular past forms in Exercise 2b.

1 take *took*	**5** go	**9** see
2 buy	**6** feel	**10** throw
3 leave	**7** sit	**11** drive
4 bring	**8** catch	**12** wake up

b Work in pairs. Which weekend do you think was the most special? Why?

4 a Match the sentence halves. Then complete the sentences with the past simple form of the verbs in brackets.

1 Last weekend, I _____ (go) ...
2 I _____ (feel) ...
3 Last week, I _____ (see) ...
4 When I was a child, I _____ (buy) ...
5 Today, I _____ (wake up) ...
6 Last month, I _____ (leave) ...

a chocolate and sweets all the time.
b to a concert with my friends.
c my job.
d early.
e very happy yesterday.
f a great film.

b Complete the first half of the sentences in Exercise 4a so they are true for you.

Last weekend, I went shopping with my girlfriend.

c Work in pairs and compare your sentences. Are any the same?

📱 Go to your app for more practice.

Grammar

5 Read the grammar box and choose the correct alternatives.

Past simple (irregular verbs)

Irregular verbs in the past simple **1** *finish / don't finish* with *-ed*.

I **had** dinner at 7 o'clock. NOT ~~I haved dinner at 7 o'clock.~~

I **woke up** early. NOT ~~I waked up early.~~

Form the negative **2** *in the same way as / differently from* regular verbs, i.e. *didn't* + infinitive.

I **didn't go** to work that day.

I **didn't feel** well last week.

6 a 🔊 6.4 **Listen and notice the pronunciation of the irregular past verbs.**

1 Last week I **bought** a new jacket.
2 I **caught** the bus at 5 p.m.
3 I **woke up** very late today.
4 I **felt** angry when he said that.
5 I **went** to her house.
6 She **left** home when she was 16.
7 I **brought** her a lovely cake.
8 I **drove** all night.

b Listen again and put the verbs in bold in sentences 1–5 in Exercise 6a in the table with verbs that have the same vowel sound.

left	brought	drove
1_____	3_____	5_____
2_____	4_____	

c 🔊 6.5 **Listen, check your answers and repeat.**

7 a Change the sentences from positive to negative, or negative to positive.

1 I left work very late last night.
   I didn't leave work very late last night.
2 I made dinner last night.
3 I didn't buy clothes last month.
4 I didn't feel happy yesterday.
5 I went to a restaurant last weekend.
6 I caught the bus to work yesterday. I didn't drive.
7 I woke up early today.
8 I saw an old friend last month.

b Work in pairs. Which of the sentences are true for you? Give more information.

Last night, I didn't leave work very late. I left at 5 o'clock

📱 Go to page 126 or your app for more information and practice.

Speaking

PREPARE

8 a 🔊 6.6 **You're going to describe a good weekend. First, listen to Tom describing part of his weekend and answer the questions.**

1 Where did he go?
2 Who did he meet there?

b Listen again and tick the things Tom describes.

- the weather
- where he went
- the clothes he wore
- who he went with
- what he did
- what he didn't do
- people he met

9 Think about a good weekend you had. Make notes. Use the ideas in Exercise 8b to help you.

SPEAK

10 a Work in pairs. Describe your special weekends.

b Report back to the class. Share two interesting things your partner told you about their weekend.

Develop your listening
page 102

6c A different world

> **Goal:** ask and answer questions
> **Grammar:** past simple (questions)
> **Vocabulary:** verbs + prepositions

Listening and vocabulary

1 a Look at the photos and the factfile. Match facts 1–5 with photos A–E. What do you know about life in your country in the 1960s?

Did you know? LIFE IN THE UK IN 1960

1 People paid just £1.30 for a music album.

2 Café culture was important for young people. Italian coffee shops became popular in the 1950s.

3 There were just two national TV channels – the BBC and ITV.

4 People went to dance halls in their lunch hour to dance. Yes, their lunch hour!

5 Young people on scooters were often called 'Mods' (short for *modernists*).

b Work in pairs and look at the photos. How was life in the 1960s different to life today? How was it the same?

2 a 🔊 6.10 Listen to Mara talking to her grandma Val. Which four things in the box does she talk about?

> clothes   free time   home   parents' work
> a Saturday job   school life

b Listen again. What does Val say about the four things in Exercise 2a?

c Listen again and choose the correct alternatives.
1 I **lived** *to/with* my parents, aunt, uncle and cousin.
2 My parents and I **moved** *at/to* our own house when I was fifteen
3 I **talked** *for/to* them nearly every day.
4 I **went** *at/to* a girls' school.
5 I **worked** *as/for* a babysitter.
6 I **walked** a mile *for/to* their house.
7 I **met up** *of/with* friends.
8 We **listened** *at/to* records.
9 We **travelled** *at/to* a dance hall.
10 We **danced** *from/with* the boys there.

3 a Complete the sentences so they are true about your life when you were young.
1 When I was young, I lived with _____ .
2 I moved to _____ when I was _____ years old.
3 I often talked to _____ .
4 I went to _____ (school).
5 I met up with _____ at the weekends.
6 I usually listened to _____ .
7 I sometimes travelled to _____ .
8 I often walked to _____ .
9 I worked as _____ .
10 I danced with _____ .

b Work in pairs and compare your sentences. Give more information.

When I was young, I lived with my parents and brother in a small town in Sicily.

c Think about teenagers in your country in the early 1960s. Do you think they did the same things as Val?

📱 Go to page 141 or your app for more vocabulary and practice.

Grammar

4 a Match questions 1–6 with answers a–f.

1 Where did you live when you were my age?
2 Why didn't they buy a house together?
3 Did you like your school?
4 Did the teachers give you a lot of homework?
5 Who did you look after?
6 What did you listen to?

a A ten-year-old boy and an eight-year-old girl.
b Because they didn't have a lot of money and houses were expensive.
c No, they didn't. We had some but not a lot.
d Yes, I did. I went to a girls' school.
e In Leeds.
f Rock and roll mostly.

b Read the grammar box and choose the correct alternatives.

Past simple (questions)

Use ¹*did/do* and the ²*past form/infinitive* to make past simple questions.

Yes/No questions

Did	Subject	infinitive + other information	Short answers	
Did	you	like your school?	Yes, I	³*did/didn't.*
Did	the teachers	give you a lot of homework?	No, they	⁴*did/didn't.*

Wh- questions

Question word	did	subject	infinitive + other information
Why	did	they	buy a house together?
Who	did	you	look after?

c Add the questions to the tables in the grammar box.

- Did he dance well?
- What did you do in your free time?
- Did they listen to records?
- Who did she live with?

5 a 🔊 6.11 Listen to the questions. What is the pronunciation of *did you?*

1 Did you watch TV last night?
2 Where did you go yesterday?
3 Which school did you go to?
4 Did you talk to Molly last week?
5 What did you do this morning?

b Listen again and repeat.

6 a Make questions about life when you were younger using the prompts and the past simple.

1 you / live in a flat?
Did you live in a flat?
2 Where / you / go to school?
3 Who / you / spend most of your time with?
4 What / you and your friends do in your free time?
5 you / listen to music?
6 What kind of films / you / watch?
7 you / do any sport?
8 What places / you / travel to?

b Work in pairs. What other questions can you ask after each question in Exercise 6a?
Did you live in a flat?
Who did you live with?

c Work with a new partner. Take turns to ask and answer the questions in Exercise 6a. Ask for more information using your questions in Exercise 6b.

📱 Go to page 126 or your app for more information and practice.

Speaking

PREPARE

7 You're going to talk about life in the 1980s and 1990s. First, think about how life was different then. Make notes. Use the ideas in the list to help you.

- clothes
- entertainment
- food
- family life
- free time
- technology

8 Work in pairs. Student A: Turn to page 153. Student B: Turn to page 158. Follow the instructions.

SPEAK

9 a Student A: Ask Student B your questions about the 1980s. Student B: Ask Student A your questions about the 1990s.

b Work in pairs. Think about life in your country in the 1980s and 1990s. How do you think it was similar or different to life in the UK?

Develop your writing
page 103

English in action

> **Goal:** give and accept an apology

1 **Look at the cartoon and discuss the questions.**

1 Where are the people?

2 What do you think they are saying to each other?

2 a 🔊 **6.12** **Listen to five conversations. Why does each person say sorry? Match conversations 1–5 with reasons a–e.**

a He took another person's thing.

b She was late.

c He is busy.

d He didn't do something.

e She needs the seat.

b **Listen again and complete the conversations with the words in the box.**

afraid	can't	problem	so sorry	worries

1 **A:** Excuse me, can I sit here?

  B: Sorry. My friend's sitting there.

  A: No _____ .

2 **A:** I'm sorry I'm late. The bus didn't come.

  B: No _____ . You're here now.

3 **A:** Excuse me, I think that's my pen.

  B: Oh, I'm _____ . I thought it was mine.

  A: That's OK.

4 **A:** I'm _____ that I didn't do the homework. Sorry!

  B: That's fine. I know you were busy.

5 **A:** Dan, can you help me with this report?

  B: I'm sorry, I _____ . I've got a meeting now.

  A: That's all right. Can you help me later?

  B: Yeah, sure!

3 a **Which phrases in Exercise 2b say sorry? Which phrases give a reply?**

b **Use the Useful phrases box to check your answers.**

Useful phrases

Saying sorry

Sorry.

I'm (really/so) sorry.

I'm sorry (that) (I'm late).

I'm afraid (that) (I didn't do my homework).

I'm sorry, I can't. I'm (busy/tired).

Replying to an apology

That's all right.

That's fine.

That's OK.

No problem.

No worries.

4 a 🔊 **6.13** **Listen to four apologies. Which are good apologies? Which are not? Why not?**

b 🔊 **6.14** **Listen and repeat the apologies. Copy the intonation.**

5 a **Make five conversations using the prompts.**

1 **A:** Let's go for a coffee.

  B: sorry / can't / busy

    I'm sorry, I can't. I'm busy.

  A: OK *That's OK.*

2 **A:** sorry / we / late. / roads / busy

  B: problem. / here now

3 **A:** Ouch. You hit me!

  B: really sorry. / not see you.

4 **A:** can / use your pen?

  B: sorry. / need it

  A: worries. / can / use Sally's.

5 **A:** afraid / not / finish the report

  B: fine. can / finish it tomorrow?

b 🔊 **6.15** **Listen and check your answers.**

c **Work in pairs. Practise having the conversations in Exercise 5a.**

6 **Work in pairs. Student A: Turn to page 155. Student B: Turn to page 157. Read the information and plan what to say.**

7 a **Work in pairs. Practise your conversations.**

b **Swap roles and practise the conversations again.**

Go online for the Roadmap video.

Check and reflect

1 a Complete the sentences with the past simple form of the verbs in brackets.

1 I _____ (dance) at a club last year.
2 I _____ (not/do) any sport last month.
3 My friends and I _____ (study) English last weekend.
4 I _____ (not/listen) to the radio this morning.
5 I _____ (not/watch) anything good on TV last night.
6 My first English course _____ (start) five years ago.
7 I _____ (not/arrive) at this lesson late.
8 Somebody _____ (call) me on my phone this morning.

b Work in pairs. Say if the sentences in Exercise 1a are true for you.

1 is false. I didn't dance at a club last year. I don't go to clubs.

2 a Choose the correct alternatives.

1 There's a table *between/under* the sofa and the chair.
2 There's a magazine *inside/on* the table.
3 *Next to/Between* the magazine, there's a coffee cup.
4 There's a box *outside/under* the table.
5 My cat's *above/inside* the box. She often sleeps there.
6 *On/Outside* the house, there's a large garden.

b Work in pairs. Tell each other where things are in your living room. Do you have similar rooms?

3 Complete the sentences with the past simple form of the verbs in the box.

buy   drive   feel   go   throw   see
sit   wake up

1 Nikki _____ a new car last weekend.
2 We _____ to a fantastic lake in the mountains.
3 I _____ the ball for my dog, but she wasn't interested.
4 Fumi always _____ to bed late when she was at university.
5 I was at work when I _____ my wife for the first time.
6 Sorry I'm late. I _____ in traffic for two hours this morning.
7 My mother always _____ sad when she was a child.
8 I _____ late and had to run to the station.

4 a Choose the correct alternatives.

1 I work *as/for* a shop assistant at a supermarket.
2 I walk *for/to* work most days.
3 I sometimes travel *for/to* my English lessons by bus.
4 I live *about/with* my family.
5 I meet up *from/with* my friends at the weekends.
6 My brother moved *at/to* Australia last year.
7 I usually listen *of/to* dance music.
8 I go *at/to* school in Bologna.

b Tick the sentences in Exercise 4a which are true for you.

5 a Make questions in the past simple using the prompts.

1 you / have a good weekend?
   Did you have a good weekend?
2 What / you / do?
3 Where / you / go?
4 Who / you / go with?
5 When / you / get home?
6 you / have a good time?
7 What / you / watch on TV?
8 you / enjoy / the TV show?

b Work in pairs. Ask and answer the questions in Exercise 5a.

A: Did you have a good weekend?
B: Yes, I did, thanks!

6 Write the question for each answer.

1 I went to the park yesterday.
   Where did you go yesterday ?
2 Ali had coffee with a friend last Saturday.
   What _____ ?
3 We saw Ed last night.
   When _____ ?
4 I watched the film with Mariana.
   Who _____ ?
5 They had dinner at a Chinese restaurant.
   Where _____ ?
6 I went to bed at ten o'clock.
   What time _____ ?
7 We had pizza for lunch.
   What _____ ?
8 We got a Hawaiian pizza.
   What kind of pizza _____ ?

Reflect

How confident do you feel about the statements below? Write 1–5 (1 = not very confident, 5 = very confident).

- I can describe an event.
- I can describe a good weekend.
- I can ask and answer questions.
- I can give and accept an apology.

Want more practice?
Go to your Workbook or app.

7A Food

> **Goal:** describe food shopping items

> **Grammar:** countable and uncountable nouns; *some, any, lots of* and a *lot of*

> **Vocabulary:** food and drink

Vocabulary

1 Work in pairs and answer the questions.

    1 How often do you shop for food?

    2 Where do you usually go to buy food: a supermarket or a market?

    3 Do you enjoy shopping for food? Why/Why not?

2 a Look at the words in the box. Which of them can you see in the photos? What other food and drink can you think of in English?

beans	chicken	coffee	eggs	fish	frozen food
fruit	ice cream	juice	meat	pasta	rice salad
soft drinks	sweets	tea	vegetables		

   b 🔊 **7.1** Listen and repeat the words in Exercise 2a.

   c Look at the underlined vowel sound in the words below. Write one word in Exercise 2a with the same vowel sound.

    1 p**a**sta *salad*   **3** b**ea**ns

    2 ch**i**cken   **4** fr**ui**t

3 Work in pairs. Tell each other about the food in the photos you like and don't like.

    I really like fruit.

📱 Go to page 142 or your app for more vocabulary and practice.

Reading

4 a Work in pairs. Look at titles A–D in the article. What do you think each person buys at the supermarket?

   b Read the article and check your ideas.

5 Read the article again and correct the mistakes by changing the underlined word.

    1 Mike buys a lot of ~~pasta~~. *soft drinks*

    2 There aren't any pizzas in Emma's basket.

    3 Simon gets some salad for breakfast.

    4 There aren't any vegetables in Simon's basket.

    5 There isn't any fish in Ryan's basket.

WHAT DOES YOUR SHOPPING BASKET SAY ABOUT YOU?

A Mike, the busy parent

'I have children who are always hungry so there's lots of food in my basket. There's some bread, pasta, meat and a lot of soft drinks. There are also some tins of tomatoes and vegetables for pasta sauce, and some sweets for when we want the children to be good. Oh, and there's some tomato ketchup, of course. My girls can't live without that.'

B Emma, the workaholic

'I work long days so I don't have any time to cook. There aren't any vegetables in my basket, and there isn't any rice or pasta. You can see that most of the food I buy is microwave food. I've got some Italian meals here and some Indian meals. There's also a pizza and cheese and bread. Oh, and I always get lots of chocolate.'

C Simon, the healthy one

'I'm really careful about what I eat so I usually buy white meat, like chicken, and vegetables, like green beans and salad. I get some eggs for breakfast, and some fruit for snacks. I also get a lot of oranges so that I can make fresh orange juice every morning. There aren't any sweets or soft drinks in my basket.'

D Ryan, the food lover

'I love food and cook every evening. At the weekends, I love making new dishes for my friends. I go shopping three or four times a week and my shopping basket is always full of different things. Today, I've got some fish, potatoes and vegetables for a delicious fish dish. I've got some fruit and ice cream for dessert, too. I don't have any frozen food in my basket. I hate it!'

Grammar

6 a Read the grammar box and choose the correct alternatives.

Countable and uncountable nouns; *some, any, lots of* and *a lot of*

Some nouns in English are countable. It's easy to count them, e.g. *an apple, two bananas, a tomato.* With plural countable nouns, use a ¹*singular/plural* verb.

There **are** some **sweets** in my basket.

Some nouns in English are uncountable because it's not easy to count them, e.g. *fruit, meat, pasta.* With uncountable nouns, use a ²*singular/plural* verb.

Fresh **orange juice is** *delicious*

Use ³*some/any* with countable and uncountable nouns in positive sentences.

There's **some bread** and cheese.

I've got **some fish** for my cats.

Use ⁴*some/any* with countable and uncountable nouns in negative sentences and questions.

There aren't **any vegetables** in my basket.

Is there **any food** for me?

Use *lots of/a lot of* when you want to talk about a ⁵*large/small* amount.

There's **lots of pasta** if you want some.

b Choose the correct alternatives to complete the titles in the table.

¹ countable/uncountable	² countable/uncountable
beans vegetables	chicken rice juice
sweets eggs	pasta salad meat
soft drinks	coffee tea fruit
	frozen food

c Add the words in the box to the table above.

> fish   bread   milk   potatoes   water   bananas

7 a 🔊 7.2 Listen to the sentences. What do you notice about the pronunciation of the /t/ and /d/ sounds in bold?

1 There aren'**t** any sweets left.
2 Have you go**t** any chocolate?
3 I don't nee**d** any sugar in my coffee.

b Listen again and repeat.

8 Choose the correct alternatives.

1 There *is/are* lots of apples in the fruit bowl.
2 This orange juice *is/are* delicious.
3 I'd like *any/lots of* salad with my burger. I don't want *some/any* chips.
4 These chocolates *wasn't/weren't* cheap.
5 Those sweets *is/are* full of sugar. Don't eat them!
6 This fruit *is/are* horrible. Can I have some chocolate?
7 I haven't got *some/any* salad – I've got *some/any* meat.
8 The milk *is/are* bad. Is it old?

9 a Think about the last time you bought food at a supermarket. Write a list of things in your basket.

b Work in pairs. Tell each other what you bought. Did you buy similar or different things? What does your shopping basket say about you?

> *I bought some fruit for breakfast. I didn't buy any milk because I had some at home.*

📱 Go to page 128 or your app for more information and practice.

Speaking

PREPARE

10 a 🔊 7.3 You're going to make guesses about a person from their shopping basket. First, listen to part of a radio show about food shopping. What does Cathy say about Robbie? Is she right?

b Work in pairs. Student A: Turn to page 155. Student B: Turn to page 157. Read your instructions and make notes.

SPEAK

11 a Student A: Tell Student B what's in your shopping basket. Student B: What can you guess about Student A? Use the Useful phrases to help you.

Useful phrases
What have you got in your basket?
I think that you're (healthy/a food lover).
I don't think that you (like sweet food).

b Swap roles and repeat.

c Report back to the class. Were your ideas correct?

Develop your listening page 104

> **Goal:** create a dish
> **Grammar:** *how much/how many?* + quantifiers
> **Vocabulary:** food containers

Reading and listening

1 Work in pairs and answer the questions.
1 Do you eat all the food you buy? Why/Why not?
2 What food do you sometimes throw away?
3 What food do you never throw away?

2 a Look at the title of the article. What do you think it is about?

b Read the article and check your answer. Would you do the same as Elias?

Don't waste it – eat for free!

It's early evening in downtown New York and it's closing time for many cafés and supermarkets. It's time to throw out all their old food for the day. A group of young people arrive and quickly start to look for any food they can find.

These people are *freegans*. They're people who think that we throw out a lot of food, so they try to use it.

'It's amazing what supermarkets throw away,' says Elias, a 24-year-old. 'Yesterday I found a box of eggs, with just one broken egg, and four frozen pizzas. They were fine, but the boxes were broken so the supermarket threw them away.'

So how much food do they find? And how many meals can they make? Elias says sometimes they find a little, and sometimes they find a lot, but they're never hungry and can always make a meal.

c Read the article again. Are the sentences true (T) or false (F)?
1 Supermarkets and cafés throw away old food in the evening.
2 Freegans throw out a lot of food.
3 The pizzas that Elias found weren't broken.
4 Elias is sometimes hungry.

3 a 🔊 7.8 Listen to Elias and Clara discussing how to cook the food they found. What food do they have?

b Listen again and choose the correct alternatives.
1 How *many/much* eggs do we have?
2 A *lot/few*. Just two, I think.
3 How *many/much* oil do we have?
4 *Lots/A little*.
5 Wow, ice cream? How *many/much* did you find?
6 Just a *few/little*, but we've got some fruit.
7 How *many/much* fruit do we have?
8 Oh, *none/lots*. Sorry. I ate it last night.

Grammar

4 Read the grammar box and choose the correct alternatives.

How much/how many? + quantifiers

Use *How much?* to ask about [1]*countable/uncountable* nouns.
How much oil do we have?
How much milk did you buy?
Use *How many?* to ask about [2]*countable/uncountable* nouns.
How many eggs did you find?
How many apples do you want?
Use quantifiers, e.g. *a few/a little, some, a lot of/lots of*, to describe the quantity/number of things.

none/not any   a few/a little   some   lots/a lot

Use [3]*a little/a few* with countable nouns. Use [4]*a little/a few* with uncountable nouns.
*There's **a little cheese**.*
*There are **a few bananas**.*

Use *none, not any, some* and *a lot of* or *lots of* with [5]*no/both* types of nouns.
*We've got **a lot of eggs**. We have**n't** got **any sugar**.*
*How much chocolate have we got? **None**.*
*How many onions have we got? **None**.*

5 a 🔊 **7.9 Listen to the questions and underline the stressed words.**

1 How much bread do we have?
2 How many tomatoes are there?
3 How many eggs did you buy?
4 How much chocolate is there?
5 How much water do you want?

b Listen again and repeat.

6 a Complete the conversations.

1 **A:** How _____ milk do you want?
   B: Just a _____ , please.
2 **A:** How _____ potatoes do we have?
   B: _____ . A whole bag!
3 **A:** How _____ oil do we need?
   B: _____ . We don't use oil in this recipe.
4 **A:** We need _____ onions.
   B: How _____ ?
5 **A:** How _____ bananas are there?
   B: Just a _____ . We need to buy more.

b 🔊 **7.10 Listen and check your answers.**

7 a Complete the questions with *many* or *much*.

1 In your family, how _____ meat do you eat?
2 In your family, how _____ cups of coffee do you drink a day?
3 In your family, how _____ rice do you eat?
4 In your family, how _____ pizzas do you eat a week?
5 In your family, how _____ chocolate do you eat?

b Work in pairs. Ask and answer the questions in Exercise 7a.

📱 Go to page 128 or your app for more information and practice.

Vocabulary

8 a Complete phrases 1–10 with the containers in the box. Then match the phrases with photos A–J.

bag	bar	bottle	box	can	carton	cup
jar	packet	tin				

1 a _____ of tea
2 a _____ of rice
3 a _____ of pasta
4 a _____ of water
5 a _____ of juice
6 a _____ of beans
7 a _____ of eggs
8 a _____ of cola
9 a _____ of chocolate
10 a _____ of coffee

b 🔊 **7.11 Listen and check your answers.**

9 Work in pairs. What other kinds of food/drink can you buy in each container?

   A: *A tin of …*
   B: *tomatoes, soup, peas*

10 Work in groups and discuss the questions.

1 Which of the things in Exercise 9 did you buy the last time you went shopping?
2 Which do you sometimes buy?
3 Which do you never buy?

📱 Go to page 142 or your app for more vocabulary and practice.

Speaking

PREPARE

11 Work in pairs. You live together. Student A is at the supermarket. Student B is at home. Look at the food in the box. Student A: Think about what food you need to buy. Student B: Think about how much food you have and don't have at home. Make notes.

cheese	chocolate	chicken	coffee	cola	eggs
juice	vegetables	water			

SPEAK

12 a Student A: Call Student B and ask what food you have got at home. Student B: Answer Student A's questions. Decide what food Student A can buy. Use the Useful phrases to help you.

> **Useful phrases**
> How many eggs have we got?
> How much coffee is there?
> We've only got two eggs in the box.
> We've got lots of cans of cola.
> Let's buy three bottles of milk.

   A: *How much juice have we got?*
   B: *We've got two cartons.*

b Work in pairs. What other food and drink would you like to buy?

> **Develop your writing**
> page 105

57

7c Unusual cafés

> **Goal:** compare places to eat
> **Grammar:** comparative adjectives
> **Vocabulary:** describing places to eat

Listening and vocabulary

1 **Look at the photos and discuss the questions.**

1 Do you prefer to eat in or out? Why?
2 How often do you eat out?
3 Do you prefer to go out for breakfast, lunch or dinner? Why?
4 Why are the cafés in the photos unusual? Would you like to go them? Why/Why not?

2 a ◀)) **7.12 Listen to Jess and Glen talking about two cafés: the Underground Café and Café Jewel. Which one do they decide to visit? Why?**

b **Listen again. Which adjectives do they use for each café? Which describe the place? Which describe the food?**

bright	cool	comfortable	crowded	dark
expensive	fresh	healthy	nice	noisy
modern	popular	small	strange	

3 a **How many syllables has each adjective in Exercise 2b got?**

b ◀)) **7.13 Listen and check your answers.**

4 a **Complete each sentence with an adjective in Exercise 2b.**

1 I like quiet places, not _____ ones like this one.
2 The menu looks OK, but that's a lot of money for a pasta dish. This restaurant's very _____ .
3 It's difficult to get a table at the Grand Café. It's really _____ .
4 The café doesn't sell chocolate or cakes. It only sells _____ food.
5 That place is so _____ ! It's difficult to see my food.
6 There's nowhere to sit and the place is so _____ there's almost no room to move.
7 Are those vegetables _____ or did they come from a tin?
8 This seat isn't very _____ . I need to stand up.

b **Work in pairs. Describe your favourite place to eat out. Use adjectives in Exercise 2b.**

I love Café Espresso on Green Street. It's really popular and the food is healthy.

📱 Go to your app for more practice.

Grammar

5 a ◀)) **7.12 Listen to Jess and Glen again. Choose the correct alternatives.**

1 Café Jewel is *good/better* than the Underground Café.
2 Café Jewel is *bright/brighter* than the Underground Café.
3 The food at Café Jewel is *nice/nicer* than the food at the Underground Café.
4 The seats at the Underground Café are *comfortable/ more comfortable* than the seats at Café Jewel.
5 The Underground Café is *more crowded/crowded* than Café Jewel.
6 Café Jewel is *expensive/more expensive* than the Underground Café.
7 The food at Café Jewel is *healthy/healthier* than the Underground Café.

b **Read the grammar box and choose the correct alternatives.**

Comparative adjectives

Use *be* + comparative adjective + *than* to compare two things.
*The Underground Café **is more crowded than** Café Jewel.*
To make comparative adjectives …
• add *-er* to **1**short/long adjectives.
*Café Jewel is **brighter** than the Underground Café.*
*The Underground Café is **smaller** than Café Jewel.*
• take away *-y* and add *-ier* to **2**one/two-syllable adjectives ending in *-y*.
*The food at Café Jewel is **healthier** than at the Underground Café.*
*The Underground Café is **noisier** than Café Jewel.*
• add *more* before **3**short/long adjectives.
*The food at Café Jewel is **more expensive** than at the Underground Café.*
*The seats at the Underground Café are **more comfortable** than those at Café Jewel.*
Some adjectives are irregular, e.g. *good – better; bad – worse.*
*Café Jewel is **better** than the Underground Café.*
*The menu at the Underground Café is **worse** than at Café Jewel.*

c **Put the adjectives in Exercise 2b in their comparative form.**

bright – brighter

6 a 🔊 **7.14 Listen to the sentences and notice the pronunciation of** *-er, -ier* **and** *than*.

1 This café is cooler than the one next door.
2 Your eggs look fresher than mine.
3 You always have a healthier breakfast than me.
4 It's noisier than usual in here today.
5 Your cooking's better than mine.
6 The brunch here is more expensive than in other places.

b Listen again and repeat.

7 Complete the sentences with the correct comparative form of the adjectives in brackets.

1 This café's _____ (expensive) than that one.
2 The coffee here is _____ (strong) than my coffee at home.
3 It's cold. We'll be _____ (comfortable) eating inside.
4 The fish here is _____ (fresh) than anywhere else in the city.
5 The café's quiet now. It's _____ (noisy) after ten.
6 Chef Smith's new restaurant is _____ (large) than his other one.

8 a Make sentences using the prompts. Add *than*.

1 Breakfast / is / delicious / lunch
  Breakfast is more delicious than lunch.
2 Italian food / is / healthy / Japanese food
3 Starters / are / good / desserts
4 Sofas in restaurants / are / comfortable / chairs
5 Cooking a meal / is / interesting / eating out
6 Cafés / are / busy / in the evening / in the daytime

b Work in pairs. Do you agree or disagree with the sentences in Exercise 8a? Why?
  I love breakfast so I think it's better than lunch.

📱 Go to page 128 or your app for more information and practice.

Speaking

PREPARE

9 a Work in pairs. Choose two cafés or restaurants you both know. Make a list of adjectives you can use to talk about each café/restaurant.

b Work on your own. Decide which café/restaurant you prefer and why. Make notes.

SPEAK

10 a Work in pairs. Imagine that you want to take your class to a café/restaurant for a meal. Compare the two cafés/restaurants and decide which one to go to. Use the Useful phrases to help you.

> **Useful phrases**
> Which café would you like to go to?
> I prefer (the Woodland Café) because …
> (The Tram Café) is cheaper than (the Woodland Café).
> So, we agree. Let's go to (the Tram Café).

b Report back to the class. Which café/restaurant did you choose? Why?

Develop your reading
page 106

> **Goal:** order in a café

1 **Discuss the questions.**

    1 How often do you buy food or drink from a café?

    2 In your country, do you usually have coffee in a café or take it out?

    3 Do you usually sit at a table and order, or pay for your drinks then sit down at cafés in your country?

2 a 🔊 7.15 **Listen to Marguerite ordering in a café and answer the questions.**

    1 What does Marguerite order?

    2 Does she have it inside the café?

    3 What does the assistant ask her about the sandwich?

    4 How much does it cost?

    5 Do they bring it to her table or does she collect it?

  b **Listen again and tick the phrases in the Useful phrases box that you hear.**

Useful phrases

Customer
I'd like (this sandwich), please.
Can I get/have (a small cappuccino), please?
I'll have (a latte), please.
How much is that?
Can I pay by card?

Assistant
Can I help?
Eat in or take out?
Would you like it hot or cold?
Any hot drinks with that?
Take a seat and I'll bring it over.
Anything else?

3 a 🔊 7.16 **Listen to the phrases in the Useful phrases box and underline the stressed words.**

  b **Listen again and repeat.**

4 a **Complete the conversations with the missing words.**

    1 **A:** _____ I have a large Americano, please?
       B: Sure. Take a seat and I'll _____ it over.

    2 **A:** Any hot _____ with that?
       B: Yes, a tea, please.

    3 **A:** Can I _____ ?
       B: I'd _____ this sandwich, please.
       A: Would you like it _____ or cold?
       B: Cold, please.

    4 **A:** Can I _____ a chicken salad, please?
       B: Sure. Eat in or _____ out?

    5 **A:** How _____ is that?
       B: Two pounds, please.
       A: Can I _____ by card?
       B: Yes, of course.

  b 🔊 7.17 **Listen and check your answers.**

  c **Work in pairs. Practise the conversations in Exercise 4a. Then, swap roles and repeat.**

5 **You're going to practise ordering in a café. Work in pairs. Look at the situations below and think about what to say.**

Student A

1 You are a customer in a café. You want a hot chicken sandwich, a glass of water and a cup of tea. Order and ask:
   • how much it is.
   • if you can pay by card.

2 You work in a café. Take the customer's order. Ask:
   • how they want to pay.
   • if they want a small or big coffee.

Student B

1 You work in a café. Take the customer's order. Ask:
   • if they want to eat in or take out.
   • if they want their food hot or cold.

2 You are a customer in a café. You want a coffee, an apple and a salad. Order and ask:
   • for your coffee without milk or sugar.
   • to eat in, but have a take-out cup for your coffee.

6 **Practise your conversations. Use the Useful phrases to help you.**

▶ **Go online for the Roadmap video.**

Check and reflect

1 a Unscramble the letters to make kinds of food.

   1 urtfi *fruit*

   2 fcoefe

   3 sbane

   4 patas

   5 cueji

   6 stewes

   7 kinecch

   8 gesg

b Work in pairs. Which of the food in Exercise 1a do you like/dislike?

2 Complete the sentences with one word.

   1 There _____ some cheese in the fridge.

   2 I don't want _____ milk in my coffee, thank you.

   3 Can I have _____ juice, please?

   4 These sweets _____ delicious – try one!

   5 We don't have _____ tea – can you buy some?

   6 I don't want _____ salad, thank you.

   7 There are _____ bananas in the fruit bowl.

   8 Would you like _____ ice cream?

3 a Correct the mistake in each sentence.

   1 I don't like any milks in my coffee.

   2 There are some chocolate in my bag.

   3 I have any pasta at home.

   4 I have some fruits every day.

   5 There is some sweets in my bag.

   6 There aren't some nuts in my kitchen.

b Work in pairs. Which of the sentences in Exercise 3a are true for you?

4 a Complete the questions with *How much* or *How many*.

   1 _____ chocolate do you eat?

   2 _____ people are in your class?

   3 _____ rooms are in your house?

   4 _____ homework do you have?

   5 _____ water do you drink every day?

   6 _____ meals did you cook last week?

b Match responses a–f with questions 1–6 in Exercise 4a.

   a A lot. I have a bottle with me all day.

   b A few. I live in a small flat.

   c A little. I'm on a diet at the moment.

   d None. I can't cook!

   e None. Our teacher didn't give us any.

   f A lot. But it's OK, we have a very big classroom.

c Work in pairs. Ask and answer the questions in Exercise 4a using the quantifiers in the box.

   a few   a little   a lot   none

   A: How much chocolate do you eat?
   B: A lot! I usually have some after dinner.

5 a Complete the phrases with a container. More than one answer may be possible.

   1 a *carton* of milk

   2 a _____ of chocolate

   3 a _____ of pasta

   4 a _____ of cola

   5 a _____ of tomatoes

   6 a _____ of sugar

   7 a _____ of coffee

   8 a _____ of eggs

b Work in pairs and discuss the questions. Which things have you got at home? Which things do you usually buy at the supermarket?

   I've got a jar of coffee at home.
   I usually buy a box of eggs when I go to the supermarket.

6 a Write sentences to compare the things. Use any adjectives you want.

   1 dinner at home / dinner at a restaurant
   Dinner at home is cheaper than dinner at a restaurant.

   2 a house / a flat

   3 chocolate / cheese

   4 my friend / me

   5 vegetables / pizza

   6 our classroom / my living room

b Work in pairs and compare your sentences. Do you agree?

7 Choose the correct alternatives.

   1 This food is *noisy/delicious*, I love it!

   2 Don't go to the restaurant at 8 p.m., it's very *busy/friendly* at that time.

   3 I can't see Mark anywhere, but it's very *dark/bright* in there.

   4 This food isn't *fresh/modern*, it looks really old.

   5 I try to eat *cool/healthy* food every day.

   6 I like *bright/modern* cafés, not old ones.

Reflect

How confident do you feel about the statements below? Write 1–5 (1 = not very confident, 5 = very confident).

- I can describe food shopping items.
- I can create a dish.
- I can compare places to eat.
- I can order in a café.

Want more practice?
Go to your Workbook or app.

8A ▷ A great time

> **Goal:** describe a travel experience
> **Grammar:** present continuous
> **Vocabulary:** geography

Vocabulary

1 Discuss the questions.

1 What do you usually do on your holidays?
2 Do you travel to different countries or stay at home?
3 What kinds of activities do you do?

2 a Work in pairs. Which of the things in the box can you see in photos A–F?

> air   beach   countryside   island   mountain
> river   sea   sky   trees   water

b Complete the sentences with the words in Exercise 2a.

1 The view from the top of the _____ is beautiful. You can see a long way!
2 There's a _____ near our hotel. The _____ looks very cold!
3 The _____ is so clean here because there are no cars.
4 It's so green here. There are _____ everywhere.
5 Cities are OK, but the _____ is so lovely and quiet.
6 Today is sunny with a clear, blue _____ .
7 We went to a really nice, sandy _____ today. We really enjoyed the sun and sea.
8 We travelled to the _____ by boat. The _____ was very calm.

3 a Complete the sentences with your ideas.

1 _____ is a very green area, with lots of trees and clean air.
2 _____ is a place with very high mountains.
3 In _____ , people often go to the beach in summer. The skies are always blue and it's very warm.
4 You can travel by boat to _____ . It's an island, and it's very pretty.

b Work in pairs and compare your sentences. Give more information.

> *In Brighton, people often go to the beach in summer. The skies are always blue and it's very warm. You can see some famous buildings, too.*

📱 Go to your app for more practice.

Listening and grammar

4 🔊 8.1 Work in pairs. Listen to a video call between Gareth and his mum. Which of photos A–F is he in?

5 Listen again and complete the sentences with the correct form of the verb *be*.

1 I _____ standing at the top of Mount Chogatake.
2 So now we _____ resting before the walk back down.
3 She _____ having something to eat.
4 _____ you having a good time at home?
5 You _____ working too hard, I hope.
6 We _____ leaving now.

6 Read the grammar box and choose the correct alternatives.

Present continuous

Use the present continuous to describe things happening [1]*now/every day*.
*We're **resting** before the walk back down.*
Form the present continuous with [2]*have/be* + verb + *-ing*.
*I'm **standing** at the top of Mount Chogatake.*
*She's **having** something to eat.*
*We're **leaving** now.*
Form negatives with [3]*do/be* + *not* + verb + *-ing*.
*You **aren't working** too hard.*
Form questions with (question word) + *be* + [4]*object/subject* + verb + *-ing*.
***What are** you and dad **doing** right now?*
***Are** you **having** a good time?*

F

9 Work in pairs. Look at the picture. Describe what one person is doing in the picture, but don't say which person it is. Listen to your partner's description and say which person they're describing.

Someone is taking a photo.

📱 Go to page 130 or your app for more information and practice.

Speaking

PREPARE

10 a You're going to have a video call from your holiday with someone back home. First, choose one of the photos in Exercise 2, or choose your own place.

b Think about what you're doing on your holiday. Make notes about:
- holiday activities
- what the person you're with is doing right now
- what you're doing/not doing right now

SPEAK

11 a Have video calls with other students. Listen and ask questions to find out more information. Use the Useful phrases to help you.

Useful phrases
Hi! Where are you?
Wow! It looks great!
What are you doing there?
Tell me about (Lake Garda)!

b Whose holiday did you like best? Why?

7 a 🔊 8.2 **Listen to the sentences. How is -*ing* pronounced?**

1 We're walking in the countryside.
2 I'm sitting on a beautiful beach.
3 They're swimming in the water.
4 He's enjoying the view.
5 She's climbing the mountain.

b Listen again and repeat.

8 Complete the sentences with the present continuous form of the verbs in brackets.

1 Hi! I _____ (sit) by this lovely river. Can you see?
2 I _____ (enjoy) the fresh air in the countryside. And you?
3 Jon _____ (read) the newspaper on the beach.
4 What _____ you _____ (do) right now?
5 Lana _____ (take) photos of the trees.
6 We _____ (have) lunch at the beach.
7 I _____ (wait) for Malcolm outside the hotel.
8 We _____ (drive) to a small beach near the hotel.
9 It _____ (not rain). That's good!
10 I _____ (not swim) in the river with the other guys. It's dangerous.
11 Teresa and Sergio _____ (wait) for me, so I need to go. Bye!
12 We _____ (travel) by boat to an island at the moment. I'm excited!

Develop your writing
page 107

63

8B Weather

B

> **Goal:** describe the weather
> **Grammar:** present simple and present continuous
> **Vocabulary:** weather

A

C

D

Vocabulary

1 Discuss the question. How many types of weather can you name?

2 a Match phrases 1–8 with photos A–H.

1	It's snowing.	**5**	It's foggy.
2	It's windy.	**6**	It's cold and wet.
3	It's raining.	**7**	It's warm and sunny.
4	It's cloudy and cool.	**8**	It's hot.

b Which of the weather words in Exercise 2a are verbs (V) and which are adjectives (A)?

3 a Put the seasons in the correct order, starting with *spring*.

> autumn   spring   summer   winter

b Work in pairs and discuss the questions.
   1 How many seasons does your country have?
   2 Which kinds of weather in Exercise 2 do you have in each season?

4 Choose the correct alternatives.
   1 Don't forget your umbrella, it's *raining/hot* outside.
   2 Let's go to the park if it's *foggy/sunny* tomorrow.
   3 It's really *hot/cool* today! Don't sit in the sun!
   4 Drive carefully, it's *sunny/foggy* this morning.
   5 Look outside, it's *snowing/cloudy*! How pretty!
   6 It's *windy/cloudy* tonight, so we can't see the stars.
   7 It's not hot, but it is *warm/cool*. You don't need a jacket.
   8 It's *wet/cloudy* outside. Be careful when you're walking.

5 Work in pairs and discuss the questions.
   1 What's your favourite kind of weather? Why?
   2 What's the weather like at the moment?
   3 Is it usually like this at this time of year?
   4 What's your favourite season?

📱 Go to your app for more practice.

Listening and grammar

6 a 🔊 8.3 Listen to a weather report about Florida, Cairo and Manchester. What's the weather like in each place?

b Listen again and complete the table with the words in the box.

> cold   dry   raining   snowing   sunny   warm

	usually	right now
Florida	It's ¹_____. People wear summer clothes.	It's ²_____. People are wearing coats and hats.
Cairo	It's ³_____. It sometimes rains a little.	It's ⁴_____ a lot. People are staying inside.
Manchester	It's ⁵_____. People don't go out much.	It's warm and ⁶_____. People are having lunch in the park.

9 Complete the sentences with the verbs in brackets in the present simple or present continuous.
1 What _____ (happen) there at the moment?
2 The children usually _____ (play) in the snow in winter.
3 We usually _____ (walk) to work, but today we're late so we _____ (drive).
4 He can't go outside, it _____ (rain) a lot.
5 I usually _____ (work) in an office, but today I _____ (work) from home.

10 a Write six sentences that are true about you: three in the present simple and three in the present continuous.

I go to work by train.
I'm studying English at the moment.

b Work in pairs and compare your sentences.

Go to page 130 or your app for more information and practice.

Speaking

PREPARE

11 a Work in pairs. You're going to prepare a weather report. Student A: you are a weather reporter. Look at the information on page 157 and choose a city to talk about. Student B: you are a news presenter. You're going to ask Student A some questions about what's happening.

b Work on your own. Student A: Imagine there is unusual weather in that city at the moment. Make notes about:
• what the weather's like
• what people usually do at this time of year
• what people are doing at the moment

Student B: Think of questions to ask the reporter about what's happening now in their city.
What are people doing?

c Share your information and prepare your news report. Practise giving the report together. Use the Useful phrases to help you.

> **Useful phrases**
> What's the weather like at the moment?
> Well, usually it's (hot and sunny), but today it's (snowing).
> What are people doing there?
> (The children) are playing outside.

SPEAK

12 a Present your news report to the class. Listen to other groups' reports.

b Vote for the best news report.

Develop your listening
page 108

7 Read the grammar box and choose the correct alternatives.

Present simple and present continuous

Use the ¹present simple/present continuous to describe things which are true in general or regular activities.
People **usually stay** inside.
This time of year **is usually** really cold.
Use the ²present simple/present continuous for things which are happening now.
People **are having** lunch in the park.
The children **are playing** in the snow.
Use adverbs of frequency (*always, usually*, etc.) with the present simple and time expressions (*today, at the moment*, etc.) with the present continuous, to make the difference clearer.
It **always rains** a little at this time of year, but **today** it**'s raining** a lot.
People **usually stay** inside at this time of year, but **at the moment** they**'re enjoying** the warm weather outside.

8 a 🔊 8.4 Listen and notice how the verb *be* is contracted in the sentences.
1 He's watching TV.
2 I'm staying inside today.
3 It's raining.
4 They're enjoying the sunny weather.
5 We're playing in the snow.

b Listen again and repeat.

8c Travel talk

> **Goal:** compare places, activities and transport

> **Grammar:** superlative adjectives

> **Vocabulary:** phrases describing travel

Reading

1 a Work in pairs. How many forms of transport can you think of?

bus, taxi …

b Look at the photos and discuss the questions.

1 How is the weather in Dubai?
2 What is it famous for?
3 What forms of transport can you use there?

c Read the travel guide to Dubai and check your ideas.

Vocabulary

2 a Complete the phrases with the verbs in the box. Use the travel guide to help you.

arrive at	arrive in	book	get back	get off
get on	go	leave	stay at	take	

1 _____ / _____ home
2 _____ a hotel/a guest house
3 _____ the city/Dubai
4 _____ the airport/the shopping mall
5 _____ a trip/a boat ride/a taxi
6 _____ a room/a table/a tour
7 _____ somewhere by bus/train/bike/metro
8 _____ the bus/train/metro/bike (=start your journey)
9 _____ the bus/train/metro/bike (=end your journey)

b Choose the correct alternatives.

1 Think about the last time you took a *travel/trip*. Where did you go?
2 What time did you leave *home/house*?
3 Did you go *by/with* car or train?
4 When did you arrive *at/to* your hotel?
5 What kind of hotel did you stay *at/to*?
6 Did you *book/get* a tour somewhere interesting? Where?
7 When did you *get back/get to* home?

c Work in pairs. Ask and answer the questions in Exercise 2b.

📱 Go to page 143 or your app for more vocabulary and practice.

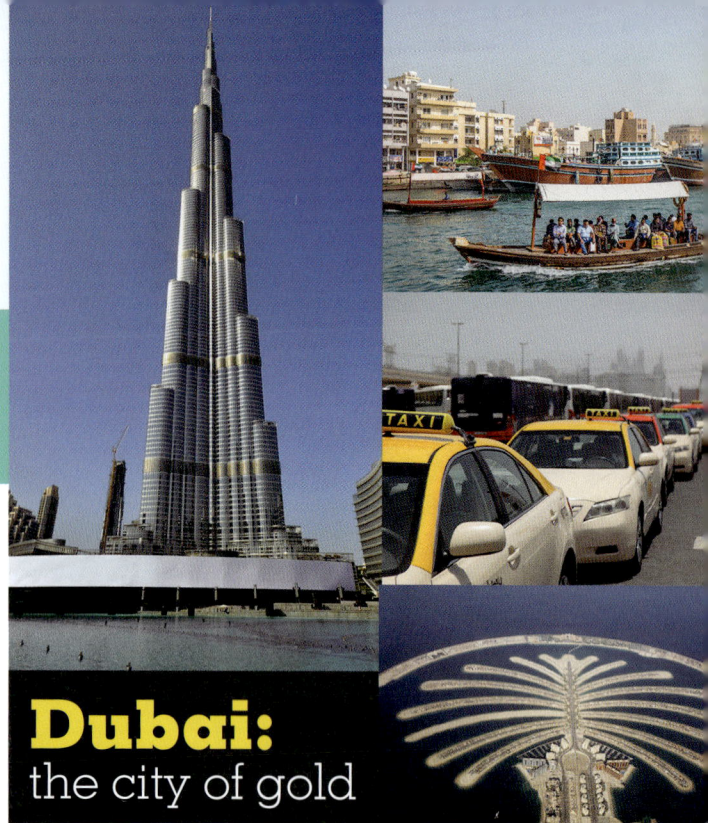

Dubai:
the city of gold

Dubai is an amazing city with fun for everyone. The beaches are lovely, the shopping centres are huge and the buildings are tall. The sun shines all year, so don't leave home without your sun cream!

The most popular places for people to stay are Jumeirah Beach and the areas in the centre. Dubai is famous for its big five-star hotels but you can stay at guesthouses, too. When you arrive in Dubai, take a taxi to your hotel. It's the easiest way to get there and it's not too expensive.

There's lots to see and do in Dubai. There's the Burj Khalifa, the tallest building in the world, and the Dubai Mall with over 1,200 shops, 150 restaurants, and lots more. There are so many restaurants, you don't need to book a table. Just make sure that you get a map from the mall so you don't get lost.

Take a trip to Dubai Creek, the oldest and friendliest part of the city. Buy gold at the markets or visit the Dubai Museum. You can also take a boat ride in a *dhow* and see the city from the water, or book a desert tour and take a camel ride.

Getting around the city isn't difficult. Taxis are the most comfortable way to travel but you can go to most places by metro. It's the best way to travel during busy times on the road. It's also the cheapest form of transport. No one goes anywhere on foot because it's too hot but you can take a bus tour around the city. Get on the bus near your hotel and get off the bus at all the places you want to visit.

Don't feel sad when you arrive at the airport or get back home. Dubai is always ready for your next visit!

Grammar

3 a Read the grammar box and choose the correct alternatives.

Superlative adjectives

Use *the* + a superlative adjective to compare three or more things.

*Taxis are **the most comfortable** way to travel.*

To make superlative adjectives:

- add [1]-*er/*-*est* to one-syllable adjectives.

*The Dubai Creek is **the oldest part** of Dubai.*

- in adjectives ending in -*y*, take away -*y* and add [2]-*ier/*-*iest*.

*A taxi is **the easiest way** to get to your hotel.*

- add *the most* before adjectives with two or more syllables (not ending in -*y*). The adjective [3]*changes/doesn't change*.

***The most popular** places to stay are Jumeirah Beach and the areas in the centre.*

Some superlative adjectives are irregular, e.g. *good – the best, bad – the worst.*

*The metro is **the best** way to get somewhere fast.*

b Write the superlative forms of the adjectives in the box.

> cheap   comfortable   friendly   old   tall

c Find the adjectives in the article and check your answers.

4 a 🔊 8.11 Listen to the sentences. What is the pronunciation of -*iest*?

1 Ranj is the friendliest person I know.
2 Seven o'clock is the earliest time I get up!
3 This is the noisiest part of the city.
4 Morning is the busiest time of day for me.
5 The metro is the easiest way to get around here.

b Listen again and repeat.

5 a Complete the text with the superlative form of the adjectives in brackets.

Getting around **Bangkok**

There are lots of ways to travel around Bangkok. The Airport Rail Link is [1]_____ (easy) way to get from the airport to the city centre. From there, you can take a taxi to your hotel. Taxis are [2]_____ (expensive) way to travel and they can be [3]_____ (slow) in bad traffic. But they're safe and comfortable. The Skytrain is [4]_____ (good) way to get around the city. It's [5]_____ (modern) form of transport and it's not expensive. The Tuk-Tuk – a motorbike with three wheels – is [6]_____ (interesting) way to travel but it's probably not [7]_____ (safe). It's also [8]_____ (noisy) because of all the cars around you.

b Work in pairs. Compare the different forms of transport where you live.

Buses are the cheapest way to travel but they're also the most crowded.

6 a Choose the correct alternatives. Then complete the sentences so they are true for you.

1 The *more bad/worst* time of day for me is *morning*.
2 The *easiest/more easy* way to travel is _____ .
3 The *most good/best* time of year is _____ .
4 The *more delicious/most delicious* food in the world is _____ .
5 The *shorter/shortest* person in my family is _____ .
6 The *more/most* interesting person I know is _____ .
7 The *most popular/more popular* restaurant in my city is _____ .
8 The *friendliest/friendlier* city in my country is _____ .

b Work in pairs and compare your sentences. Give more information.

The worst time of day for me is morning. I hate getting up early for work.

📱 Go to page 130 or your app for more information and practice.

Speaking

PREPARE

7 a 🔊 8.12 You're going to give a short talk about a city. First, listen to two tourist information officers talk about Cambridge. Put the topics in the order you hear them.

a What to see and do
b How to get around
c What it's famous for
d The best time of year to go
e Where to eat

b Listen again. What forms of transport do they talk about?

8 a Work in pairs. Student A: Turn to page 151. Student B: Turn to page 157. Read the information.

b Prepare to give a presentation about the city or prepare a talk about your own city. Make notes and practise your presentation.

SPEAK

9 a Student A: Give your presentation to Student B. Student B: Decide if you want to visit the city. Use the Useful phrases to help you.

Useful phrases

I'd like to tell you about (things you can do).
Getting around the city is (easy).
The (most interesting) activity is (a boat ride).
The (best) places to visit are (the colleges).

b Swap roles and repeat.

Develop your reading
page 109

English in action

A

> **Goal:** make a phone call

1 Look at the photos. What's happening in each one?

2 🔊 **8.13** Listen to Will make four phone calls. Which two conversations match photos A–B? Why does Will make each phone call?

3 a Listen again and choose the correct alternatives.

1 Hello, New Street Surgery. Maddie *speaking/talking*.
2 *Can/Do* I make an appointment with Dr Bell, please?
3 *Thank/Thanks* for your help.
4 *Are you/Is that* The Blue Hat restaurant?
5 Do you *know/mean* the table near the window?
6 Lizzie? *I'm/It's* Will.
7 Sorry, I didn't *hear/listen* that.
8 *Meet/See* you soon.
9 *Could/Do* I book a taxi, please?
10 Sorry, can you say that a*gain/more*?

b Use the Useful phrases box to check your answers in Exercise 3a.

B

Useful phrases

Making plans and appointments on the phone
Hello, (New Street Surgery). (Maddie) speaking.
Hello, is that (The Blue Hat restaurant)?
Hi, it's/this is (Will).
Can I (make an appointment with Dr Bell)?
Could I (book a taxi), please?
Thanks (very much) for your help.
Goodbye./Bye.
See you (soon/on Thursday at four fifteen).

Asking someone to repeat information
Sorry, I didn't hear that.
Sorry, can you say that again?

Asking for clarification
Is that (the 12th)?
Do you mean the table near the window?

4 a 🔊 **8.14** Listen to the question below. Does the speaker's voice go down and up, or up and down at the end?

Is that The Blue Hat restaurant?

b 🔊 **8.15** Listen to the questions. Mark the intonation at the end of each one.

1 Sorry, can you say that again?
2 Is that the 12th?
3 Do you mean the table near the window?
4 Can I make an appointment with Dr Bell?
5 Could I book a taxi, please?

c Listen again and repeat.

5 a Put the words in the correct order to make conversations.

1 **A:** Hello. [1]Smith's taxis / that / is ?
   B: Yes, it is.
   A: [2]the Forest Hotel, / book / can I / from / please / a taxi ?
   B: Where do you want to go?
   A: To the airport.

2 **A:** Hi. [3]could / please / an appointment with the dentist, / book / I ?
   B: How about 3 o'clock?
   A: [4]today / for / that / is ?
   B: Yes, it is.
   A: OK then.
   B: What's your name, please?
   A: It's Seb Carter.
   B: [5]you /again / say that / sorry, / can ?
   A: Seb Carter.
   B: OK, thanks. That's all fine.
   A: Great. [6]your help / very much / for / thanks .
   B: [7]at 3 o'clock / you / see .

b 🔊 **8.16** Listen and check.

c Work in pairs and practise the conversations. Then, swap roles and repeat.

6 You're going to practise making phone calls. Work in pairs. Student A: Turn to page 156. Student B: Turn to page 152. Read your instructions.

7 a Practise your conversations. Use the Useful phrases to help you.

b Swap roles and repeat.

> **Go online for the Roadmap video.**

Check and reflect

1 Complete the messages with the present continuous form of the verbs in the box.

lose   play   ride   sit   sleep   talk
watch   write

1 I _____ some emails to my friend.
2 Max _____ golf with his friends.
3 Roger Federer _____ the match at the moment. He usually wins so it's a bit strange!
4 The children _____ their bikes to the park.
5 Sam and Tom _____ to each other because they're angry. It's so quiet!
6 Dad _____ a film on TV at the moment so I can't watch the football.
7 The dog _____ on the sofa. He's on the floor.
8 Be quiet! The baby _____ and I don't want her to wake up.

2 Read the definitions and complete the geographical features. You have the first letter to help you.

1 birds often live in these tall plants – **t**_____
2 water that goes from the mountains to the sea – **r**_____
3 what we can see when we look up – **s**_____
4 land with water around it – **i**_____
5 the place next to the sea – **b**_____
6 land outside the city with fields and forests – **c**_____

3 a Put the letters in the correct order to complete the sentences.

1 It was so *tho* last night. I don't sleep well when it's very *rmaw*.
2 I can't see the road. It's really *gyfog*.
3 It's *wnisgon* outside. The roads are white already.
4 There's no sun today. It's really *ydocul*.
5 I didn't take an umbrella so now I'm all *tew*.
6 You can't use your umbrella today. It's really *dyiwn*.

b Work in pairs. What do you think the weather is like in these places now?

- Moscow
- Sydney
- Mexico City
- Iceland

4 Complete the sentences with the present simple or present continuous form of the verbs in brackets.

1 We _____ (watch) a film at the moment.
2 What time _____ Richard _____ (get up) on Mondays?
3 What book _____ your sister _____ (read)?
4 It _____ (not/rain) now. It's dry.
5 I can't hear you. Maria _____ (play) her music very loud.
6 I _____ (meet) Jack for lunch every Friday.
7 My brothers _____ (not/like) coffee.

5 Choose the correct alternatives.

1 The Smiths are the *friendliest/friendly* people in the town.
2 This is the *best/good* restaurant in the area.
3 Jack is a really *funniest/funny* person.
4 Sit on that chair. It's the *comfortable/most comfortable* one in the room.
5 This song is terrible. It's really *bad/worse*.
6 At 89, my grandma's the *old/oldest* person in my family.

6 a Complete the phrases with the superlative form of the adjectives in brackets.

1 *the prettiest* (pretty) place in my town/city
2 _____ (exciting) day of the year
3 _____ (cold) month of the year
4 _____ (good) café or restaurant
5 _____ (busy) street
6 _____ (expensive) shops
7 _____ (noisy) part of my town/city
8 _____ (interesting) thing to do in my town/city

b Work in pairs. Think of one place or thing for phrases 1–8 in Exercise 6a.

I think the park is the prettiest place in my town.

7 Complete the blog post with the past simple form of the verbs in the box.

arrive   get back   get off   get on   leave   take

A trip to Beijing

I went to Beijing for a short work trip. I **1**_____ home on Tuesday and **2**_____ in Beijing on Wednesday. On Saturday, I got up early and went to the Summer Palace. I **3**_____ the metro near my hotel and **4**_____ ten minutes later near the palace. There are lots of different buildings around a pretty lake. I **5**_____ a boat trip across the lake. It was a lovely day. I left Beijing on Sunday morning and **6**_____ home on Sunday afternoon.

Reflect

How confident do you feel about the statements below? Write 1–5 (1 = not very confident, 5 = very confident).

- I can describe a travel experience.
- I can describe the weather.
- I can compare places, activities and transport.
- I can make a phone call.

Want more practice?
Go to your Workbook or app.

9A Good advice

> **Goal:** give advice

> **Grammar:** *should/shouldn't*

> **Vocabulary:** health

A

B

Vocabulary

1 **Look at the photos and discuss the questions.**

   1 What's happening in the photos? Which of the activities do you do? When do you do them?

   2 Which of the activities are good for you/bad for you?

2 a **Work in pairs. You're going to listen to a radio show about ways to live a long life. Look at the four topics in the box. What do you think the people say about them?**

> exercise   food   sleep   work

  b 🔊 **9.1** **Listen and check your ideas.**

3 a **Complete the phrases with the words in the box.**

> do   eat   go   join   keep   move   sit   stand
> stay   walk (x2)

   1 _____ **well**. Don't have a lot of unhealthy food.

   2 To _____ **healthy**, we shouldn't eat a lot of sugar.

   3 It's important to _____ **fit**, too.

   4 You don't need to _____ **a gym** but you should _____ some **exercise**

   5 _____ **up** the stairs at work.

   6 Don't _____ **down** all day.

   7 _____ **up** and _____ **around** the office.

   8 The app also tells you to _____ **around** every hour.

   9 Relax before you _____ **to sleep**.

  b **Listen to the show again and check your answers.**

4 a **Complete the sentences with a verb phrase in bold in Exercise 3a. More than one answer may be possible.**

   1 I always _____ the stairs. I hardly ever take the lift.

   2 I try to _____ every day. I eat a lot of vegetables and I don't eat chocolate.

   3 I _____ most days. I go running or swimming.

   4 I don't _____ every day, but I often play badminton so that I can _____ .

   5 I _____ at a desk most days. I don't _____ a lot during the day.

   6 I don't want to _____ . I don't like exercise bikes or running machines.

   7 I _____ before 11 every night and wake up before 7 a.m.

  b **Work in pairs. Change the sentences in Exercise 4a so they are true for you. Then compare your sentences with your partner.**

    I never walk up the stairs. I'm very lazy.

📱 Go to page 144 or your app for more vocabulary and practice.

Grammar

5 a 🔊 **9.2** **Listen to the sentences and choose the words you hear.**

   1 We *should/ shouldn't* eat a lot of sugar.

   2 You *should/ shouldn't* do some exercise.

   3 *Should/ Shouldn't* we think about rest, too?

   4 I *should/ shouldn't* watch a great film every day then.

  b **Work in pairs. Which sentences in Exercise 5a talk or ask about a good idea? Which sentence talks about a bad idea?**

  c **Read the grammar box and choose the correct alternatives.**

> ### should/shouldn't
>
> Use [1]*should/shouldn't* + infinitive to say that something is a good idea or to give advice about what to do.
> *You **should try** and be positive in life.*
> Use [2]*should/shouldn't* + infinitive to say that something is a bad idea or to give advice about what not to do.
> *You **shouldn't sit** down all day.*
> Use *should* to ask for advice. *Should* and the subject change places to make a [3]*negative/question*.
> *A: **Should** we **think** about rest, too?*
> *B: Yes, we should./No, we shouldn't.*
> *What **should** we **do**?*

6 a 🔊 **9.3** **Listen to the sentences. Which letter in *should/ shouldn't* is silent?**

   1 You should come for a walk with us.

   2 We should do some exercise tomorrow.

   3 He shouldn't eat all that chocolate.

   4 You shouldn't use the lift.

   5 Should I take an umbrella with me?

  b **Listen again and repeat.**

7 Complete the sentences with *should/shouldn't* and a verb in the box.

book	buy	go	join	play	walk

1 You _____ netball to keep fit. It's a great sport.
2 I want to make some new friends. _____ I _____ a club or something?
3 Marta _____ home at night on her own. It's not safe.
4 You _____ any new clothes. You want to save money, remember?
5 It's your birthday. You _____ out and have fun.
6 _____ we _____ a table at the restaurant?

8 a Make sentences using the prompts. Add *should/shouldn't*.

Eight ways to
sleep well!

1 No coffee before bedtime.
   You shouldn't drink coffee before bedtime.
2 Turn off your mobile phone.
3 Do exercise.
4 No work before bedtime.
5 No sleep in the daytime.
6 Go to bed and get up at the same time every day.
7 Don't eat before you go to bed.
8 Have a hot bath 90 minutes before you go to sleep.

b Work in pairs and compare your sentences in Exercise 8a. What other advice can you give for sleeping well?

Go to page 132 or your app for more information and practice.

Speaking

PREPARE

9 a Work in pairs. You're going to give a presentation on one of the following topics:
  - how to be less lazy
  - how to feel OK on a plane journey
  - how to be less stressed at work
  - how to be a good student
  - how to be happy
  - how to have a good day every day

b Think of advice you can give and agree on the best ideas. Think of at least eight different ideas.

c Prepare your presentation. Use the Useful phrases to help you.

> **Useful phrases**
> Here are eight ways to (have a good day every day)
> Number 1 is … / Number 2 is …
> You should (take lots of breaks).
> You shouldn't (stay at home all the time).
> Don't (work all the time).

SPEAK

10 a Work in pairs. Present your advice to the class.

b Vote on the most useful presentation. Why is it useful? What is the best idea in the presentation?

Develop your listening
page 110

9B My goals

> **Goal:** discuss your goals for the future
> **Grammar:** *be going to*
> **Vocabulary:** future plans

Listening

1 **Look at the vision board and discuss the questions.**
  1 What can you see on the board?
  2 What do you think this person's goals are?

2 a 🔊 9.10 **Listen to Petra telling her friend Dave about her vision board and check your ideas in Exercise 1.**

b **Listen again and complete the sentences with the verbs in the box**

buy	do	eat	get up	have

  1 Petra's going to _____ some new running shoes.
  2 She's going to _____ at 5 a.m. every morning.
  3 Petra and Sally are going to _____ yoga twice a week.
  4 Petra's going to _____ healthy food.
  5 She isn't going to _____ chocolate.

3 **Work in pairs and discuss the questions.**
  1 Do you think a vision board is a good idea? Why/Why not?
  2 What would you like to make a vision board for?

Grammar

4 **Read the grammar box and choose the correct alternatives.**

be going to

Use *be* + *going to* + infinitive to talk about
¹*future/past* plans and intentions.
I'm going to eat healthy food.
She's going to do yoga.
Use ²*be/do* to make negative sentences and questions with *be going to*.
She isn't going to eat chocolate.
Are you going to run?
Change the position of the subject (*I, you, he,* etc)
and ³*be/going to* to make a question.
What are you going to do?

5 a 🔊 9.11 **Listen to the sentences. What is the sound of the second 'g' in *going*?**
  1 They're going to eat less junk food.
  2 I'm going to buy a car.
  3 He's going to try to meet new friends.
  4 We're going to write a book together.
  5 Are you going to get married this summer?

b **Listen again and repeat.**

6 **Complete the text with *be going to* and the verbs in the box.**

be	(not) be	do (x2)	finish	start	write

- Decide on your goals. What ¹_____ you _____ this year? Write down your goals.
- Tell people your goals. Help from other people ²_____ very important.
- Make a plan. Think of smaller things you ³_____ by the end of each week or month. For example, my son wants to write a book next year, so he ⁴_____ a little every weekend.
- Begin! How ⁵_____ you _____? What ⁶_____ you _____ first?
- Stay positive. It ⁷_____ easy, but try to enjoy it!

7 a **Write two things you're going to do in the next 12 months and two things you're not going to do.**
  I'm going to visit India.
  I'm not going to get a new job.

b **Work in small groups and compare your plans. Does anyone else have the same plans?**

📱 Go to page 132 or your app for more information and practice.

MOVE

Healthy food

You can do this!

Vocabulary

8 a Complete the phrases with the verbs in the box.

buy   decide   do   get   learn   look for   save   talk to

1 _____ a new language/how to
2 _____ a bonus/a new job
3 _____ a course/exercise
4 _____ what to do/where to go
5 _____ a camera/a book
6 _____ information/a job
7 _____ money/time
8 _____ friends/people

b Work in pairs. Add one more thing to each of the phrases in Exercise 8a.

learn a recipe
get a new dog
do sport

9 Choose the correct alternatives.

1 I need to *buy/save* money every month.
2 I'm going to join a football club because I want to *do/make* more sport.
3 We want to learn *how to/what to* ski next year.
4 I've got some news. Mike and I are going to *get/go* a new car!
5 Sarah always has to work at weekends. She wants to *decide/look for* a new job.
6 The best thing about my job is that I *talk to/write* people all the time.

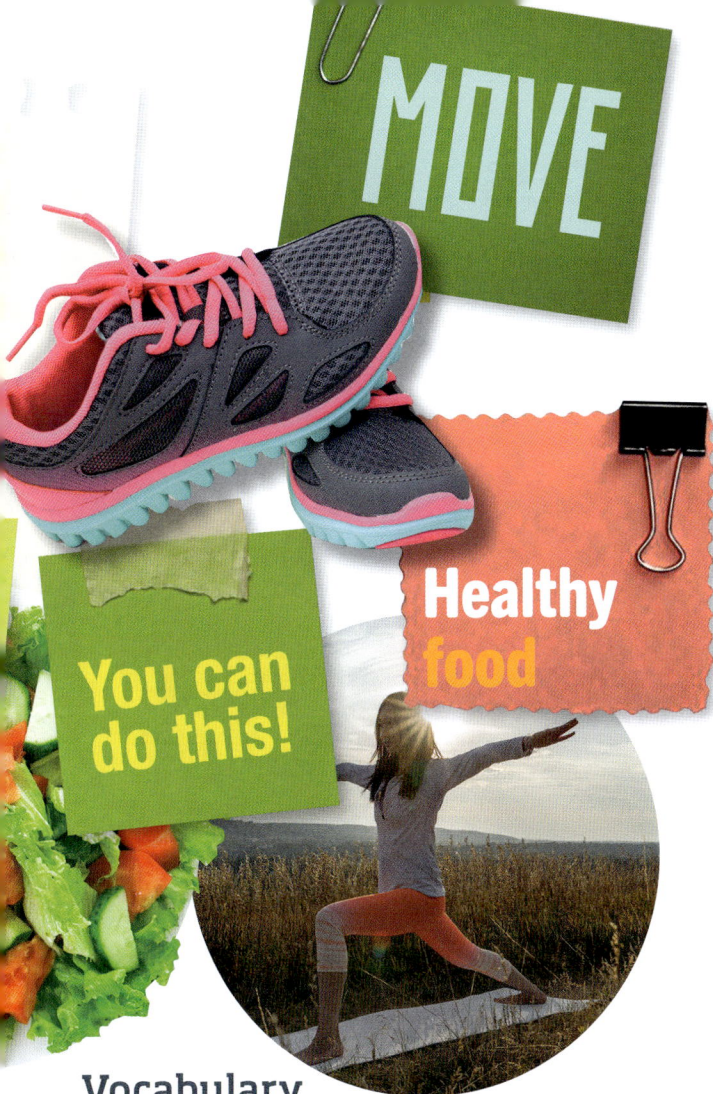

10 Look at the goals below. What small steps can you take?

1 Buy a house
talk to my parents
look for information about house prices
2 Learn a new language
3 Travel around the world

📱 Go to your app for more practice.

Speaking

PREPARE

11 a You're going to tell other people about a goal you have and what you're going to do. First, decide what your goal is. Choose one of the ideas below or your own idea.

• buy a house/car/new computer
• get fit/be healthy
• get a new job
• start a new business
• work less
• go travelling
• save money (for something)

b Decide what your plans are for your goal. Think of at least four things.

go travelling: save money, decide where to go, read about the places I want to visit

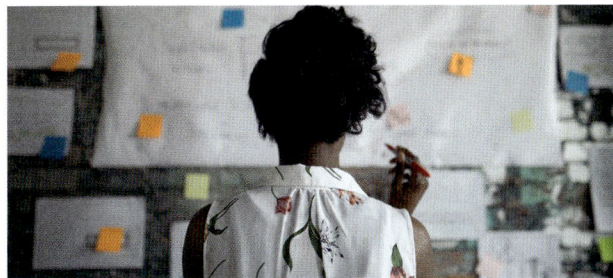

SPEAK

12 a Work in pairs. Share your goal with a partner and tell them how you are going to do it. Give your partner advice about his/her goal.

A: *I'm going to get fit. I'm going to buy some sports shoes and join a gym.*
B: *Are you going to run every day?*

Useful phrases

First, I'm going to ...
You should (join a gym).
Are you going to (save money)?
How often are you going to (go to the gym)?
That's a great plan!

b Report back to the class. What was the best advice you heard?

Develop your writing
page 111

⟩ **Goal:** describe what you want to do

⟩ **Grammar:** *would like/want*

⟩ **Vocabulary:** activities with *go*

Reading and vocabulary

1 Look at the photos and discuss the questions.
1. Do you like doing new things?
2. Do you often do new things?
3. What new things did you try last year?

2 a Read the article and answer the questions.
1. What did the writer do for 30 days?
2. What activity examples does he give?
3. Did the writer think it was easy to do?
4. How did it change the writer's life?

Try something new every day for **30** days

Are you bored with life? Do you want to change things? If so, then try doing something new every day for 30 days. I did it and it changed my life.

Start by making a list of 30 activities and write each one on a different day of the calendar. You don't need to make big changes. Small things can make your life more interesting. For example, I walked a different way to work, cooked a new meal, learnt to say 'hello' in ten languages, visited a new park and did yoga.

It wasn't easy. Some days, I didn't want to do my activity. I wanted to do the same things I do every day – get up, go to work, get home, cook dinner, watch TV and go to bed. But I tried hard, and I did all 30 things.

How did it change my life? Well, those days were special. I remember many of those 30 days more than any other day this year. Because of that, I still do new things today. Not every day, but every week. When I do new things, I make more memories.

So, what are you waiting for? Make a 30-day plan now and give it a try!

September
MON TUES WED THUR FRI SAT SUN
1 2 3 4 ~~5~~ 6 7
8 9 10 11 12 13 (14)
18 19 20 21

b Work in pairs. Would you like to try something new every day for 30 days? Why/Why not?

3 a Match activities 1–10 with photos A–J.
1. go horse riding
2. go swimming
3. go climbing
4. go surfing
5. go skiing
6. go snowboarding
7. go shopping
8. go cycling
9. go sightseeing
10. go bowling

b 🔊 9.12 Listen to the activities and underline the stressed syllable(s).

c Listen again and repeat.

d Work in pairs and discuss the questions.
1. Which activities in Exercise 3a do you sometimes or often do?
2. Which activities do you never do?
3. Which activities would you like to do in the future?

📱 Go to your app for more practice.

Listening and grammar

4 a 🔊 **9.13 Listen to Adam and Lily planning some new activities. Which activities in the box do they talk about?**

> bake a chocolate cake go skiing go surfing
> learn a musical instrument look at the stars
> sing in public take a dance class take photos

b **Listen again. Which of the activities do Adam and Lily both decide to do?**

5 **Read the grammar box and choose the correct alternatives.**

would like/want

Use *would like to/want to* + a noun or infinitive to talk about [1]*past/future* wishes.

I'd like to look at the stars. My friend from work **would like to do** it, too.

My mum **wants to teach** me her recipe.

Use [2]*be/do* to make negative sentences and questions with *want to*.

I **don't want to go surfing**.

Do you **want to come** to dance lessons with me?

When **do you want to go**?

Would and the [3]*subject (you, he, etc.)/like* change places to make questions with *would like*.

Would you **like to try** it next month?

When **would** you **like to go**?

6 a 🔊 **9.14 Listen to the sentences. Is *to* stressed or unstressed?**

1 I'd like to do yoga.
2 We'd like to make something.
3 She'd like to learn how to paint.
4 They want to go to an art gallery.
5 I want to see more of my city.

b **Listen again and repeat.**

7 a **Put the words in the correct order to make sentences.**

1 learn / language / like / a new / They'd / to
2 don't / to / We / a salsa class / want / go to
3 I'd / a new / make / like / friend / to
4 like / grow / you / your own vegetables / Would / to ?
5 how to cook / she / learn / want / Does / to ?
6 don't / join / want / I / a gym / to

b **Complete the sentences so they are true about next weekend for you.**

1 I want to _____ .
   I want to visit my grandparents.
2 I'd like to _____ .
3 I don't want to _____ .

c **Work in pairs and compare your sentences. Give more information.**

> *I want to visit my grandparents. It's my grandma's birthday and I've got her a present.*

📱 Go to page 132 or your app for more information and practice.

Speaking

PREPARE

8 **You're going to make a plan with a partner to do one new activity each day for a week. Write down some new activities you'd like to do.**

SPEAK

9 a **Work in pairs. Tell each other about the new activities you'd like to do. Agree on seven activities to do together every day for one week. Use the Useful phrases to help you.**

Useful phrases

Would you like to do that?
Yes, I would. /That sounds great. Let's do it!
No, I don't want to do that.
When do you want to do that?

b **Work with another pair. Tell each other your plans. Did you choose the same or different activities?**

> *One day, we're going to take a cooking class. We both want to learn how to cook Thai food.*

> Develop
> your
> reading
> page 112

> **Goal:** make arrangements and invitations

1 Look at the photo and discuss the questions.

1 What do you think the people are celebrating?

2 In your country, do people celebrate …
* the end of a course?
* leaving a job?
* passing a driving test?
* the end of a project at work?
* moving home?

3 How do they celebrate them?

2 a 9.15 Listen to Pavel, Erica and Rosa discussing how to celebrate something and answer the questions.

1 What do they want to celebrate?

2 How do they want to celebrate it?

b Listen again and tick the phrases in the Useful phrases box that you hear.

Useful phrases

Making arrangements and invitations
What shall we do (to celebrate)?
What time shall we meet?
Where shall we meet?
Let's (have a party).

Responding to suggestions
Good idea!
I don't think it's a good idea.
I'm not sure.

Inviting people
Would you like to come?
Do you want to join us?

Responding to invitations
Yes, please!
Sorry I can't, I'm busy.

3 a 9.16 Listen to the phrases in the Useful phrases box and underline the stressed words.

b Listen again and repeat.

4 a Complete the conversations with one word.

1 **A:** We're going to have a party next Saturday. Would you _____ to come?
   B: _____ , please!

2 **A:** What time _____ we meet?
   B: Four o'clock?

3 **A:** It's John's last day at work next Tuesday. What shall we _____ to celebrate?
   B: _____ take him to a restaurant.

4 **A:** We going to have a picnic in the park at the weekend. Do you want to _____ us?
   B: Sorry, I _____ . I have to work then.

5 **A:** _____ we do something special for the design team?
   B: I _____ think it's a good idea. We can't do something special for only one team.

6 **A:** _____ shall we meet for lunch? Do you want to go to Gando's?
   B: I'm not _____ . They only have meat options and Penny doesn't eat meat.

b 9.17 Listen and check.

c Work in pairs and practise the conversations. Then swap roles and repeat.

5 a Answer the questions. Use your own ideas.

1 Would you like to come to my party on Saturday?

2 What shall we do to celebrate dad's 50th birthday?

3 Where shall we meet?

4 I'm having a barbecue on Sunday. Would you like to come?

b Work in pairs. Take turns to ask and answer the questions in Exercise 5a.

6 a Work in pairs. You're going to celebrate something. First, choose one of the things to celebrate in Exercise 1, or think of your own idea.

b Discuss the details. Agree on:
* how to celebrate.
* where/when to meet.

7 a Walk around the class and invite people to your celebration. Make a note of who is coming.

b Report back to the class. Who's having the biggest celebration?

Go online for the
Roadmap video.

Check and reflect

1 Complete the conversations with *should/ shouldn't* and the verbs in the box.

eat   go   leave   see   watch

1 **A:** I need to lose weight.
    B: You _____ unhealthy food.

2 **A:** I don't feel well.
    B: You _____ the doctor.

3 **A:** The film starts at 4 o'clock.
    B: We _____ at 3.30.

4 **A:** I'm always tired.
    B: You _____ to bed so late every night.

5 **A:** She wants to learn English.
    B: She _____ TV programmes in English.

2 a Match verbs 1–8 with a–h to make phrases.

1	keep	a	down
2	sit	b	to sleep
3	join	c	healthy
4	eat	d	fit
5	walk	e	well
6	go	f	up the stairs
7	do	g	some exercise
8	stay	h	a gym

b Complete the sentences with the phrases in Exercise 2a.

1 I want to _____ a _____ and go every morning before work.

2 I have a bath in the evening because it helps me _____ to _____.

3 Try not to _____ _____ at your desk all day. _____ _____ _____ at least once an hour.

4 Avoid junk food and don't eat too much if you want to _____ _____.

5 I always _____ up _____ _____ in my apartment building. I don't use the lift.

6 Isla has junk food every day. She really doesn't _____ _____.

3 Correct the mistakes in the sentences.

1 She's isn't going to get a new job.

2 Fiona and I going to get married!

3 Are you going learn a new skill this year?

4 I'm going eating more healthy food this week.

5 We're going to travelling in South America next summer.

6 They aren't go to buy a house.

4 Complete the text with the missing verbs.

> I've got lots of plans for this year. First, I'm going to ¹_____ a course. I'd like to ²_____ a new language, maybe French? I'm also going to try and ³_____ money, because my wife and I also want to ⁴_____ a house this year. If we have enough money after that, we want to go on holiday, but we need to ⁵_____ where to go. Maybe France!

5 Rewrite the sentences so that they are negative.

1 I want to visit Greece this year.
    I don't want to visit Greece this year.

2 She'd like to climb a mountain.

3 We'd like to go bowling at the weekend.

4 He wants to learn another language.

5 You want to go skiing in January.

6 I'd like to learn how to drive.

6 a Choose the correct alternatives.

1 I'd like *learn/ to learn* another language in the future.

2 I don't *want/ like* to join a gym – ever!

3 I *not/ wouldn't* like to visit the Antarctic.

4 My parents want *me to/ to* speak to me more often.

5 I'd like *to climb/ climbing* a mountain.

6 I *don't/ 'm not* want to watch TV tonight.

b Work in pairs. Discuss which of the sentences in Exercise 6a are true for you.

7 Complete the sentences with the correct form of *go* and the verbs in the box.

bowl   cycle   sightsee   ski   surf

1 We always _____ when we visit a new city.

2 At the weekend, I _____ along the cycle paths around the city.

3 Do you ever _____ in the mountains in winter?

4 Let's _____ tonight! There's a new bowling alley in town.

5 We _____ for the first time on holiday. The waves were huge!

8 a Complete the sentences with a phrase with *go* so that they are true for you.

1 I'd like to go _____ next summer.

2 I'm not going to go _____ this week.

3 I never go _____ .

4 I want to go _____ this year.

b Work in pairs and compare your answers.

Reflect

How confident do you feel about the statements below? Write 1–5 (1 = not very confident, 5 = very confident).

- I can give advice.
- I can discuss my goals for the future.
- I can describe what I want to do.
- I can make arrangements and invitations.

Want more practice?
Go to your Workbook or app.

Living together

> **Goal:** interview people
> **Grammar:** verb patterns
> **Vocabulary:** housework

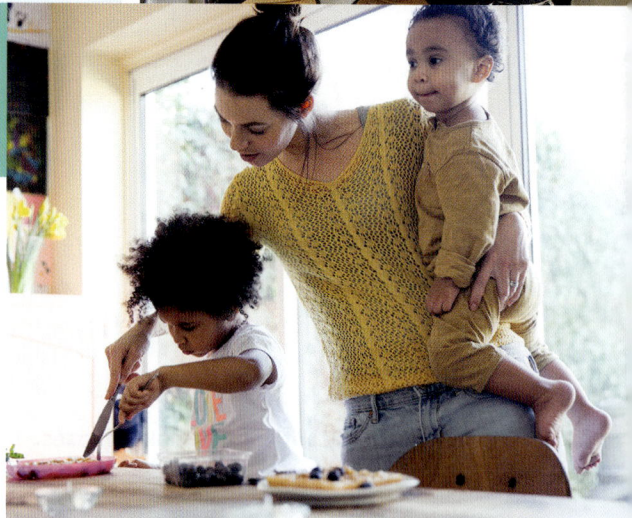

Reading and vocabulary

1 Discuss the questions.

1 Do people in your country usually share a house or flat with other people who are not their family?

2 What are the good things about living alone or with other people?

3 Do you think you're an easy person to live with? Why/Why not?

2 a Read the quiz. Match the phrases in bold in the quiz with pictures A–G .

b Do the quiz, then turn to page 158 to find out what your answers mean.

Are you EASY to LIVE with?

1 How long do you leave your **washing up** after you cook a meal?
a I don't like washing up, so I don't do it.
b One day.
c I hate leaving dirty dishes. I finish eating then I wash up.

2 How do you feel about **sharing bills**?
a I don't want to pay anything. I need my money for other things.
b I only want to pay for the things I use.
c I don't mind sharing the bills.

3 It's the weekend and you're free. What do you do?
a Sit around, watch TV, do nothing.
b Go out with my friends.
c **Tidy my room, clean the bathroom,** kitchen and windows.

4 Your clothes are dirty and you need to **do the laundry.** What do you do?
a Leave my dirty clothes in the washing machine. Someone else can do it.
b Do my own laundry.
c Ask if anyone else has any dirty clothes and wash them with mine.

5 The fridge is broken. What do you do?
a I don't want to pay for a new one – I didn't break it!
b Share the cost of fixing it.
c Fix it myself. I like **fixing things.**

6 How do you feel about cooking for other people?
a I don't like cooking. I can buy you a burger, maybe.
b I don't mind cooking today, but you should cook tomorrow.
c I like **cooking for people.** I always ask people to share my food.

3 a Complete the sentences. Use the phrases in bold in the quiz to help you.

1 We _____ all the bills in our house.
2 I never _____ the windows – I just pay someone to do it.
3 I always _____ things when they're broken.
4 I _____ my room every morning before work.
5 It's nice to _____ meals for other people.
6 When I need clean clothes, I _____ for everyone in the house.
7 I usually do the _____ when there are no more clean dishes.

b Change the sentences so they are true for you.

c Work in pairs and compare your sentences.
  A: I do the washing up when I finish a meal.
  B: Really? I do it once a week.

Go to your app for more practice.

Grammar

4 Read the grammar box and choose the correct alternatives.

Verb patterns

After *love, (don't) like, don't mind, hate,* use verb +
-ing or [1]*a noun/an adjective* to express your feelings.
I **hate leaving** *dirty dishes*.
I **don't mind sharing** *the bills*.
I **love going** *to parties*.
I **love parties**.
Ask about likes and dislikes with
[2]*What do you like doing?/What are you liking?*
Ask questions with *Do you mind/like/hate* +
verb + *-ing*.
Do you mind cleaning?
Do you like cooking?

5 a 🔊 10.1 Listen to the sentences and underline the stressed words.

1 I hate cleaning!
2 I don't mind working at the weekend.
3 I don't like getting up early.
4 I love staying at home.
5 I like shopping.

b Listen again and repeat.

6 a Make questions with *you* using the prompts.

1 mind / clean / house?
   Do you mind cleaning the house?
2 hate / clean / bathroom?
3 like / live / alone?
4 What / love / do / your free time?
5 mind / tidy / room?
6 What / hate / clean / most?

b Work in pairs. Take turns to ask and answer the questions. Ask for more information.
  A: Do you mind cleaning the house?
  B: I hate it.
  A: What do you hate cleaning the most?
  B: I hate cleaning the kitchen.

Go to page 134 or your app for more information and practice.

Speaking

PREPARE

7 a 🔊 10.2 You're going to interview people to be your new housemate. First, listen to Natalia and Hailey interviewing two people. How are they different?

b Listen again. Does each sentence describe Julia (J) or Maria (M)?

1 She doesn't like sharing the bills.
2 She works near to Natalia and Hailey's house.
3 She likes cleaning.
4 She doesn't have a job.
5 She has pets.
6 She goes out a lot.

c Work in pairs. Who is better for the house, Julia or Maria?

8 Work in pairs. Student A, you are renting a room in your house. Think of questions to ask someone who wants to move in. Student B, you want to rent a room. Think of questions to ask about:

- housework
- likes/dislikes
- pets
- free-time activities

SPEAK

9 a Work in pairs. Ask and answer questions. Use the Useful phrases to help you.

Useful phrases

Do you mind cleaning the house with us?
What's your job?
Can I bring my pet(s)?
How often do you cook?

b Report back to the class. Would you like to live with each other? Why/Why not?

Develop your writing
page 113

10B Formal or casual?

> **Goal:** play a guessing game
> **Grammar:** *have to/don't have to*
> **Vocabulary:** clothes

Vocabulary

1 **Look at the photos and discuss the questions.**

   1 How many of the people's clothes can you name?

   2 What do you think the people's jobs are? Why?

2 **Find the clothes in the box in photos A–F. Who is wearing each thing? Which things can't you see in the photos?**

> boots cap coat dress helmet jeans shirt
> shorts smart clothes suit tie trainers
> trousers uniform

3 a 🔊 10.3 **Listen to the words and underline the stressed syllable. Which syllable is always stressed?**

   b **Listen again and repeat.**

4 **Work in pairs and discuss the questions.**

   1 Which of the clothes in Exercise 2 do you wear …
     • at work?
     • at school?
     • in your free time?

   2 Which of the clothes do you never wear? Why?

📱 Go to your app for more practice.

Reading

5 a **Read the introduction to a survey. What is it about?**

   b **Read four people's responses in the survey. Where does each person work?**

> **What do you wear to work?**
> Can you wear what you want at work? Or do you have to wear a uniform? We asked some people on the street.
>
> **1** *I work for a small IT company and I usually wear jeans and a shirt, with trainers. We don't have to wear a suit or smart clothes.*
>
> **2** *I work for a big supermarket in the centre of town. We have to wear a uniform – I really hate it. The uniform is blue trousers, a white shirt, black shoes and a red tie. Oh, and we also have to wear a silly cap!*
>
> **3** *Well, I'm a sports teacher, so I have to wear sports clothes. I usually wear shorts, a T-shirt and trainers. I love my job and I always feel comfortable in these clothes!*
>
> **4** *I'm a manager at an office near here. I can wear what I want, but I like wearing smart clothes, so I usually wear a nice dress. Today, it's cold so I'm wearing my warm boots, too!*

6 **Read the responses again and answer the questions.**

Which person or people …

a can wear what they want?

b doesn't like what they wear?

c is wearing something because of the weather?

d doesn't wear smart clothes?

Grammar

7 **Read the grammar box and choose the correct alternatives. Use the responses in Exercise 5 to help you.**

> ### have to/don't have to
>
> Use *have to* + infinitive to describe something which is [1]*necessary/not necessary*.
> *We **have to wear** a uniform.*
> *I **have to wear** sports clothes.*
> Use *don't have to* + infinitive to describe something which is [2]*necessary/not necessary*.
> *You **don't have to wear** trainers to wear (but you can if you want to).*
> *Office workers **don't have to wear** smart clothes nowadays.*
> Use [3]*has to/have to* + infinitive with *he/she/it*.
> *My husband **has to wear** a uniform for his job.*
> *She **doesn't have to work** at weekends.*
> Use [4]*be/do* to make questions with *have to*.
> *What do you **have to wear** at work?*
> *Do you **have to wear** a uniform?*

C

D

E

F

8 a 🔊 10.4 **Listen to the sentences with *have to*. How do we pronounce *have to* and *has to*?**

1 We don't have to be there early.

2 She has to wear a uniform.

3 I have to work at the weekend.

4 He has to do homework every day.

5 You don't have to wear formal clothes to the party.

b Listen again and repeat.

9 Rewrite the sentences using *(don't) have to* + infinitive.

1 It's necessary for you to wear smart clothes.
   You have to wear smart clothes.

2 It's not necessary to take a present to the party.

3 Is it necessary for us to buy a ticket?

4 It's necessary for the manager to wear a suit.

5 They don't need to be early.

6 You need to have a passport to travel abroad.

7 We need to wear a uniform.

8 We can wear what we want, so we don't wear smart clothes.

10 a Complete the sentences to talk about rules at your work/school.

1 We have to _____ .

2 We don't have to _____ .

3 My teacher/boss has to _____ .

4 Workers/students don't have to _____ .

b Work in small groups and compare your answers. Does anyone have the same answers?

📱 Go to page 134 or your app for more information and practice.

Speaking

PREPARE

11 a 🔊 10.5 **Listen to three friends playing a game. What's James's job?**

b Listen again. Which of these rules are true?

1 You have to take one card.

2 You can show your card to other people.

3 Other people have to ask *yes/no* questions.

4 You don't have to answer the questions.

5 Other people have to guess the job on the card.

12 You're going to play the same game in small groups. First, think of a job and make notes. Use the questions below to help you. Do not show your information to other students.

• What do you have to do? *cook food*

• What do you have to wear at work? *a hat*

• Where do you have to work? *a restaurant*

• When do you have to work? *in the evenings*

SPEAK

13 Work in groups and play the game. Remember to only ask *yes/no* questions. Can you guess each other's jobs?

Useful phrases
Do you have to wear (a uniform)?
No, I don't have to wear (a hat).
Are you a (police officer)?

Develop your reading
page 114

> **Goal:** talk about past experiences
> **Grammar:** present perfect simple
> **Vocabulary:** technology

Vocabulary

1 Discuss the questions.

1 What kind of technology do you use the most? Why?
2 Is there any technology you don't like? Why?
3 Are there any problems with using technology?

2 a Which things in the box can you see in the photos?

app file laptop tablet program
online game printer screen smartphone
speakers (text) message the internet (web)site
multiplayer game

b Complete the verb phrases with the words in the box in Exercise 2a.

1 download a/an _____ /_____ /_____
2 read/write/send a _____
3 open/close a/an _____ /_____ /_____ / _____
4 save a _____
5 go on _____ /online
6 play a/an _____ /_____
7 own (a) _____ /_____ /_____ /_____ /_____
8 visit/look for a _____

c Complete the questions with the words in Exercises 2a and 2b.

1 What _____ do you visit the most?
2 Do you ever need to print anything on a _____?
3 How many hours a day do you look at a _____?
4 When do you usually first _____ online each day?
5 How many text _____ do you send every day?
6 Do you prefer to listen to music on headphones or through _____?
7 How do you usually share _____ with friends?

d Work in pairs. Take turns to ask and answer the questions.

📱 Go to page 145 or your app for more vocabulary and practice.

Reading

3 a Read the article. What is it about?

a Good things about technology
b The differences between people of different ages
c Problems between people of different ages

b Read the article again and complete the sentences.

1 Marc has never sent anyone a _____ .
2 He has never printed a _____ .
3 Marc has made his own _____ .
4 Marc's grandfather has never talked to anyone _____ .
5 Marc's grandfather hasn't used a _____ .
6 Marc's father owns a _____ and a _____ .
7 Marc's father has downloaded a lot of _____ .
8 Marc's father has never played games _____ .

Our world is changing so fast, isn't it? My grandfather, my father and I live in the same world, but our lives are very different. One of the biggest differences is how we use technology.

I haven't sent a letter to anyone. I send text messages, I sometimes write emails but I haven't written to anyone on paper. I'm a little sad about that, because it's a great way to communicate. Also, I've never printed photos. I take them with my phone and upload them to social media.

Of course, I have done many things with technology that my father and grandfather haven't done. I've played multiplayer games online, I've recorded music on my computer and I've even made my own website. These things are normal for people of my age.

And there are many other things that they haven't done. My grandfather has never chatted to anyone online or bought anything online. And he hasn't used a smartphone. My father has a tablet and a laptop and he downloads apps all the time but he's never played games online (he still plays his old video games from 1985!), and he met my mother in a disco, not online.

So, we're different but we're not so different. We do the same things but in different ways. **– Marc**

Grammar

4 a Read the grammar box and choose the correct alternatives.

Present perfect simple

Use the present perfect simple to talk about a
[1]*present/past* experience in our lives. We [2]*say/
don't say* when it happened. Form the present
perfect simple with *have/has/haven't/hasn't* + past
participle.
I've printed photos.
She's chatted to friends online.
I haven't played a multiplayer game.
He hasn't used a smartphone.
Form regular past participles by adding [3]*-ing/-ed* to
the infinitive, e.g. *download - downloaded,
own - owned.*
Some past participles are irregular, e.g. *have - had,
make - made, do – done.*
Use [4]*never/ever* to make a verb negative.
I've never bought a DVD.
Use [5]*never/ever* to make a question.
A: Have you ever watched TV in black and white?
B: Yes, I have./No, I haven't.
A: Has he ever owned a Nokia phone?
B: Yes, he has./No, he hasn't.

b Write the past participles of the verbs in the box.
Use the article in Exercise 3 to help you. Which are
irregular?

| buy | chat | do | make | play | print | record |
| send | write |

5 a 🔊 10.6 Listen to the sentences and notice the
pronunciation of the contractions of *have.*
1 I've never downloaded an app.
2 He's written letters to his family.
3 They haven't played video games.
4 She hasn't had a mobile phone.

b Listen again and repeat.

6 Complete the conversations with the correct present
perfect form of the verbs in brackets.
1 **A:** My cousin _____ (never/own) a computer.
  B: Really? How does he do his homework?
  A: He uses a tablet.
2 **A:** _____ you _____ (ever/share) a photo online?
  B: Yes, I have. Why?
  A: I _____ (never/do) it. Can you show me how?
3 **A:** Ben _____ (make) a short film.
  B: Has he? I _____ (not/see) it.
  A: It's really good.
  B: _____ he _____ (be) in a film before?
  A: Yes, I think he has.

7 a Make sentences that are true about you using the
phrases in the box.

> break my mobile phone screen   buy a DVD
> own a laptop   read a blog   watch a film on my phone
> write a letter by hand

I've never broken my mobile phone screen.

b Work in pairs and compare your sentences. What do
you have in common?
A: I've never broken my mobile phone screen.
B: Me neither./I have.

📱 Go to page 134 or your app for more information and practice.

Speaking

PREPARE

8 🔊 10.7 You're going to interview your classmates
about technology. First, listen to Freddie and Ali and
answer the questions.
1 Have they ever made a website?
2 Have they ever sent a text message to the wrong
person?

9 Think of questions about technology with *Have you
ever ...?*
Have you ever written a program?
Have you ever printed photos?

SPEAK

10 a Talk to your classmates. Ask your questions in
Exercise 9. Ask extra questions to find out more.
A: Have you ever made a website?
B: No, I haven't. Have you?
A: Yes, I have.
B: What website did you make?

b Work in pairs and discuss what you have learned
about your classmates.

Develop
your
listening
page 115

> **Goal:** give a compliment

1 a Look at the pictures and answer the question. What do you think the people are saying in each one?

b Match captions 1–3 with pictures A–C.

   1 'You did a great job.'
   2 'You play really well.'
   3 'This room is beautiful.'

c 🔊 **10.11** Listen to three conversations and check your answers.

2 a Complete the conversations with one or two words.

   1 A: The house _____ fantastic, Steve. You did a _____ job.
      B: Thanks. I'm _____ you like it.
   2 A: You play really _____ .
      B: Oh, thanks. That's _____ of you to say.
   3 A: Wow, this room is _____ ! It's really modern.
      B: _____ . I like it.

b Listen again and check your answers.

c Which sentences in Exercise 2a give a compliment? How do the speakers reply to the compliments?

d Use the Useful phrases box to check your answers in Exercise 2c.

Useful phrases

Giving compliments
I love/like your bag/car.
The house looks great/fantastic/lovely.
Your new sofa looks great/fantastic/lovely.
This room/food is lovely/beautiful/fantastic.
You're so funny/kind/helpful/interesting.
You always tell the best stories/make me laugh.
You play/sing/dance really well.
You did a good/great/fantastic job.

Replying to compliments
Thanks./Thank you.
That's kind/nice of you (to say).
I'm pleased/glad you like it.

3 a 🔊 **10.12** Listen to the pairs of compliments. Which one is better, A or B? Why?

   1 Your cooking is fantastic. *A/B*
   2 You played well today. *A/B*
   3 You did a great job with the garden. *A/B*
   4 You're so clever. *A/B*

b 🔊 **10.13** Listen and repeat the compliments. Copy the intonation.

4 a Read the situations. What compliment can you give in each one? Use the Useful phrases box to help you. More than one answer is possible.

   1 You think your friend's new TV is good.
   2 Your friend is very kind.
   3 Your friend invited you to a great party.
   4 Your friend repaired your bike for you.
   5 Your brother played well in a football match.
   6 Your friend baked a cake. It looks lovely.

b 🔊 **10.14** Listen and compare your ideas.

c Work in pairs. Take turns to give and reply to the compliments in Exercise 4a.

5 You're going to practise giving compliments. Work in pairs. Student A: Turn to page 158. Student B: Turn to page 156. Read the instructions.

6 a Work in pairs and role play the conversation in Exercise 5.

b Work in pairs and discuss the questions.

   1 Do you enjoy getting compliments? Why/Why not?
   2 What kind of compliments do people give you?

Go online for the Roadmap video.

Check and reflect

1 Complete the likes and dislikes with the correct form of the verbs in the box.

> do   go   cook   read   ride

1 Amy doesn't like _____ books very much.
2 I like _____ Italian food.
3 My brother loves _____ to the beach.
4 Susie doesn't mind _____ the laundry.
5 We love _____ our bikes to the river.

2 a Match the sentences halves.

1 Sammy, go and tidy
2 We should clean
3 My husband cooks
4 I cooked. You can wash
5 I need someone to fix
6 I don't have any clothes. I need to do
7 Everyone in the house shares

a this clock. It's not working.
b the bathroom. It's really dirty.
c up the dishes.
d meals for the family every day.
e the laundry.
f your room, please!
g the bills.

b Work in pairs. Tell your partner which things in Exercise 2a you do.

3 Correct the mistakes in four of the sentences.

1 My parents doesn't have to work these days.
2 I don't have get up early tomorrow.
3 Sammy have to tidy her room today.
4 We don't have to go anywhere today.
5 My brother doesn't have to doing any housework.
6 Richard has to work all day tomorrow.

4 a Choose the correct alternatives.

> I work in a small office. It's on the other side of the city so I ¹*has to/have to* get up early and take the bus there. I ²*don't have to/doesn't have to* start until 9 a.m. but I often get there at 8 a.m. because it's quiet. I have lunch with a colleague Andy at midday. I ³*have to/don't have to* eat with him but I enjoy it.
> The office is quite relaxed. No one ⁴*has to/have to* wear a uniform but we all ⁵*have to/don't have to* look smart. My day finishes at 5 p.m. but once a week, I ⁶*have to/don't have to* work until 7 p.m. I don't mind that. Andy ⁷*has to/don't have to* work one Saturday a month but he ⁸*doesn't have to/don't have to* work on Sundays.

b Work in pairs. Tell each other about three things you have to do in the next 24 hours.

5 Write the names of the items of clothing. Which things do you own?

1 Things you wear on your feet when you do sport.
2 Short trousers.
3 Clothes that a police officer or a nurse wears to work.
4 Something a man wears around his neck with a shirt.
5 Something baseball players wear on their head.
6 A pair of trousers and a jacket which go together.

6 Correct the mistakes in each sentence.

1 I never have been to Chicago.
2 He have read every Harry Potter book.
3 Have you ever visit the history museum?
4 We never seen the Eiffel Tower.
5 She haven't eaten Mexican food.
6 Has Ellie ever had a job? No, she haven't.

7 a Complete the conversations with *has(n't)/have(n't)* and the correct form of the verbs in brackets.

1 **A:** _____ you ever _____ (visit) Egypt?
   B: No, I _____ but I'd like to.
2 **A:** _____ Alicia _____ (try) sushi?
   B: No, she _____ . She doesn't like fish very much.
3 **A:** I _____ never _____ (be) to the theatre.
   B: I have. I _____ (be) a few times.
4 **A:** _____ Carlos _____ (see) the new James Bond film?
   B: Yes, he _____ . He enjoyed it.

b Work in pairs. Tell each other two things you've done and two things you haven't done in your lives.

8 Complete the sentences with a technology word. You have the first letter to help you.

1 Don't look at your phone **s**_____ for long.
2 Who's that text **m**_____ from?
3 I need to email a **f**_____ to my boss but it's 100MB.
4 You should **d**_____ this app. It's free.
5 Can I use your **p**_____ , please? I need a paper copy of my plane ticket.
6 Can you play the music through your **s**_____ ?

Reflect

How confident do you feel about the statements below? Write 1–5 (1 = not very confident, 5 = very confident).

- I can interview people.
- I can play a guessing game.
- I can talk about past experiences.
- I can give a compliment.

Want more practice?
Go to your Workbook or app.

Develop your writing

> **Goal:** write an online message
> **Focus:** using capital letters and full stops

1 a Discuss the questions. What's a study group? Do you think it's a good idea?

b Read the conversation in an online study group. Which person/people ...
1 likes sports?
2 is a songwriter?
3 are parents?
4 is from another country?
5 are teachers?

Patrick Smith

Hi, everyone. Welcome to the study group for our course. Let's introduce ourselves! I'm Patrick Smith. I'm from Chicago. I'm an English teacher at a high school there. I'm a big music fan. I play the guitar and write my own songs.

Mona Galotti

It's nice to meet you, Patrick. My name's Mona and I'm a university student. I'm from a small town in Texas called Palmer. It's about 30 minutes from Dallas. I'm a soccer player and I'm in a really great team in my town. My best friend is my dog, Bertie. He's big, brown and really friendly.

Steven Welsh

Hi, Patrick. Hi, Mona and everyone else. I'm Steven. I'm from Denver in Colorado. I'm a taxi driver and I'm married with five children. Five! 😳 They're all girls, too! Every room in my house is noisy. The only quiet place is the garden. It's my favourite place at home!

Annika Petrov

Hello, everyone! I'm Annika. I'm Russian but I'm here in the US now. I'm a teacher at the University of California. Nice to meet you all. I speak three languages – Russian, English and French. I love books and read all kinds of books from all over the world. My favourite author is Haruki Murakami. His books are amazing!

Maria Martinez

Hi! I'm Maria. I'm from Charlotte, a city in North Carolina. I'm a receptionist at a big hotel in Tryon Street on Fridays, Saturdays and Sundays and I'm a mother, too. My children are four and five so life is busy and I'm always tired. I like books, TV and films. I think all stories are interesting – I love them all.

2 a Read the Focus box. Find one example of each use of capital letters in the online group in Exercise 1b.

Using capital letters and full stops

We use capital letters (e.g. A, B, C) at the beginning of a sentence. We use a full stop (.) at the end of a sentence.
I'm a big music fan.
Hi everyone. Welcome to the group.
We also use capital letters for:
- the subject *I*
- people's names, e.g. *Natasha, Leo*
- road or street names, e.g. *Park Road, Oxford Street*
- names of towns, cities, states and countries, e.g. *Sheffield, Florida, Argentina*
- nationalities, e.g. *Japanese, Turkish*
- languages, e.g. *English, Spanish*
- names of companies and universities, e.g. *Samsung, the University of Cambridge*
- days and months, e.g. *Friday, October*

b Rewrite the message below. Add capital letters and full stops.

hello everyone i'm kelvin and i'm canadian i'm a doctor at the south west hospital here in los angeles i'm married with two children, sam and maggie my wife is a manager at the california water company she is at work all week, but i am only at the hospital on mondays, wednesdays and thursdays

Prepare

3 You're going to write an online message to introduce yourself to your classmates. Make notes about:
- your name
- your town/city
- your job
- your family
- something else about you

Write

4 Write your message. Use capital letters and full stops.

1B Develop your listening

> **Goal:** understand a simple conversation

> **Focus:** understanding question words

1 🔊 **1.8 Listen to a conversation between two people, Marco and Eva. Answer the questions.**

1 Who are they?

2 Where are they?

3 Where are they from?

2 a Read the Focus box. What do question words do?

Understanding question words

To help to understand a question, listen for the question word. It tells you what information the speaker wants. For example:

When is your first lesson? = Time

Where is your first lesson? = Place

What is your first lesson? = Type (e.g. writing, speaking)

b Match question words 1–6 with meanings a–f.

1	What	a	time
2	Where	b	age
3	When	c	thing
4	Who	d	person
5	How old	e	reason
6	Why	f	place

c 🔊 **1.9 Listen to the pronunciation of the question words. When does the speaker pronounce the sound /h/?**

3 a 🔊 **1.8 Listen to Marco and Eva again. Write the question word in each question. If there is no question word, write –.**

1 _____ 's your name?

2 _____ are you from?

3 _____ are you here for nine months?

4 _____ are you a student?

5 _____ 's your job?

6 _____ 's your first lesson?

7 _____ is it?

8 _____ 's the teacher?

b 🔊 **1.10 Listen to Marco and Eva's questions. Match answers a–h with questions 1–8 in Exercise 3a.**

a In classroom 6b.

b Monza.

c Eleven o'clock.

d I'm a university student.

e Marketa.

f Marco.

g Yes, I am.

h No, I'm not. I work for a bank.

4 a You're going to listen to Marco talking to another student. What information is missing? What question word can help us to get that information?

1 Her name is __*(Name - e.g Linda, Michell)*__ . *What*

2 She's from _____ .

3 She's in class _____ .

4 She's here with _____ .

5 She works for an _____ company.

6 Her next lesson is at _____ o'clock.

b 🔊 **1.11 Listen to the conversation and complete the sentences in Exercise 4a.**

5 a 🔊 **1.12 Work in pairs. Student A: Listen to the questions and say your answers. Student B: Listen and write down Student A's answers.**

b 🔊 **1.13 Student B: Listen to the questions and say your answers. Student A: Listen and write down Student B's answers.**

6 Work in pairs. Look at your answers. Can you remember the question words?

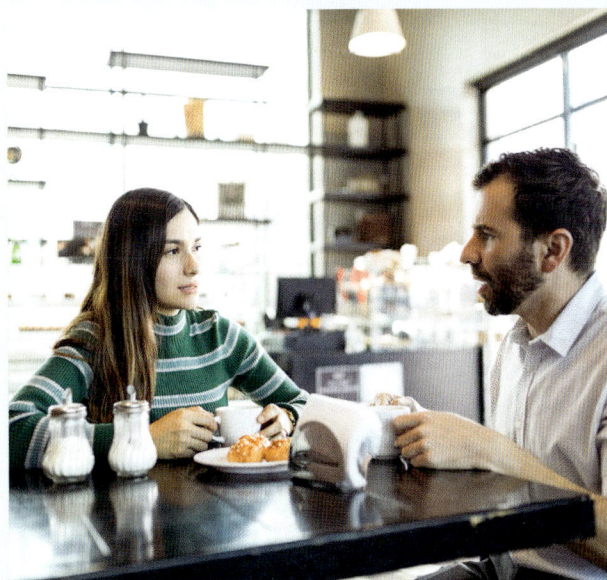

Develop your reading

> **Goal:** understand adverts
>
> **Focus:** identifying specific information

1 Read the website quickly and choose the correct option.

This website is for …

a making friends.

b buying and selling things.

c watching videos.

Korean laptop
This laptop is two years old. It's good but I need a tablet for work.
It's black with white lines on the side.
€100

Red dress from a lovely shop in Paris
It's three years old but I never wear it because it's a bit small for me now.
€1,500

Children's book from the 1950s
A lovely story book for young readers.
€300

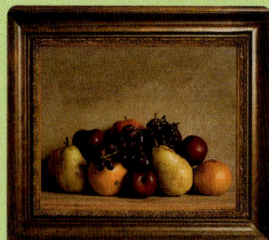

Picture by Carla Weber, a German artist
I love it but my new house is very small and there's no space.
2 metres x 1.5 metres
€75

Mobile phone with wifi and 4G
Ready to use with any phone company.
Only three months old! Unwanted gift.
€500

Sports bag from the US
Good for running or cycling.
This is a very good bag at a very good price!
€5

2 Read the Focus box, then find the prices, places, ages and sizes in the adverts in Exercise 1.

Identifying specific information

To find information quickly in a text, don't read everything.

- To find a price, look for symbols, e.g. £, €, $, etc. and a number.
- To find where something or someone is from, look for place names with a capital letter, e.g. *France, Spain, Rome,* etc.
- To find age, look for *years old* or years in numbers, e.g. *50 years old, from the 1970s,* etc.
- To find size, look for *cm, m, metres* with numbers, e.g. *35 cm x 1.5 m*, etc.

3 a Read the adverts in Exercise 1 again and answer the questions.

Which object is …

1 almost new?	4 expensive?
2 from the US?	5 big?
3 from Asia?	6 old?

b Work in pairs. Which words in each advert gave you the answers in Exercise 3a?

4 Read adverts 1–4 quickly and find the information.

Which object is …

1 small?	5 cheap?
2 old?	6 free?
3 quite new?	7 good for a student?
4 from Spain?	

[1]**Men's racing bike**
This bike is twenty years old.
It's a really great bike.
Only €100!

[2]**Large suitcase for sale**
This is a strong suitcase and only six months old.
76 cm x 48 cm
€50

[3]**White desk lamp**, 30 cm tall
Perfect for work or homework!
€5

[4]**Spanish guitar**, made in Madrid. I don't have time to play it now. Free to good home.

5 Work in pairs. Which things on the page do you like?
I like the bike!

2A Develop your listening

> **Goal:** understand a conversation about family

> **Focus:** *and*, *too* and *but*

1 a Discuss the questions. Does everyone in your family live in the same place? If not, where do they live?

b 🔊 2.4 Listen to the conversation and answer the questions.

1 Do Teresa's family all live in the same place? *no*

2 How many different countries and cities does Teresa mention? *five countris*

2 Read the Focus box and complete the sentences with *and*, *but* or *too*.

---

and, *too* and *but*

Some words help us understand the connection between things/actions.

And and *too* introduce extra information:

*My parents live in Madrid, **and** my brothers live there, too.*

*My grandparents live there, **too**.*

But introduces different information:

*My husband's from Australia, **but** his family all live in London.*

---

1 My cousin's from France, *but* she lives in India.

2 My parents live there, *and* my sister, too.

3 My parents live there, and my grandparents live there *too*.

3 a Complete the conversation with *and*, *but* or *too*.

A: Do your family all live in Rio?

B: My parents live there, [1] *but* my brother lives in Washington.

A: Washington, wow!

B: Yeah, my uncle and aunt live there, [2] *too*.

b 🔊 2.5 Listen to the conversation and check your answers.

4 a 🔊 2.6 Listen to the conversation and choose the correct alternatives.

1 His dad lives in *England*/ Spain.

2 His brother lives in *England*/ Spain.

3 His mother lives in England /*Spain*.

b Listen to the conversation again. How do the speakers pronounce the words *and* and *but* in these sentences?

1 ... my dad is here, and my brother.

2 ... but my mum lives in Spain, in Alicante.

5 🔊 2.7 Listen to the conversation and write the family members next to the correct places.

Map of Poland showing: Toruń — *parents*; Poznań; Warsaw — *brother*; Krakow. **POLAND**

6 a 🔊 2.8 Listen to the conversation. Are the sentences true (T) or false (F)?

1 The woman lives in Edinburgh. *T*

2 Her sister and brother live in the same place. *T*

3 Her parents live in Edinburgh. *F*

b Listen to the conversation again. How many times do the speakers use *and*, *but* and *too*?

7 a 🔊 2.9 Listen to the conversation. Which members of her family does Emma talk about?

b Listen again and answer the questions.

1 Where is Emma from? *Italy*

2 Which members of her family live in the same place?

3 Which member of her family is a student? *her sister*

4 Who does her brother live with? ~~Toyth~~ *his wife and son.*

Develop your reading

> **Goal:** understand online posts
> **Focus:** understanding the important words

1 Read the sentences. Are they true for you?
   1 I keep all my old things.
   2 I sell old things I don't use.
   3 I give old things to other people.

2 Read posts 1–5 from a website where people offer things they don't want for free. Match them with photos A–E.

1 I've got various pieces of jewellery – earrings, necklaces, etc. Some of them are old and some are quite new. They're all free!

2 I've got a handbag which I don't want. It's quite new and looks nice. It's blue (see the photo).

3 Fastech 2.6 laptop. The screen is broken but it works. Collect it from Friar's Street on Thursday or Friday.

4 These chargers are for various different types of phones. There are more than 30 here! Good for anyone?

5 I've got lots of new bottles of perfume from different companies. Some of the bottles are three or four years old but the perfume still smells nice. I don't want them because I need the space.

A
B
C
D
E

3 Read the Focus box, then underline the important words in the posts in Exercise 2.

Understanding the important words

Look for **nouns**, **verbs** and **adjectives** to find the important information in a sentence.
For example:
I've got a **handbag** which I **don't want**. It's quite **new** and looks **nice**.
We can understand the meaning using only these words:
I've got - handbag - don't want - new - nice

4 Underline the important word(s) in these sentences.
   1 The laptop's screen is broken.
   2 It's a new sweater.
   3 I've got an old, blue necklace. It's free!
   4 It's old but it works fine.
   5 I don't want these sunglasses. I don't like them.

5 Match posts 1–4 with posts a–d. Use important words to help you.

1 I've got a child's bike, quite old, but it works fine. It's for ages 5–7 but my son is too big for it.

2 I've got a beautiful old clock from the 1950s – interesting for collectors. It's broken so you will need to repair it.

3 I don't want my bike any more. It's a racing bike, quite new, but I think it needs a new wheel. Is anyone interested?

4 I've got an old camera from the 1990s. It's old but it's not broken.

a Does anyone have old things out there? I collect interesting, beautiful or useful objects from around the mid-twentieth century. Broken things are fine!

b I need an adult bike. Mine is broken and I need it to go to work every morning.

c My daughter wants her first bike! We'd like a bike for her to learn to ride. She's six years old.

d I'm a photographer and I use old cameras with paper photos. Does anyone have a camera? I can collect.

6 Work in pairs. Do you get things from websites like these? What do you get?
   I get old clothes, like jackets and shoes.

2c ▶ Develop your writing

> **Goal:** write a review of a product
> **Focus:** using *and, but* and *so*

1 **Look at the website and discuss the questions.**

1 What things are for sale on the website?
2 Is there anything you would like to buy?

Today's top buys

Wailers brown wallet £19.99	**GoGym trainers** £29.99
A Pookiechoo teddy bear £20.00	**Timewell Green wall clock** £15.22
Novelet tablet computer £259.00	**A pair of Sunbrow sunglasses** £33.50
K-T digital watch £45.00	**Berrychan scarf** £15.00

2 a **Read reviews 1–4 about things for sale in Exercise 1. Complete the reviews with headings A–D.**

A Fantastic trainers!
B Don't buy these sunglasses
C A great clock!
D A useful wallet

Customer reviews (358)

1 _____

I love it! It's a beautiful green colour. It's small but it looks great in our kitchen. It's modern and it works well.

2 _____

These are terrible. In the photo they look black but they're not – they're brown. They're heavy on your nose so they aren't comfortable at all. They're OK for about an hour but that's it. Don't buy them.

3 _____

It's not cheap but it's large so I can put all my money in it. The colours are nice. It's brown on the outside and a lovely orange colour on the inside. It's a good buy.

4 _____

These are great for the gym. They're light and comfortable. They're only £29.99 so they're a good price. I'm happy with them.

b **Read the reviews again. Which are positive? Which are negative? What tells you this information?**

3 **Read the Focus box. Underline more examples of *and, but* and *so* in the reviews in Exercise 2a.**

Using *and, but* and *so*

Use *and* to add information.

*They're light **and** comfortable.*

*It's an old watch **and** it's broken.*

Use *but* to give opposite or different information.

*It's soft **but** heavy.*

*It's not cheap **but** it's large.*

Use *so* to give a result.

*They're heavy **so** they aren't comfortable.*

4 a **Join the two sentences with *and, but* or *so*.**

1 They're cheap. They aren't great.
2 They're over £50. They aren't cheap.
3 It's good. It's heavy.
4 They're yellow. They're bright.
5 They're expensive. They're not popular.
6 It's soft. It's not comfortable.

b **Work in pairs. Are your sentences the same or different?**

5 **Complete the sentences with your own ideas.**

1 These shoes are really comfortable and …
2 The sunglasses are expensive but …
3 The suitcase is large and …
4 The book is long but …
5 I love these boots. They're big and …
6 This sofa is really soft so …

Prepare

6 a **You're going to write a review. Choose an item in Exercise 1. Do you want to write a positive review or a negative one?**

b **Make notes and write some adjectives you can use. Think about:**

* cost   *expensive/cheap*
* size
* looks
* colour
* feel

c **Write three sentences about your item. Include *and* in one sentence, *but* in the second and *so* in the third.**
The trainers are not expensive and they look good.

Write

7 **Write your review. Use the reviews in Exercise 2a and your notes in Exercise 6 to help you.**

91

Develop your writing

> **Goal:** write an online profile
> **Focus:** using commas and apostrophes

1 Read the sentences. Are they true or false for you? Give more information.

1 I use social media.
2 I have a blog or website.
3 You can find information about me online.

2 a Read Lacey's online profile. Which information in the box does she give?

age   family   favourite music   free-time activities
home   job   name   studies

Hi! I'm Lacey Brown and I'm a student. I'm from Leeds but I live in London. I study history at King's College. Most days, I take classes, study in the library and spend time with my friends. At the weekends, I work in a little café near college. I live with my two best friends in a small flat. My friends' names are Isabella and Alice and they're also students. We all love history so we try to visit a different museum every month. It's my favourite activity. I cook for my friends every Sunday. I usually make pasta, rice dishes and curries. In the holidays, I go home and spend time at my parents' house. I don't often cook there but I eat a lot of my mum's cakes. Chocolate, lemon and banana are my favourites. Yum!

b Read Lacey's online profile again. Answer the questions.

1 Where is Lacey from?
2 Where does Lacey live now?
3 What's Lacey's job?
4 What does Lacey do in her free time?
5 What does Lacey do in the holidays?

3 a Read the Focus box. Do we use a comma or an apostrophe to show that a letter is missing?

Using commas and apostrophes

Use a comma (,) …
- after a time expression at the beginning of a sentence.

At the weekends, I work in a little café.
- in a list.

I take classes, study in the library and spend time with my friends.

Use an apostrophe (') …
- in contractions to show a letter is not there.

*I **don't** cook there.* (do not)
It's my favourite activity. (It is)
- in possessives.

King's College (the college of the king)
*My **mum's** cakes.* (the cakes my mum has)

A regular possessive plural noun is followed by an apostrophe.

*My **friends'** names are Isabella and Alice.*

Don't use an apostrophe in the possessive pronoun *its*.
*I love New York and **its** tall buildings.*

b Read Lacey's profile again and find more examples of commas and apostrophes. Why are they used?

4 a Add a comma where necessary in each sentence.

1 I study English French and Spanish.
2 On Fridays I work in a restaurant.
3 I've got a dog a cat and a rabbit.
4 I read listen to music and go for a walk on Sundays.
5 At the weekend I go for coffee with my friends.
6 I like basketball volleyball and baseball.

b Add an apostrophe where necessary in each sentence.

1 Im always tired in the evenings.
2 I love my brothers new car. I want one myself!
3 Were students at the University of Barcelona.
4 I love my town and its fantastic cafés.
5 I really like my job. Its always interesting.
6 My cousins names are Paul and Ava.

Prepare

5 a You're going to write an online profile.
- Choose six topics from the box in Exercise 2a.
- What can you say about each one? Make notes.

b Decide on the order of information in your profile.

Write

6 Write your online profile. Use the profile in Exercise 2a to help you. Use correct punctuation.

> **Goal:** understand a factual text

> **Focus:** using headings to find information

1 Which of these sentences are true about schools in your country?

1 Children wear a uniform.
2 The school year starts in September.
3 Children start school at six years old.
4 The school day starts at 8 a.m. and finishes at 2 p.m.
5 Most children walk to school.
6 Children learn foreign languages at school.

2 a Look at the headings in the article about schools in Australia. Match sentences 1–6 in Exercise 1 with paragraph headings A–E.

School in *Australia*

A Important dates

Children start school at six years old in Australia and study at their first school until they're twelve. Then from 13–17 they study at high school, but they can finish school at 15 if they want to. The school year starts in January, after a four-week summer holiday.

B The school day

School starts at 8.30 in most places but some schools start at 9.00. The day finishes at around 3.30. Classes are 40 or 90 minutes long with some breaks in between.

C Clothes

Children wear a school uniform in most high schools, in the school colours. In summer, it gets very hot so there's a 'No hat, no play' rule. This means children must wear a hat to play outside at break time.

D Getting to school

Many children go to school by 'walking bus'. Some parents walk to school with the children, who join the 'bus' (a line of children who walk together) when they walk past their house.

E Foreign languages

Most children study Indonesian as a foreign language. Some schools also teach Mandarin Chinese and Japanese.

b Read the article and check your answers. If necessary, change the sentences in Exercise 1 so they're true for Australian schools.

3 Read the Focus box. Why is it good to look at headings in a text?

Using headings to find information

Before you read a text, look at the **headings** to help you find the information you want. For example, you want information about what clothes your child needs for school and you look at these headings:

Important dates
The school day
Clothes
Getting to school

You see the heading *Clothes*. You read that section because you can find information about *school uniforms* there.

4 a You're going to read an article about schools in Singapore. Match the headings in the box with questions 1–5.

A typical day   Clothes   Homework
Important dates   Languages

1 When does the school year start and finish?
2 What do students do in the afternoon?
3 What do students wear on their shirts?
4 How many languages do students and teachers speak in the school?
5 What do students do in the evening?

b Read the article and answer the questions in Exercise 4a.

School in *Singapore*

Important Dates

The school year in Singapore starts in early January and finishes in the middle of November. Children have a six-week summer holiday at the end of the year.

A typical day

School starts early at 7.30 a.m. Classes continue until around 1.30 p.m. then children have lunch. After lunch, they do Co-Curricular Activities (CCA), such as sport or art. This finishes around 5 p.m.

Clothes

All schools have school uniforms. Children also have a name tag on their shirts so everyone can see their name.

Languages

Teachers and students use English in all classes to learn different subjects. They also learn Mandarin Chinese, Malay or Tamil in separate classes.

Homework

The day doesn't end when students get home. In the evening, they do around two hours of homework before or after dinner.

5 Work in pairs and discuss the questions.

1 What things are the same/different about schools in Australia and Singapore?
2 Which schools do you prefer? Why?

3c ▶ Develop your listening

> **Goal:** understand short talks
>
> **Focus:** understanding key words

1 a Look at the people in the photos and make guesses about their lives.

1 What are their jobs?

2 What do they do every day?

3 What do they do in their free time?

I think Dorothy usually stays in and spends time with her family.

I think Simon studies a lot. He rarely goes out.

b 🔊 3.6 **Listen to one of the people talking about his/her life. Which person is it? Are your ideas about his/her life correct?**

2 Read the Focus box. What types of words are key words?

Dorothy   Simon

Understanding key words

When we speak, we usually stress words which give the most important information. These words are usually nouns (like *man* or *dog*), verbs (like *eat* or *run*) or adjectives (like *good* or *hot*).

People often **think** that at my age we **stay home** every **night** and **relax** with a **book** or something, but for me that's **not true**.

Negatives are also stressed because they give important information.

I **don't like** this film.

She **hasn't got** a sister.

When you listen, you don't always need to understand every word. Listen to the stressed words to get the general idea.

3 Listen to Dorothy again and choose the correct alternatives.

1 People think she stays home with a *book/film*, but that's not right.

2 She sings *once/twice* a week.

3 Her group is called The *Music/Song* Birds.

4 The group meets at the town *centre/hall*.

5 At the weekend, she has *coffee/lunch* with friends from the group.

4 🔊 3.7 **Listen to the sentences and underline the key words.**

1 I rarely go to the cinema.

2 My old friends often come to my house.

3 We don't stay at home much in the evenings.

4 I don't like crazy parties.

5 We have a cup of tea every day at 11.

6 I often go for a walk at the weekend.

7 My house is near the sea so I swim a lot.

8 We work for a big company.

Rana

5 🔊 3.8 **Listen and complete the sentences with one or two words.**

1 I start work at _____ o'clock every morning.

2 My favourite thing is _____ . I love it!

3 I'm a shop assistant at that _____ over there.

4 I've got three _____ but I haven't got any sisters.

5 I play badminton three times a week with my _____ .

6 We love _____ . We watch a different one every evening.

7 We enjoy _____ food and have it every week.

8 My favourite thing in the world is _____ but I only watch it!

6 a 🔊 3.9 **Listen to Rana and Simon and answer the questions.**

1 Who talks about meeting new people everywhere?

2 Who talks about chatting online?

b Listen again and answer the questions. Use the key words to help you.

1 Where does Rana never go?

2 How many books does she read a week?

3 Who does she talk to about books?

4 Who does Simon often go out with?

5 What three places does he meet people?

6 What two words does he use to describe people?

7 Work in pairs and discuss the questions. Are Dorothy, Rana and Simon similar to you? Why/Why not?

> **Goal:** write a description
> **Focus:** using word order correctly

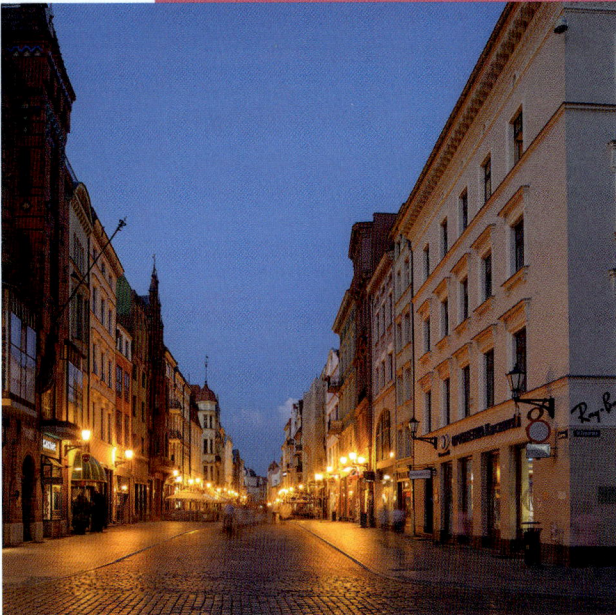

1 Look at the photo and discuss the questions.

1 Where do you think this town is?

2 What things can you see in the photo?

2 a Read about the city in the photo and check your ideas in Exercise 1.

Toruń – my home town

I live in a small city called Toruń, in the north of Poland. It's about three hours from Warsaw, the capital city.

Toruń is a very old city – over a thousand years old! There's a castle in the old town and it's nearly 800 years old. There are a lot of attractive buildings in the city and it looks really beautiful at night.

There's a big train station and from here the trains go all over Poland. There's also a bus station near the old town. The buses go to many European cities, so it's easy to visit here. There's a famous speedway (motorbike racing) stadium and people go there with their families at the weekend. There are a lot of theatres, too: two drama theatres, two children's theatres, two musical theatres and several other theatre groups.

My favourite thing in Toruń is the gingerbread. People come from many different places in Poland to eat it. There's even a gingerbread museum.

Toruń is a great place to live and visit. Come and say hello!

b Read the article again. Are the sentences true (T) or false (F)?

1 Toruń isn't a big city.

2 The city is nearly 800 years old.

3 Toruń has many nice buildings.

4 It's difficult to get to Toruń.

5 The writer's favourite thing about Toruń is the theatres.

6 There's a museum for a special type of food.

3 a Read the Focus box. Where do we put adjectives?

Using word order correctly

Basic word order is:
Subject + verb + object
    I   like   my home town.
Adjectives come before nouns.
old buildings NOT ~~buildings old~~
a great place NOT ~~a place great~~
Or after the verb *be*.
*The hotel **is lovely**.*
The usual word order in long sentences is:
who? + what? + where? + who with? + when?
People go there with their families at the weekend.

b Find more examples of the word order in the Focus box in the article.

4 Put the words in the correct order to make sentences.

1 live in / city / I / an / interesting
   I live in an interesting city.

2 live and work / People / there

3 beautiful / in the city / There / some / parks / are

4 have lunch / in summer / in the parks / People

5 every weekend / a museum or gallery / I / with my friends / visit

6 with his partner / Jamie / to the theatre / after work / goes

7 is / The city centre / beautiful

5 Complete the sentences about your town or city.

1 There are a lot of _____ .

2 I don't like _____ .

3 _____ is a great place.

4 _____ new buildings.

5 People _____ at the weekends.

6 The city centre _____ .

Prepare

6 a You're going to write a description of your favourite city. First, make notes about:

- where it is
- its size (small or big town/city)
- who lives there
- transport
- places and buildings
- things people do at the weekend
- who visits the town/city and why

b Decide the order of the information for your description.

Write

7 Write your description. Use the article in Exercise 2 to help you.

Develop your reading

> **Goal:** understand social media posts
>
> **Focus:** guessing new words

1 Look at the photo and answer the questions. Where is the person? Why do you think they like this place?

2 Work in pairs. Read the first three social media posts. Which one describes the place in the photo?

---

¹@Mel

I'm lucky, I have the sea on my doorstep. In the evenings, I walk five minutes and I arrive at the beach. I go there and watch the <u>sunset</u>. Other people go there to look at the sunset, too. We all enjoy the beautiful red and orange sky above the water. I love it! What place do you love? #theplaceIlove

---

²@Sam

My husband and I stay in a cottage every winter. It's in a pretty village in the countryside and it's very quiet there. The cottage is tiny. It's only got one very small bedroom, but it's old and beautiful. Every evening, we sit in front of an open fire and read books. We leave our phones and other technology at home. It's wonderful. #theplaceIlove

---

³@Lou

My job is stressful and I have a lot of things to think about. It's tough for me to relax in the evenings so I go to the gym. I love it there. I quickly relax and stop thinking about work. I go home and sleep well. #theplaceIlove

---

⁴@Carl

#theplaceIlove is a big tree in a park. I go there in my lunch hour at work. I have a picnic under the tree – two or three different types of food, nothing special. I read my messages and listen to the birds. It's lovely, except when it rains!

---

⁵@Andy

There's a fantastic café called Molly's. I go there every Saturday at 11 a.m. and have brunch. The people there are friendly and the brunch is great. I sit at a table in the window and people watch. It's fun! #theplaceIlove

---

3 a Read the Focus box. Use the questions and answers in the box to guess the meaning of *sunset* in the first post.

Guessing new words

If you see a word you don't understand, you can try to guess the meaning. Ask these questions to help you:

- What kind of word is it, e.g. a noun, a verb, an adjective?
  For example, *sunset* is a noun. It comes after *the*.
- Are there any more examples of the word? Underline them.
  For example, *watch the sunset / look at the sunset*
- Look at the word. Do you understand any part of it? Is it like an English word you know or a word in your language?
  For example, you probably know the word *sun* in *sunset*.
- Look at the words around the word. Can they help you understand the meaning?
  For example, *in the evenings / enjoy the beautiful red and orange sky*

b Underline the word *cottage* in post 2 and the word *tough* in post 3. Answer each question in the Focus box about each word.

c Answer the questions. Use your answers in Exercise 3b to help you.

  1 What does *cottage* mean?
    a a country home
    b a kind of room in a house
  2 What does *tough* mean?
    a easy
    b difficult

4 Read posts 1–3 again. Are the sentences true (T) or false (F)?

  1 Mel's home is near the beach.
  2 Mel watches the sunset alone.
  3 Sam's cottage is small.
  4 Sam spends time using a computer at the cottage.
  5 Lou has an easy job.

5 a Read posts 4–5. Write a list of words you don't know. For each word, answer the questions in the Focus box.

b Guess the meaning of the words in Exercise 5a. Then, check your ideas in a dictionary.

6 Use your understanding of the vocabulary in posts 4–5 to answer the questions.

  1 What kind of lunch does Carl have?
  2 When does Carl not like going to the tree?
  3 Why does Andy like Molly's café?
  4 What does Andy do at the café when he's eating?

7 Work in pairs and discuss the questions.

  1 What's your favourite place to be?
  2 Why is it special?

> **Goal:** understand a short radio programme

> **Focus:** understanding weak forms

1 a Look at the photo and discuss the questions.

1 Where do you think the people are?
2 Is life easy or difficult in this place? Why?

b 4.11 **Listen to a radio programme about life in very cold places. Are the sentences true (T) or false (F)?**

1 It's sometimes -40˚C in Calgary.
2 People in Calgary need to wear sunglasses in winter.
3 You can walk around Calgary for eight kilometres without going outside.

2 a Read the Focus box. How do you think we pronounce the words in bold?

Understanding weak forms

When we speak, we don't pronounce every word clearly. They often include a sound called schwa /ə/. For example:

Articles

*I work in **an** office.*
*People live in all kinds of unusual places around **the** world.*

Prepositions

*I walk **from** the train station **to** my office inside.*

Verb *be* and *do/does* in questions

*How **are** the streets?*
*How **do** people live?*

and/but

*It's warm **and** comfortable.*
*It's cold here in winter **but** it's also sunny.*

b 4.12 **Listen and check.**

3 4.13 Listen to the sentences and select the words you hear.

1 of/an
2 a/the
3 to/for
4 the/those

4 a 4.14 Listen to the next part of the radio programme and answer the questions.

1 What does the man do every day in winter?
2 Why is there no snow on some roads in Reykjavik?
3 How many hours of sunlight are there in Reykjavik in winter?
4 How many hours of night are there in Reykjavik in summer?
5 How long do people stay outside for in Yakutsk?
6 What clothes does the man wear?
7 What transport sometimes doesn't work in winter – trains or cars?

b 4.15 **Listen and complete the sentences.**

1 People don't need to pay _____ warm homes in winter.
2 I go outside every day and sit in _____ hot pool.
3 The hot water also helps with _____ roads.
4 It's not easy _____ drive around Iceland.
5 Natural hot water goes under some _____ our roads.
6 Some days it's -40˚C here _____ people live normal lives.
7 _____ don't stay outside for very long.
8 Clothes _____ important in cold places.
9 Shops _____ schools usually stay open in winter.
10 One big problem is our cars. _____ don't always start in winter.

5 Work in pairs and discuss the questions.

1 Would you like to live in a very cold place? Why/Why not?
2 What do you need to live in a cold place?

5A ▶ Develop your writing

> **Goal:** write a description of a person

> **Focus:** using paragraphs

1 **Discuss the questions.**
1 Who are your favourite people?
2 What do they do that you like?
3 Is there anything they do that you dislike?

2 a **Read Jodie's description quickly. Why is her grandmother special to her?**

1 My grandmother is very special to me. She's 76 but she looks young. She's short and she's very attractive, I think. She has beautiful blue eyes and long, dark hair.

2 Every day my grandmother gets up early and works in the garden with her plants and flowers. It always looks so beautiful, even in the winter. She loves nature and helping things grow.

3 My grandmother's special to me because she always listens to me when I have a problem. Sometimes I don't want to talk about my problems, but when I do, she listens to everything I say. My grandmother is my best friend.

b **Read the entry again and answer the questions.**
1 How old is Jodie's grandmother?
2 What does she look like?
3 What does she do in the morning?
4 Why does she like it?
5 What does Jodie like about her?
6 What does her grandmother do when Jodie has a problem?

3 **Read the Focus box. How many paragraphs does each topic have?**

Using paragraphs

Use paragraphs to introduce different topics. In Jodie's description in Exercise 2a, Jodie writes about three topics:
* a description of her grandmother
* what her grandmother does in the day and in her free time
* why her grandmother is her favourite person.

4 **Read a description of Craig. Match descriptions a–c with paragraphs 1–3.**
a What Craig looks like ____
b What Craig and Marcus do together ____
c Why Craig is special to Marcus ____

1My friend Craig is special to me. He's the same age as me and he's tall and thin. He's got short, brown hair and brown eyes.
2Craig goes to university near me, so we often meet at lunchtime and eat together. He works very hard but he doesn't talk much about his studies.
3Craig is special to me because he's an old friend. We were at school together at five years old and we're still friends. I like him because he always helps me when I have problems or just need advice. He's my best friend. - **Marcus**

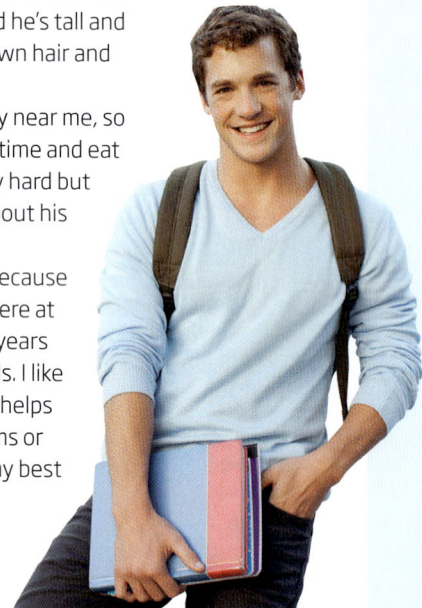

Prepare

5 a **You're going to write a description of a person who is special to you. First, decide who you're going to write about.**

b **Make notes on what to include in each paragraph. Use the following ideas to help you.**
* Paragraph 1: a description of the person (their name, age, appearance, job, nationality)
* Paragraph 2: what they do in the day and in their free time
* Paragraph 3: why they are special to you

Write

6 **Write your description. Use your notes in Exercise 5 to help you.**

5B ▶ Develop your listening

> **Goal:** understand a story
> **Focus:** linking between words

1 Look at the children in the photos. How old are they? Where are they?

2 a 🔊 5.7 Listen to part of a radio show about memories. Tom is talking about his first memory. Is it a happy memory?

b 🔊 5.8 Read the Focus box and listen to the linking in the examples. When do we link words together?

Linking between words

Sometimes we connect the sounds of two words in English.

- When a word ends with a consonant sound and the next word starts with a vowel sound.

in a car
I was about three years old.

- When a word ends in the sound /r/ and the next word starts with a vowel sound.
  /r/
near a mountain

3 a Mark the linking between words that end with a consonant sound and words that begin with a vowel sound.

1 my parents and my brother
2 We were in a car in Italy.
3 It was a little white Fiat.
4 I was in the front of the car.
5 I wasn't happy at all.

b 🔊 5.9 Listen and check your answers. Then, listen and repeat. Copy the linking.

4 🔊 5.7 Listen to Tom's memory again and answer the questions.

1 How old was he?
2 Where was he?
3 Who was there?
4 How was Tom?

5 a You're going to listen to three more people talk about first memories. First, look at some of their phrases. Mark the linking between words.

1 I was outside
2 we were on holiday
3 at a hotel
4 at the bottom of the pool
5 I was at school
6 we were all on the floor

b 🔊 5.10 Listen and check your answers.

6 a 🔊 5.11 Listen to Felicity, Greg and Tiffany talk about their first memories. Were they happy?

b Listen again and answer the questions for each speaker.

1 How old was he/she?   3 Who was there?
2 Where was he/she?   4 What was there?

c Listen again and complete the sentences with one or two words.

1 Felicity was at _____ .
2 Felicity was with _____ .
3 Greg and his family were at a hotel with _____ pool.
4 Greg's favourite toy was _____ toy car.
5 Tiffany was in _____ the classrooms.
6 There was something _____ Tiffany's shoes.

7 Work in pairs. What was your first memory? Discuss the questions.

1 How old were you?
2 Where were you?
3 Who was there?
4 What was there?

Develop your reading

> **Goal:** understand information in a brochure

> **Focus:** understanding *it, they* and *them*

1 Work in pairs. Look at the picture. What kind of information do you need before you start studying in a school or university?

2 Read the brochure for a language school and match headings 1–8 with paragraphs A–H.

1 Getting started *A*
2 Free-time activities
3 Buying reading material
4 Cheap transport
5 Borrowing books
6 Your details
7 Help your teacher, help yourself
8 Study times

A On your first day, you'll do a test to check your level of English. You need to take it before you can start your classes with us. It usually takes about 20 minutes. You can do it on the computers in the reception. Please ask the reception staff and they will be happy to help you.

B You can buy your coursebooks in the reception. When you finish your course, you can sell them back to the school if you want to. They usually cost £25.

C The library is on the fifth floor. It's open between 10 a.m. and 4 p.m. every day. You can borrow books for seven days but please bring them back on time!

D Please don't use your phones or tablets during classes – it's not good for you, or for your teacher! Your teacher will ask you to turn them off before the lesson starts. Also, please do the homework that your teachers give you. It really helps you improve your English!

E Do you want to spend less money on the train or the bus? You can find a travel card form in the reception. Fill it in and give it to the reception staff. They usually take two to three weeks to arrive.

F Remember to give us your new phone number and your address if you change them! You can tell us at reception. It's open from 9 a.m. to 5 p.m. Monday to Friday.

G Every month we organise parties and trips and lots of our students enjoy them! Please look at our posters or talk to the social team. They will be happy to tell you what's happening this month.

H You can take classes every day from Monday to Friday. They last three hours and you can choose to do them in the morning from 9 a.m., or from 1 p.m. in the afternoon.

3 Read the Focus box. When do we use *it, they* and *them*?

Understanding *it, they* and *them*

When we don't want to repeat words, we can use *it* for singular nouns and activities.

*Please fill in **the form** for new students. **It's** very easy to complete.*

Use *they* for plural nouns when they replace the **subject** of a verb.

***Classes** are three hours long. **They** start at nine …*

Use *them* for plural nouns when they replace the **object** of the verb.

*You can borrow **books** … You can take **them** for …*

4 Replace the words in bold with *it, they* or *them*.

Every week we have conversation classes. [1]**Conversation classes** start at 12 p.m. and finish at 3 p.m. You can book [2]**conversation classes** at the reception. Speaking English can be easy if you practise [3]**speaking English** every day!

We have a special class on Fridays. [4]**The class** is called 'cultural exchange'. You can meet people from other countries and exchange information with [5]**people from other countries**. [6]**People from other countries** will tell you lots of interesting things about their country! If you want to take the class, you can ask your teacher about [7]**the class**. [8]**The class** is useful and fun!

5 a Look at the brochure in Exercise 2 again and underline the words *it, they* and *them*. What words do they replace in the text?

b Read the brochure again and answer the questions.

1 When do you need to take your test?
2 What can you sell to the school?
3 How long is the library open for every day?
4 What helps you improve your English?
5 What's open from 9 to 5 every day in the week?
6 How long is a class?

6 What other information do you think students need to know about the school in Exercise 2?

Develop your reading

> **Goal:** understand reviews
> **Focus:** understanding adjectives

1 Look at the photos and discuss the questions.

1 Which of these events would you like to go to?

2 Do you ever read reviews before you decide what to do? How can they help you decide?

2 a Read the reviews. Are they good or bad? Do you want to go to this event? Why/Why not?

¹ There were lots of different kinds of food, but most of it was boring. There weren't many other things to do, either, just eat. We didn't have a very good time – **Chris**

² The area was very small and it was very crowded because there were lots of people. The food was alright, but we waited a long time to buy anything. It was noisy and a bit dirty, too, because people threw their rubbish on the ground. We don't want to go there again – **Emily**

³ The food wasn't bad but there wasn't anything we liked. It's a good place to try different types of food from around the world but we didn't like it – **Vicky**

b What words and phrases helped you answer the questions in Exercise 2a?
boring, didn't have a good time

3 a Read the Focus box. Then find adjectives in the reviews in Exercise 2.

Understanding adjectives

To get the main idea of reviews, we can look for …
* positive adjectives, e.g. *It was **fantastic**.*
* neutral adjectives, e.g. *The place was **OK**.*
* negative adjectives, e.g. *Quite **boring**.*
* words which make the adjective stronger or weaker, e.g. *The area was **very** small. It was **quite** boring.*

Sometimes we can use a positive adjective to say something negative.
*The film was **not interesting**.*

b Are the adjectives in the reviews positive, negative or neutral?

4 a Read the reviews below. Find positive adjectives (+), neutral adjectives (N), and negative adjectives (-).

Summer Pop-up Cinema

My girlfriend and I went to this last week for my birthday. It was an OK film but the screen was small so we couldn't see much. The sound was really bad, too, so we didn't hear much. – **Darren**

It was very crowded, so there wasn't enough space to be comfortable. It's expensive, too. There are different things you can do for the same price, so I don't recommend this. Do something different. – **Sunit**

It was very cold that evening and we didn't bring any warm clothes. There was a group of people near us talking all the way through, which was horrible. We didn't stay until the end. – **Alexei**

High Life: The Musical

The start was a bit boring but then it improved a little bit. It was an average night out overall. – **Sveta**

The singing and dancing were beautiful and the story was amazing! We loved the whole thing, from start to finish. – **Ed**

The story was terrible. The show was very expensive, too. Save your money and go to the cinema! – **Lisa**

Science Fair

We visited the science fair with our two children. We all had a wonderful time and there were things for both the children and the adults to do. Fantastic! – **Penny**

The event was awesome and the people working there were really friendly. There were lots of experiments to do and we all learnt something. – **Rich**

It was brilliant! The area was really big so there was lots of space to move around. We all want to go again next year. – **Greg**

b Work in pairs and give each review up to 5 stars (1 star = very bad, 5 stars = excellent).

5 a Work with another pair. Compare your answers in Exercise 4b.

b Which event would you like to go to most? Why?

Develop your listening

> **Goal:** understand a narrative

> **Focus:** understanding the order of events

1 Discuss the questions.

1 When was the last time you had a good day out?
2 Where did you go?
3 What did you do?
4 Why was it good?

2 a 🔊 **6.7 Listen to Aiden talking about a good day out with his girlfriend. Which places in the box did they visit?**

> the countryside   a museum   a park

b Listen again and put the events in the correct order.

a It rained.
b They went to the museum.
c He decided to go to the park.
d They went to the park.

3 Read the Focus box. What do words like *before* and *after* tell us?

Understanding the order of events

When we listen to a story, we can listen for words that tell us the order that things happened:

- An earlier event: *before (that)*
  Before *I went out, I called Kenneth.*
- A later event: *after (that), then*
  We had lunch, **then** *we walked in the park.*
- Two events happening together: *at the same time*
  We arrived at the party **at the same time**.
- The end of the story: *in the end*
  In the end, *we were OK.*

---

4 🔊 **6.8 Listen to the sentences. Which action happens first, a or b?**

1	**a** we met	**b** I was alone
2	**a** did some work	**b** relaxed
3	**a** called my mum	**b** cleaned the flat
4	**a** was worried	**b** it was OK
5	**a** asked me my name	**b** told me hers
6	**a** came here	**b** saw Peter
7	**a** lived in Berlin	**b** moved to Stockholm
8	**a** had lunch	**b** played golf

5 a 🔊 **6.9 Listen to Tonia describing a good day out she had. Put the events in pictures A–H in the order they happened.**

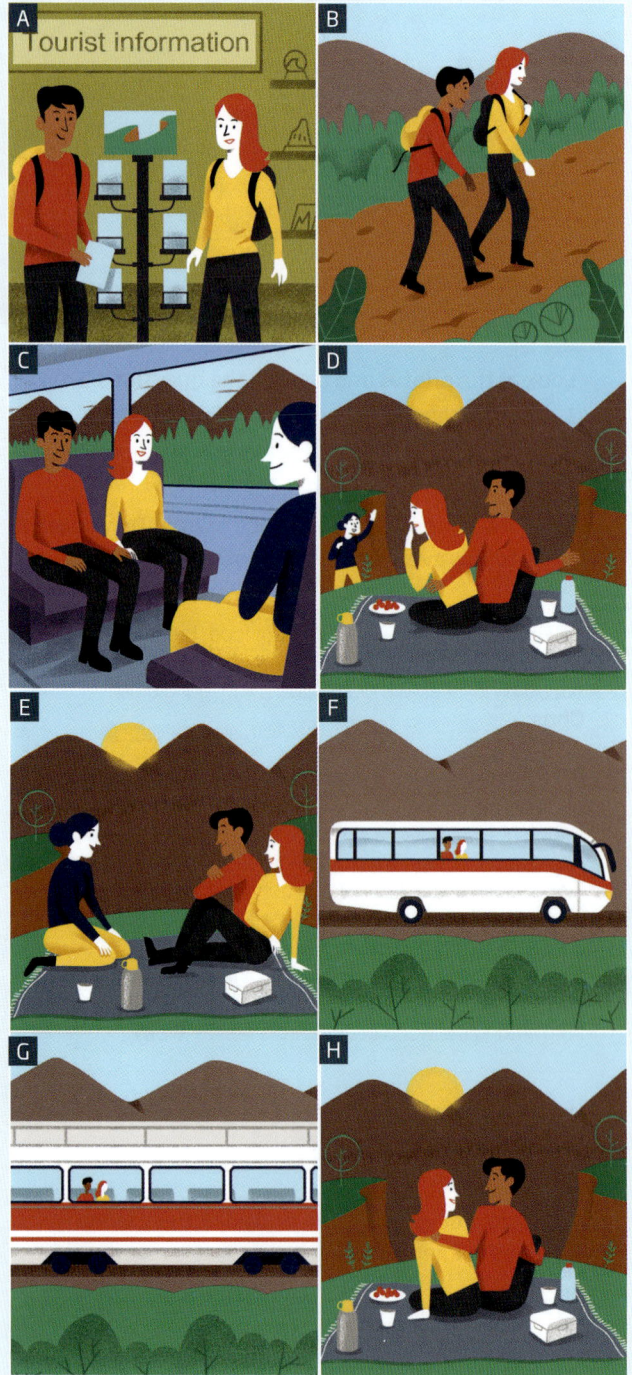

b Listen again and answer the questions.

1 What can you see there?
2 How far away are the Mendip Hills?
3 How did they get there?
4 What did they do when they arrived?
5 Why was meeting her friend a surprise?
6 What did they do after they met?

6 Discuss the questions.

1 Who do you think had the best day out: Aiden or Tonia? Why?
2 Would you like to do what they did? Why/Why not?

Develop your writing

> **Goal:** write a short story
>
> **Focus:** using subject pronouns

1 **Look at the photo and answer the questions.**

  1 What are the people doing?

  2 Would you like to do this?

2 a **Read the story. Why was the night in 1965 special?**

When I was young, I loved the dance hall. I went three times a week and danced for hours. Thursday night was my favourite because it was rock and roll night.

One night in 1965, I saw a tall, handsome man near the door. He looked at me and smiled. I smiled back. I saw him every week for two months but he never spoke to me. Finally, one evening, he came over and asked me to dance.

He was a terrible dancer but he tried hard. After two songs, we sat down and talked. His name was Henry and he was a postman. I knew he was special. We got married exactly one year later and had our first child a year after that. Today, we have four children, eight grandchildren and three great grandchildren.

b **Read the story again and choose the correct alternatives.**

  1 The *man/woman* visited the dance hall a few times a week.

  2 The *man/woman* started a conversation after two months.

  3 The *man/woman* wasn't a very good dancer.

  4 The *man/couple* worked for the post office.

  5 The *man/couple* got married twelve months later.

  6 The *woman/couple* have eleven grandchildren and great grandchildren in total.

3 a **Read the Focus box. Then look at the story in Exercise 2 again. Find examples where the writer doesn't repeat the subject pronoun.**

Using subject pronouns

Subject pronouns are words like *I, you, he, she, we* and *they*.

A clause is a group of words that includes a subject pronoun and a verb.

I went to the dance hall three times a week.

Sometimes we connect two clauses with words like *and* and *but*.

*He looked at me **and** he smiled.*

A clause can only have one subject.

Henry smiled at me. NOT *Henry he smiled at me.*

When a sentence has two clauses and the subject is the same, we don't need to repeat the subject pronoun.

He looked at me and smiled.

Both subject pronouns are necessary when the subject in each clause is different.

I saw him every week for two months but he never spoke to me.

b **Make sentences with *and*. Delete the second subject pronoun if you can.**

  1 I put on my best clothes/I went to the party.

   I put on my best clothes and went to the party.

  2 I met Rachel at the party/We talked for hours.

  3 My friend came to my house/We ordered pizza.

  4 Carl got home/He went to bed early.

  5 My friends and I went to the cinema/We saw a great film.

  6 The cat came into the room/It sat on the sofa.

  7 We went to the theatre/We got tickets to the show.

  8 Anna and I went to London/We walked along the river.

Prepare

4 **You're going to write about when you met someone who is important to you. First, make notes about what happened. Use the questions to help you.**

  • When did you meet?

  • Where did you meet?

  • What did you do there?

  • How was the weather?

  • Did someone introduce you?

  • Were other people there?

  • What did you talk about?

  • Did you go anywhere together?

  • Did you like each other the first time you met?

Write

5 **Write a description of how you met someone. Use your notes in Exercise 4 to help you.**

6 **Read your description. Can you take out any of the subject pronouns?**

   We went to the theatre and we saw 'The Mousetrap.'

Develop your listening

> **Goal:** understand announcements
> **Focus:** listening for specific information

1 Discuss the questions.

1 How often do you travel by train?

2 Do you prefer travelling by plane or by train?

3 Do you ever travel in English-speaking countries? Which ones?

4 Do you ever listen for travel information in English? Is it easy or difficult?

2 a 🔊 **7.4 Listen to the two announcements. Which one is for …**

a a train?

b a plane?

b Listen again. Which of these words do you hear? Which can we use to talk about planes (P), trains (T) or both (B)?

arrive   depart   flight   gate   platform

3 Read the Focus box. Listen to the announcements again and answer the questions.

1 When does the flight to Barcelona leave?

2 What platform does the train to Manchester leave from?

Listening for specific information

You don't need to understand everything when you listen. You can listen just for the information you need.

For example, you want to know the time of the next train to Birmingham, and you hear this announcement:

*The 12:30 train to Bradford will depart from platform 4 in 5 minutes. The next train to **Birmingham** will leave **in twenty minutes** from platform 9. The train to Broadstairs has been cancelled.*

You only need to listen for the time expression near to *Birmingham*.

4 You want to know the time of the next train to London. Look at the announcement below and underline all the important words.

This is an announcement from Network Rail. The next train to Manchester has been delayed due to problems with signalling, and will not depart on time. We will keep you updated on the revised time for departure as soon as we have more information. The next train to London will leave from Platform 5 at 19:30 as planned.

5 a 🔊 **7.5 Listen to the announcements. Which of the pairs of words are stressed more strongly?**

1 London/five	train/depart
2 Munich/thirty	flight/leave
3 next/to	thirty/Belfast
4 gate/flight	Malaga/19

b Look at the information which was pronounced more strongly. What was the announcement?

London – Five.
Maybe the train for London leaves in five minutes?

c Listen again and check.

6 🔊 **7.6 You are at the airport. You need the following information. Listen and make notes about the information.**

1 the time of the flight to Berlin

2 the gate that it departs from

7 🔊 **7.7 You are at the train station. You need the following information. Listen and make notes about the information.**

1 the time of the next train to Liverpool

2 the platform it departs from

8 Work in pairs and discuss the questions.

1 If you don't understand a travel announcement, what can you do?

2 Do you always arrive on time for your flight or train?

3 Do you ever miss flights or trains?

4 Are travel announcements easy or difficult to understand in your country?

7B Develop your writing

> **Goal:** write a social media post
>
> **Focus:** giving opinions and reasons

1 Discuss the questions.

1 What social media apps and sites do you use?
2 What things do you write about on social media?
3 Do you ever write in English on social media?

2 a Look at the photo Lilly posted on social media. What do you think she wrote about?

b Read Lilly's description and check.

> I just tried this at my friend's house – what a great sandwich! At first, I didn't want to eat it because it looked strange, but I tried it and it tasted really nice. Banana, cheese and chocolate are amazing together.
> I don't think everyone will like it, but I think everyone should try it once!

3 Read the Focus box. Then find Lilly's opinions and reasons in her social media post.

Giving opinions and reasons

To give opinions, you can use the phrases *I think* and *I don't think* to introduce your ideas.

I think that sandwich is strange.

When you talk about past experiences use *thought/didn't think*:

I didn't think the film was good, but my boyfriend loved it.

You can also give opinions using positive and negative adjectives like *good, bad, exciting, boring, lovely, amazing, horrible, awful* or *interesting*.

That's a lovely jacket.

I thought the film was amazing.

That sofa is horrible.

I think sushi is awful.

Use *because* to give a reason for the opinion.

I don't think that café is good for lunch because it's too crowded.

I think shopping online is great because it's easy

---

4 a Match opinions 1–8 with reasons a–h.

1 Nurses are amazing
2 I think they didn't come
3 Noisy cafes are not good
4 I think he feels a little sad
5 I think running is popular
6 The film was amazing
7 The weekend was great
8 I don't think you should stay at home today

a because it's difficult to hear each other.
b because they work so hard.
c because they were tired.
d because anyone can do it.
e because the weather was lovely.
f because he doesn't know anyone at his new school.
g because it's hot and sunny.
h because it had all my favourite actors in it.

b Complete the sentences with your own ideas.

1 I think ___dogs___ are great, but I don't like ___cats___ because *they are less friendly* .
2 I don't think _____ is a good place to go for lunch because _____ .
3 People think _____ is amazing, but I don't like it because _____ .
4 My friend thinks _____ is awful, but I think it's _____ because _____ .

c Work in pairs and compare your opinions and reasons. Do you agree?

Prepare

5 a You're going to write a social media post giving your opinion. Choose one of the following.

- a restaurant
- a food you tried
- a film
- a day out
- a party

b Think of opinions, and your reasons for your opinions. Make notes.

Write

6 a Write your social media post. Use your notes in Exercise 5 to help you.

b Work in pairs and share your posts. What comment would you write on their post?

Develop your reading

1 a Discuss the question. In what order do you usually do these things in a restaurant?

> find a table   get the bill   get food   get a menu
> order food   pay the bill

b Read the menu instructions for how to order. Do you usually order food in this way in your country?

HOW TO ORDER FOOD

THE HOT CHICKEN RESTAURANT

- Find a table and take a seat. You can sit anywhere that's free. The menus are on your table.
- Choose your meal and then order and pay at the counter. Don't forget to look for your table number before you go to the counter and give it to your server.
- After you order, take knives, forks and spoons from the Sauce Station. You can choose from our amazing hot sauces in the same area.
- Enjoy your food!

2 Read the Focus box. Find more examples of instructions in The Hot Chicken Restaurant menu.

Understanding instructions

When you read instructions, you will often see:
- the infinitive + object

Find a table and ***take a seat***.
- *You can* + infinitive

You can sit *anywhere that's free.*
- Words like *First, then, next, before, after*

After *you order, take knives, forks and spoons from the table.*

3 a Read the instructions again. Put these actions in the correct order.

- **a** Pay for your food.
- **b** Order your food.
- **c** Decide what to eat.
- **d** Sit down.
- **e** Look for your table number.
- **f** Get knives, forks and spoons.

b Are the sentences true (T) or false (F)?

1 The waiter takes you to a table.
2 The waiter brings you a menu.
3 You order from the waiter at your table.
4 There are no knives and forks on the table.
5 You can find sauces in another place.
6 You pay at the end of your meal.

4 a Read the instructions for a different restaurant. Do customers order in the same or a different way to the Hot Chicken Restaurant? What is similar and what is different?

SHOTOKU ROBOT RESTAURANT

HOW TO ORDER FOOD

Our robots are here, ready to serve you. When you arrive, tell a robot how many people are in your group. Remember the table number the robot gives you. Then, find your table and sit down.

The menu is on the tablet computer on the table. Choose the dishes you want. You can order your own dish or a meal with many different dishes for your group. After you choose, tap in your credit card information and pay.

Before your food arrives, use the tablet to read the news or watch funny cat videos with your friends. Your meal arrives between ten and twenty minutes after you order it. At the end of your meal, give your dirty plates to one of the robots. You can then order one of our delicious desserts.

b Read the instructions again. Underline examples of the language in the Focus box.

c Which action, A or B, happens first?

1 A Say hello to the robot.
B Sit at a table.
2 A Give your credit card information.
B Choose what you want to eat.
3 A Get your food.
B Use the tablet for entertainment.
4 A Order dessert.
B Return your plates to a robot.

5 Discuss the questions.

1 Would you like to go to the robot restaurant? Why/Why not?
2 What other unusual restaurants do you know about?

Develop your writing

> **Goal:** write a guide
> **Focus:** using adjectives

1 a Look at the photos and discuss the questions.
1. What can you see in each photo?
2. Where do you think each place is?
3. Which of the places would you most like to visit? Why?

b Read the article and check your ideas.

2 a Read the Focus box. How can we make our writing more interesting?

Using adjectives

Use adjectives to make your writing more interesting:

- Use 'strong' adjectives, e.g. *delicious, wonderful, awesome, amazing, fantastic, beautiful.*
  *... famous for its **delicious** Balinese food.*
- Use words like *very* and *really* to make weak adjectives (like *good, bad, nice, interesting, exciting*) stronger.
  *... in a **very nice** atmosphere.*

b Find more adjectives and the words *very* and *really* in the article in Exercise 1b.

3 Use the words in brackets to make each sentence more interesting. More than one answer may be possible.
1. Visit the old centre of town. (beautiful)
2. You can walk along the beach in the afternoon. (quiet)
3. Summer is a nice time to visit the forest. (really)
4. Try the food. (delicious)
5. There's an island in the middle of the lake. (very pretty)
6. Watch the dancers perform a dance on the beach. (wonderful, amazing)

Prepare

4 a You're going to write a list of the top five things to do in your area or a place you have visited. First, choose which five things to write about.

b Think about which adjectives and intensifiers to use and make notes about the following:
- where the place is
- what you can do there
- the type of people it's popular with

Write

5 a Write your guide. Use your notes in Exercise 4 to help you.

b Read your description. Can you make it more interesting?

TOP FIVE THINGS TO DO IN *Bali*

1 HAVE BREAKFAST AT THE TOP OF MOUNT BATUR
Leave your hotel very early in the morning and walk to the top of Mount Batur to have breakfast while the sun comes up. Watch the beautiful sky change colour from blue, to pink, to orange.

2 LEARN TO COOK IN UBUD
Have a cooking lesson in Ubud. It's famous for its delicious Balinese food. Learn to cook traditional food in a very nice atmosphere. After cooking, enjoy your meal with friends.

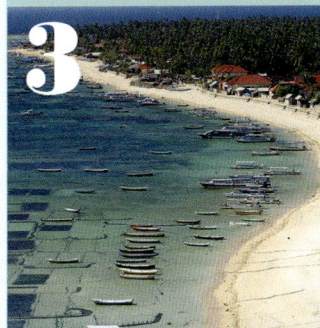

3 VISIT NUSA LEMBONGAN ISLAND
Travel to this wonderful island by boat. At Nusa Lembongan, you can lie on the beach, swim in the peaceful sea, or walk around the island. It's all really relaxing.

4 WATCH A PERFORMANCE AT ULUWATU TEMPLE
Visit this awesome temple and have a really delicious seafood dinner while dancers perform a traditional 'Kecak' dance for you.

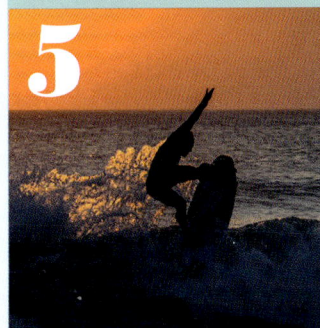

5 GO TO KUTA BEACH
Visit Bali's most popular beach with young people. You can surf in the sea during the day and party at night.

Develop your listening

> **Goal:** understand a news report
> **Focus:** understanding connected speech

1 Work in pairs and discuss the questions.
1 How often do you watch or listen to the news?
2 Where do you watch or listen to it?

2 🔊 8.5 Listen to a news report. Which photo in Exercise 1 is it about?

3 Read the Focus box. When do two words join together in speech?

Understanding connected speech

When a word ends with a consonant sound and the next one starts with the same consonant sound, the sounds 'join together'.

southwest town

When a word ends with a consonant sound and the next word starts with a vowel sound, they join together.

town of

4 a Work in pairs. Practise saying the extracts from the news report in Exercise 2 in pairs. How do the words join together?

1 storm arrived
2 storm made
3 fall into
4 came into
5 fire and
6 move out of
7 school in
8 next town

b 🔊 8.6 Listen and check. Then listen again and repeat.

5 a 🔊 8.7 Listen to the sentences from the next part of the news report and mark where the words join together.

1 It's hot today, which is unusual for October.
2 It's sunny and people are having a great time.
3 It's a really nice Sunday afternoon!

b 🔊 8.8 Listen to the whole of the second part of the report and answer the questions.

1 Why is the weather unusual?
2 What are the children doing?
3 What are the families doing?
4 What day is it?

6 a Read the next part of the news report and mark where the words join together.

> In other news, the government wants to put a new tax on food and drink with a lot of sugar. The tax will make these kinds of food and drink 10 percent more expensive.
>
> Finally, the prime minister met the Greek president today. It was the first time in London for the Greek president after he won last year's election.

b 🔊 8.9 Listen and check.

7 🔊 8.10 Listen to a report about a lost dog and choose the correct option, a or b.

1 How did Gareth feel when his dog escaped?
   a sad   b angry
2 What is Gareth's dog's name?
   a Saatchi   b Archie
3 How long did it take for the dog to come back?
   a one week   b one year
4 Does Gareth know where the dog went?
   a yes   b no
5 How did it feel to have his dog back home?
   a grey   b great

8 Work in pairs and discuss the questions.
1 What is in the news at the moment?
2 Look at the list below. What kinds of news stories do you listen to/watch? Why?
   • stories about famous people
   • sports news
   • politics
   • stories about problems in the world

Develop your reading

> **Goal:** understand a short article
>
> **Focus:** understanding paragraph topics

Transport around the world

The Philippines

¹ Travel in the Philippines is sometimes difficult. In some places, the roads are bad so it's hard to travel by car. People need a fast form of transport with space for a family and bags and that can drive along poor, small roads. So, they use the *habal habal*.

² The *habal habal* is a motorbike, but it's not the usual type of motorbike. It's popular with families but you can also use it like a taxi. Up to seven people can sit on it because it has extra seats. These seats are on the back or on the side of the *habal habal*.

³ It's always good to try something different and a trip on a *habal habal* is not the same as a trip in a car or taxi. You can see places that you can't visit by car because the *habal habal* travels down smaller roads and it's an unusual and fun way to get around.

⁴ The *habal habal* isn't always safe, it can be dangerous. You can fall off, and not every driver drives slowly and carefully on the poor roads. Accidents are common!

A

Hong Kong

⁵ A junk boat is a traditional type of Chinese boat. For hundreds of years, people used these wooden boats to travel around parts of Asia and buy and sell things. We can still see junk boats in Hong Kong today. In fact, they're one of the most exciting ways to see Hong Kong.

⁶ The best time to go on a junk boat is at night. You can see the amazing lights of Hong Kong and look up and see the stars in the night sky. In the daytime you can visit the beach and enjoy time in the water. Night tours are four hours long and day tours are about seven hours long. The day tours are usually more expensive.

⁷ Junk boat tours are very popular so you need to book one or two months before the day. It's not usually possible to call on the same day, so book early! There are many tour companies online so look for a company there and read the reviews from other users. It's the easiest way to book.

⁸ There are many different tours so you need to choose the best one for you. Some tours include food and drink; others ask you to bring your own. On some tours, you can do water sports and on others there's even a DJ! These tours usually cost more, but you can always find a tour at the right price for you.

B

1 a Look at photo A and discuss the questions.
 1 Where do you think the people are?
 2 What transport can you see?
 3 What's unusual about this transport?

b Read the first part of the article and check your ideas.

2 a Read the Focus box. Then choose a topic (A–D) to describe paragraph 1 of the article in Exercise 1b.
 A Problems with the *habal habal*
 B Problems with travel in the Philippines
 C How the *habal habal* is different to other transport
 D What the *habal habal* is

Understanding paragraph topics

A text usually has several paragraphs. Each paragraph has a topic. To understand what the topic is:
* Read the first sentence and look at the important words.
 *Travel in the **Philippines** is sometimes **difficult**.*
* Look for words with a similar topic.
 *Travel in the Philippines is sometimes **difficult**. The **roads** are **bad** so it's **hard** to **travel** by **car**.*

b Match paragraphs 2–4 with the other topics.

c In which paragraphs can you answer these questions?
 1 How many people can sit on a *habal habal*?
 2 Why is it dangerous for passengers on a *habal habal*?
 3 What are the two good things about a *habal habal*?
 4 Where do people sit on a *habal habal*?
 5 Why is not every *habal habal* driver safe?

d Read the first part of the article again and answer the questions.

3 a Read the second part of the article. Underline important words and circle repeated words/words with the same meaning.

b Match paragraphs 5–8 with topics A–D below. Use your underlined and circled words to help you.
 A The best time to go on a junk boat
 B Different types of junk boat tours
 C Booking a junk boat tour
 D What is a junk boat?

4 a In which paragraphs can you answer these questions?
 1 What do some junk boat tours include?
 2 What activities can you do on a junk boat?
 3 How long are day tours and night tours?
 4 When did people start using junk boats?
 5 When do you need to book a junk boat tour?
 6 What is the best way to book a junk boat tour?

b Read the article again and answer the questions.

5 Would you like to use these types of transport?

Develop your listening

> **Goal:** understand a short talk
>
> **Focus:** dealing with unknown words

1 Look at the photos and discuss the questions.

1 What do you know about the food and drink in the photos? Are they good or bad for you?
2 What other food and drink is good for you? And bad for you?

2 🔊 9.4 **Listen to the beginning of a radio programme. Which food and drink does the speaker talk about?**

3 a Read the Focus box. Which things in the box do you already do?

Dealing with unknown words

When we listen, we often hear words we don't understand. When you listen in English:

• Don't worry when you hear words you don't know. Continue to listen.

*Many **wise** parents tell their children that carrots help them to see in the dark like **foxes, rabbits** or **owls**.*

• Pay attention to the words you DO understand.

*Many wise **parents tell** their **children** that **carrots help** them to **see in the dark** like foxes, rabbits or owls.*

• Use the words you know to guess the speaker's meaning e.g. *carrots make our eyes better.*

• Use information you already know, e.g. who the speakers are, where they are, what you know about the topic.

I know that people think carrots help us to see in the dark. Maybe he's talking about that.

b 🔊 9.5 **Listen to Mark talking about carrots. Note down any important words.**

c Think about the words you noted down in Exercise 3b and what you already know about carrots. What is Mark's message, a or b?

a Carrots help us see better in the dark.
b Carrots don't help us see better in the dark.

4 a 🔊 9.6 **Listen to Mark talking about orange juice. Note down any important words.**

b Think about the words you noted down and what you know about orange juice. What is Mark's main message, a or b?

a Orange juice can stop you getting a cold.
b Orange juice can't stop you getting a cold.

5 a 🔊 9.7 **Listen to Mark talking about coffee. Note down any important words.**

b Think about the words you noted down and what you know about coffee. What is Mark's main message, a or b?

a Some coffee is probably fine.
b Coffee is usually bad.

6 a 🔊 9.8 **Listen to Mark talking about breakfast. Note down any important words.**

b Think about the words you noted down and what you know about breakfast. What is Mark's main message, a or b?

a We should all eat breakfast.
b It's not always important to eat breakfast.

7 🔊 9.9 **Listen to the whole talk again and answer the questions.**

1 What vitamin do carrots have in them?
2 What does orange juice have in it that is bad?
3 When is it OK to miss breakfast?

8 Work in pairs. What other things do people believe about our health that aren't true?

Develop your writing

> **Goal:** write an informal email

> **Focus:** organising an email to a friend

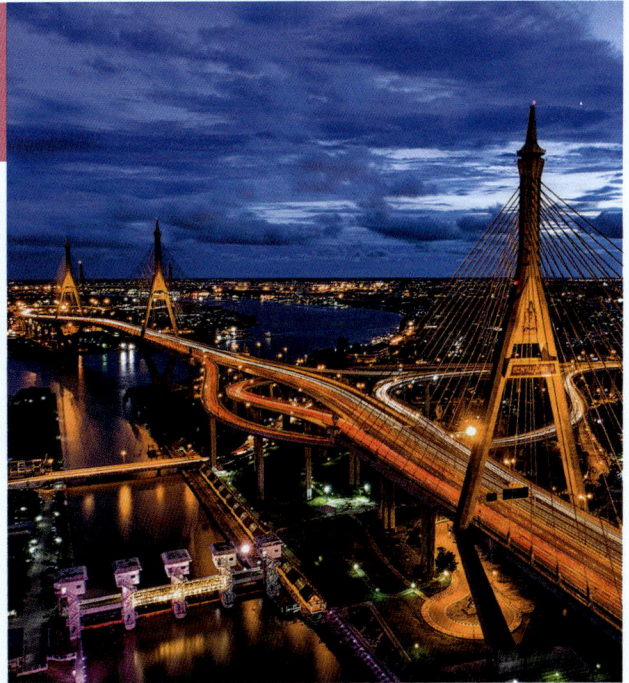

1 **Discuss the questions.**

1 How often do you contact friends?

2 How do you contact them, by email, on social media or in some other way?

2 a **Read Patrick's email to a friend. Why is he writing?**

To: evansky@newmail.com
From: pat01@email.com
Subject: Happy New Year!

Hi Evan

How are you? Hope you had a good new year. We had a great time in Berlin. Did you see my photos?

Anyway, I have some news. In March, Alissia and I are going to leave our jobs and go travelling for six months in Asia. We're so excited! First, we're going to fly to Bangkok in Thailand but after that we're not sure where we're going to go next. We might go to one of the islands but I really want to see the elephants in the north. We're going to go to Cambodia, Laos and Vietnam, too. When we get back, Alissia's going to start her MA at university and I'm going to start a new job in the city. I can't wait!

What about you? Do you have any exciting plans for this year?
All the best
Patrick

---

b **Read the email again and answer the questions.**

1 What did Patrick do at new year?

2 What are his and Alissia's plans in March?

3 What are their plans for later in the year?

4 What does he ask Evan to do?

3 **Read the Focus box, and underline points 1–5 in the email in Exercise 2a.**

Organising an email to a friend

1 Begin with a greeting, e.g. *Hi Evan, Hello Charlotte!*

2 Ask an opening question or comment, e.g. *How are you? Hope you had a good weekend/new year/holiday. Good to hear from you!* (if your email is a reply)

3 Introduce your news, e.g. *Anyway, I have some news.*

4 Ask more questions or make requests, e.g. *Please write and tell me your news. Let me know (when you're free).*

5 End with a closing phrase, e.g. *All the best, Bye for now, See you soon, Love to the children/Fiona/your mum.*

---

4 **Match phrases a–e with points 1–5 in the Focus box.**

a See you soon.

b I have some exciting plans to tell you about.

c How are things with you?

d Hello, Kim.

e What about you?

5 **Put parts A–E of the email in the correct order.**

A Are you going to be there? If so, do you want to meet us? Let me know.

B Hello, Charlotte!

C Bye for now!
Cassie

D So, we have some travel plans. Mike is going to be in Edinburgh with work for two weeks from 14th August. We really want to go to the Edinburgh Festival, so I'm going to join him for a weekend.

E How are things with you? Hope you and the family are well.

Prepare

6 a **Imagine you are Evan. You're going to write a reply to Patrick's email in Exercise 2 and tell him about your plans for the year. First, think of three or four plans you want to tell him about. Make notes. Use these ideas to help you:**

- Say hello to Patrick.
- Ask a question or make a comment.
- Tell him your plans.
- Ask another question.
- Close the email.

b **Decide which of the phrases in the Focus box you want to use.**

Write

7 **Write your reply. Use your notes to help you.**

Develop your reading

My *30-day* habit

Changing your life
Did you know that it takes 30 days to make a new habit? If you do one activity every day for 30 days, it becomes a regular activity for you. I always wanted to write but I didn't because I didn't have the time. I decided to change that …

What is NaNoWriMo?
National Novel Writing Month (or NaNoWriMO for short) happens in November every year. People write a 50,000-word book in one month. They start with a plan and share it with other authors. Then, in November, they write 1,666 words a day for 30 days. They write every day so they don't have too much to write at the end of the month.

How was it for me?
On 1st November two years ago, I sat at my computer after work and started my very first book. I had a lot of ideas in my head so the words came easily and I wrote over 2,000. The next day, I wrote 1,700 words and the day after that I wrote 1,800. At first, it seemed very easy.

After a week, it became difficult because it was hard to write every evening after a long day at work. On the ninth day, I didn't have time to write because it was my sister's birthday party. The next day, I needed to write 3,332 words so I wasn't late. I almost stopped because it was so hard, but I'm glad that I didn't.

Was I successful?
On 30th November, I finished my first book. I was really pleased. Of course, the book was not great because you can't write a good book in 30 days but I was now a writer. Last year, I wrote a second book. This time, I spent six months on it so it was a lot better. I then published it online and I sold 202 copies. It's not a lot but I can say that I'm a published writer!

1 **Discuss the questions.**
   1 Would you like to write a book? Why/Why not?
   2 Do you think it's easy to write a book? Why/Why not?

2 a **Read the headings and first line of the blog post. What do you think it's about?**

   b **Read the blog post and answer the questions.**
   1 What did the blogger do for 30 days? Why?
   2 What happened at the end of the 30 days?
   3 What happened next?

3 **Read the Focus box and find examples of *so* and *because* in the blog.**

Understanding *because* and *so*
- Introduce reasons with *because and so*. They answer the question *why?*

I never wrote a book **because** *I didn't have time.* (Why didn't you write a book?)

They write every day **so** *they don't have too much to write at the end of the month.* (Why do they write every day?)

- Introduce the result of something with *so.*

I had a lot of ideas **so** *the words came easily.* (Result: a lot of ideas = words came easily)

4 **Match the sentence halves.**
   1 I'd like to be a writer
   2 I didn't know much about the subject so
   3 It's good to meet other writers because
   4 I am going to join a writing group
   5 The book is about my favourite country so
   6 I want to finish my book soon because

   a I am enjoying it a lot.
   b so I can meet other writers.
   c we can help each other with ideas.
   d so I can work from home.
   e I want to start my next one.
   f it was difficult to write about it.

5 **Read the blog post again and answer the questions. Underline the words in the blog post that help you.**
   1 Why did the blogger not write before November two years ago?
   2 What is National Novel Writing Month?
   3 Why was the writing easy at first?
   4 What made it difficult for the blogger?
   5 Why did the blogger almost stop writing?
   6 Why was the book bad?
   7 Why was the blogger's second book better?

6 **Work in pairs and discuss the questions.**
   1 Do you think that you can change a habit in 30 days? Why/Why not?
   2 What new habit would you like to make?
   3 How can you make that new habit?

Develop your writing

> **Goal:** write a personal profile
> **Focus:** expressing likes and dislikes

1 **Discuss the questions.**
1 How can you find somewhere to live?
2 What kinds of things are important in a place to live?
3 What things are important about the people you live with?

2 a **Read the profile. What does Alex want?**

Hi, everyone. I'm Alex and I'm 27. I'm a professional engineer. I work all over the country, but I spend a few days per week in London. I'm looking for a double room in the North London area from 14th September.

I'm a big fan of sport (watching and playing), so great if you like it, too. I'm not really into cooking but am happy to help. I'm OK with sharing all the bills and I'm clean and tidy, I promise! I'm fine about most things (pets, music, doing the washing up!) but I can't stand smoking, so non-smoker housemates only, please.

Please contact me through the website.

b **Read Alex's profile again and put the information in the order he writes about it.**
a his likes and dislikes
b information about himself
c contact information

3 **Read the Focus box. What things does Alex like and dislike in Exercise 2a? What things doesn't Alex mind?**

Expressing likes and dislikes

a expressing likes, e.g. *I'm a big fan of, I'm into …*
b saying you don't mind something, e.g. *I'm OK with …, I'm fine about …*
c expressing dislikes, e.g. *I can't stand …, I'm not really into …*

4 **Match sentences 1–6 with categories a–c in the Focus box.**
1 I'm not into music.
2 I don't mind pets.
3 I really like modern art.
4 I'm really into tennis.
5 A small room is not a problem.
6 I really hate cleaning.

5 **Rewrite the sentences. Use the words in brackets.**
1 I like football. (into)
   I'm into football.
2 Washing up is not a problem. (OK)
3 I really like American action films. (fan)
4 I'm fine about sharing bills. (mind)
5 I don't like rock music (into)

6 **Complete the personal profile.**

Hi, everyone. I'm Naomi. I'm 34 and I'm a singer. I work evenings and weekends. I'm looking for a room from next month.
I'm ¹_____ into music, but don't worry, I'm a quiet person! I'm not really ²_____ watching TV, but I don't ³_____ watching it with other housemates. I'm a big ⁴_____ of Italian food and happy to cook for everyone. I'm ⁵_____ with sharing bills and cleaning.
Please message me through the website.

Prepare

7 a **You're going to write a personal profile for a house-sharing website. First, make notes and think about:**
• information about you
• what you're looking for
• your likes and dislikes
• things you don't mind

b **Think about which phrases from the lesson you can use to write your profile.**

Write

8 a **Write your profile. Use your notes to help you.**

b **Share your profile with the class. Do you have the same likes and dislikes?**

> **Goal:** understand an opinion article

> **Focus:** identifying opinions

1 **Discuss the questions.**

1 What do you wear . . .

- at work/school?
- at the weekend?
- at a wedding?
- for an interview?

2 Do you think it's more important for employees to look smart or feel relaxed? Why?

2 **Read the article quickly. Which statement best describes the writer's opinion?**

a The writer thinks people dress well for work.

b The writer thinks people are too casual at work.

c The writer thinks people should wear the same clothes at work as they wear at home.

NEW STYLES AT WORK

Last week, I was in a meeting at work. During the meeting, I looked round at people's clothes. There were no suits or ties, just jeans, T-shirts and sweaters. One man even had shorts on! Are we becoming too casual at work? In my opinion, we are and it's not a good thing.

Only 10 percent of office workers wear a suit to work nowadays, and over half wear casual clothes. These days, the workplace is relaxed. Many companies now have dress codes that say workers don't have to wear a suit or similar smart clothes. It's now OK to wear jeans, trainers and a sweater.

'We don't want our workers to look bad, they have to look quite smart,' says Mark Wirrell, manager of a computer company in London, 'but it's important that they feel comfortable. Any company that wants to be successful and keep good workers has to do this.'

A few years ago, many companies started 'Casual Friday', where workers don't have to wear their usual work clothes to work every Friday. Nowadays, every day is casual day, and I think this is wrong. It gives a terrible impression of a company.

3 a **Read the Focus box, then underline two opinions in the article in Exercise 2.**

Identifying opinions

To give their opinions, writers often use phrases like *I think* or *In my opinion*.

I think this is wrong.

In my opinion, we should wear smart clothes to work.

The adjectives that writers use often tell us their opinions.

*In my opinion, we are, and it's **not** a **good** thing.*

*It gives a **terrible** impression of a company.*

b **Work in pairs and compare your answers. Do you agree with the opinions?**

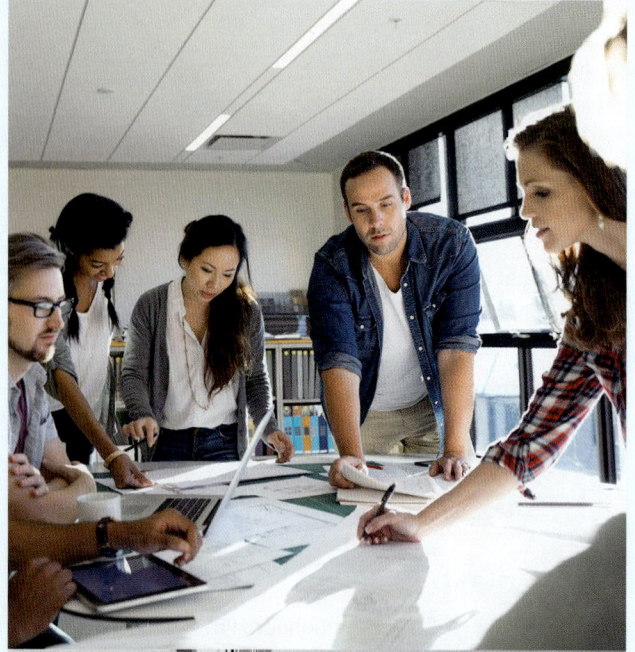

4 **Read the article again and answer the questions.**

1 What item of clothing was the writer surprised to see in a meeting?

2 How many office workers wear a suit to work?

3 How many workers wear casual clothes?

4 What clothes can people wear to work these days?

5 How does Mark Wirrell want his workers to dress?

6 How does he want his workers to feel?

7 What is 'Casual Friday'?

8 Does the writer think wearing casual clothes every day is a good idea?

5 **Work in pairs and discuss the questions.**

1 Is your workplace/school becoming more or less casual?

2 Do you have a Casual Friday?

3 Do you have any days at work/school where you wear special clothes? What are they for?

> **Goal:** understand an interview
> **Focus:** understanding time expressions

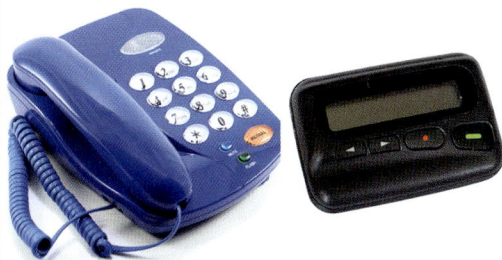

1 a Discuss the questions.

1 What technology do you use to chat to your friends and family?
2 What's the oldest technology you have used?

b 🔊 10.8 Listen to a radio interview about technology and communication. What types of communication do they talk about?

a using messaging apps
b calling on the telephone
c sending birds with messages
d writing letters
e writing emails
f sending telegrams
g talking face to face

2 a Read the Focus box. Add the time expressions in the box under the correct headings.

in a few months   right now   when I was young

Understanding time expressions

Time expressions can help us understand if someone is talking about the past, the present or the future.
You can often hear time expressions at the beginning of a sentence:
Ten years ago, we used emails more than now.
These days, we send messages instead of sending emails.
You can also hear them at the end of a sentence or clause:
We're not going to use text messaging in the future.
People used to call each other more often in the past.
Some common time expressions are:
Past time
ten years ago, in the 1980s, in the past, last year
Present time
these days, now, at the moment, today, at this time
Future time
in (the) future, in ten years
The tenses which someone uses can also help you decide if they are talking about the past, present or future.
In the 1950s, people wrote letters to each other. – Past
We're not going to call each other in the future. – Future

b 🔊 10.9 Listen and complete the sentences with the time expressions you hear. Is each one about the past, present or future?

1 _____ ,technology changes every year.
2 I got my first mobile phone _____ .
3 _____ , I'm going to get a new laptop.
4 I dropped my mobile phone down the toilet _____ .
5 I'm using my old phone _____ .
6 I chatted to my friends online _____ .
7 I don't go online very often _____ .
8 _____ , technology companies are going to give us something completely new.

3 🔊 10.10 Listen to eight sentences. Write the sentence numbers in the correct place in the table.

Time	Sentence number
Past	_1_ , _____ , _____ ,
Present	_____ , _____ ,
Future	_____ , _____ , _____ ,

4 a 🔊 10.8 Listen to the radio interview again. Does Zoe say these activities are in the past, present or future?

1 Letters
2 Everybody and email
3 Use of chatting apps
4 Use of text messages
5 Use of phone calls
6 Use of telegrams
7 Use of a digital assistant to communicate

b Listen to the interview again. Are the sentences true (T) or false (F)?

1 Zoe says that nobody writes letters today.
2 Young people use email to chat.
3 People used phones to send messages a hundred years ago.
4 Telegrams were quicker than today's text messages.
5 Zoe doesn't know about the future of chatting apps.
6 Technology companies want to make better digital assistants in the future.

5 Discuss the questions.

1 What technology from the past was great? Should we use it again?
2 What technology from the present don't you like? Why?
3 What technology would you like to see in the future?

Grammar bank

1A Verb *be* – positive and negative

Use *be* ...
- with names, e.g. *I'm Sofi.*
- with ages, e.g. *He's 60.*
- with nouns, e.g. *She's a waitress. It's a dog.*
- with adjectives, e.g. *They're tall. The town is big.*
- to say where a person or thing is from, e.g. *It's from China.*
- to say where a person or thing is, e.g. *Jon's in Moscow.*
- with prices, e.g. *It's £2.50.*
- to say the time, e.g. *It's six o'clock.*

You is both singular and plural.
Jane, you're late.   Jane and Tom, you're late.
Use contractions when speaking. Use an apostrophe (') to show the missing letter.
Hi, I'm Rachel. I'm American. ~~Hi, I am Rachel. I am American.~~

be positive

I'm = I am	Italian.
You're = You are	Turkish.
He's = He is	
She's = She is	Russian.
It's = It is	from Paris.
We're = We are	from Mexico City.
They're = They are	from the US.

be negative

I'm not = I am not	Italian.
You aren't = You are not	Turkish.
He isn't = He is not	Russian.
She isn't = She is not	
It isn't = It is not	from Paris.
We aren't = We are not	from Mexico City.
They aren't = They are not	from the US.

's not can be used with *he/she/it* in the negative.
She's not here.
're not can be used with *we/you/they* in the negative.
They're not from Munich.

1B Questions with *be*

The subject (e.g. *I, he, they*) and verb *be* change places to make a question.
She's a policewoman. Is she a policewoman?

Yes/No questions			Short answers
Am	I	Italian? Australian?	Yes, I am. No, I'm not.
Is	he/she/it	Greek? from the US?	Yes, he/she/it is. No, he/she/it isn't.
Are	we/you/they	from Spain? from Mexico?	Yes, we/you/they are. No, we/you/they aren't.

Add a question word to ask a *wh-* question.
What/Which = thing
Who = person
Where = place
When = time
How old = age
How much = money

Who are you? I'm Lizzie.   **How much** is it? It's £5.
Where is he? He's over there.

Question word	be	subject
How old	are	you?
When	is	our lesson?
What	is	your name?
Where	are	the shops?

1C *This, that, these* and *those*

Use *this* and *these* with things near to you.

Use *this* for one thing.
This mobile phone.

Use *these* for two or more things.
These mobile phones.

Use *that* and *those* with things far from you.

Use *that* for one thing.
That mobile phone.

Use *those* for two or more things.
Those mobile phones.

To say something is near, use *here*.
*This pen **here**. These pens **here**.*

To say something is far away, use *over there*.
*That pen **over there**. Those pens **over there**.*

PRACTICE

1A

A Complete the sentences with the correct form of *be*.

1 Masha ___is___ (+) Russian. She _____ (+) from Moscow.
2 We ___aren't___ (-) Australian. We _____ (+) from New Zealand.
3 The orange juice _____ (+) £2.50.
4 It _____ (-) cheap in this restaurant. It _____ (+) expensive.
5 I _____ (-) tall. I _____ (+) short.
6 Helen _____ (+) 45 years old.
7 Jim and Pippa _____ (+) married. They _____ (+) really happy.
8 They _____ (-) Spanish. They _____ (+) from Mexico.

B Make sentences using the prompts and the positive (+) or negative (-) form of *be*.

1 Sam / a teacher. (+)
  Sam is a teacher.
2 Mel and her friend Sue / 33 years old. (+)
3 My watch / from Switzerland. (-)
4 Zak and his brother / doctors. (+)
5 It / ten o'clock in the morning. (+)
6 We / very happy about the news. (-)
7 A cup of coffee / £2.99. (+)
8 The clothes in this shop / very nice. (-)
9 This coffee / good. (-)
10 The school / very nice. (+)

1B

A Put the words in the correct order to make questions.

1 from / where / you / are ?
2 your email address / is / what ?
3 you / are / a student ?
4 when / your next lesson / is ?
5 your job / is / what ?
6 over there / the woman / is / who ?
7 you / married / are ?
8 your favourite colour / is / what ?
9 friend / from / where / is / your ?
10 your / class / how / is ?
11 how old / brother / your / is ?
12 teacher's name / what / our / is ?

B Write questions for each answer.

1 Megan's <u>six years old</u>.
  How old is Megan?
2 My phone number is <u>07395 229309</u>.
3 That man's <u>William</u>.
4 I'm <u>a teacher</u>.
5 They're from <u>the UK</u>.
6 Your keys are <u>over there</u>.
7 It's <u>three o'clock</u>.
8 A cup of tea is <u>£2.40</u>.
9 Yes, she's <u>French</u>.
10 I'm <u>at home</u>.

1C

A Correct the mistakes in six of the conversations.

1 **A:** How much are that sunglasses?
  B: They are ten pounds.
2 **A:** Is these your pen?
  B: No, that's my pen.
3 **A:** This picture is nice.
  B: Yes, I like it.
4 **A:** Hi Joanne.
  B: Hi Alice, these is my friend Ken.
5 **A:** That's a nice clock.
  B: Thank you! Those clock is from China.
6 **A:** Do you like these bags here?
  B: No, I don't.
7 **A:** Is this Sally over there?
  B: No, that's Jane.
8 **A:** I like those laptop.
  B: Yes, it's a great

B Put the words in bold in the correct place in the sentence.

1 **A:** How much are bags over there? **those**
  How much are those bags over there?
  B: The blue bag is £10 and red bag is £20. **that**
2 **A:** Do you prefer bike over there or bike here? **this, that**
  B: I prefer one. **that**
3 **A:** I don't like shoes, but I like jacket. **those, this**
  B: Oh, really? I like pink shoes. **those**
4 **A:** Skateboard is expensive, but board games are cheap. **that, those**
  B: How much are board games? **those**
5 **A:** Look at plates here. They're really nice. **these**
  B: Plates are nice. Plates over there are really pretty too. **these, those**
6 **A:** How much is umbrella in the window? **that**
  B: It's £25. One here is £15. **this**

Want more practice? Go to your Workbook or app.

117

2A Possessive adjectives and possessive 's

Possessive adjectives

Use possessive adjectives before a noun to show ...
• who a family member is related to.
*That's **my** mother.   Chris is **her** brother.*
• who something belongs to.
*Are these **your** glasses?   That's **their** car.*

Subject pronoun	Possessive adjective
I	my
you	your
he	his
she	her
it	its
we	our
you	your
they	their

Possessive 's

Use possessive 's with names in the same way as possessive adjectives.
*She's Susan**'s** grandmother.* NOT ~~The grandmother of Susan.~~
*They're Pete**'s** glasses.* NOT ~~The glasses of Pete.~~
To describe something that belongs to two or more people, add possessive 's to the last name.
*It's John and Nick**'s** book.*
*They're Angela, Joanna and Steve**'s** games.*
Note that 's shows possession and is not a contraction of *is*.
Charlotte's husband. NOT ~~Charlotte is husband~~.
Rob's car. NOT ~~Rob is car~~.
If the noun is plural, an apostrophe without s comes after the plural -*s*.
*That's my parent**s'** car.*
*They're my grandparent**s'** children.*

2B *whose* and possessive pronouns

Possessive pronouns

Use possessive pronouns when we know who the person or people are.
*That isn't Katy's cap, it's **mine**.   It's not **yours**, it's **mine**.*

Subject pronoun	Possessive pronoun
I	mine
you	yours
he	his
she	hers
it	its
we	ours
you	yours
they	theirs

Also use possessive pronouns in short answers.
A: Are these Phil's glasses?
*B: Yes, they're **his**.*
A: Is that your neighbour's car?
*B: No, it's **ours**.*
In short answers when we disagree, it's not necessary to repeat the noun.
A: Is this Linda's bike?
B: No, it's Graeme's.

Whose

Use *whose* to ask about possession.
***Whose** phone charger is this?*
***Whose** gloves are those?*

2C *have got*

Use *have got* to talk about things we have, e.g.:
• our family *I**'ve got** two sisters and a brother.*
• our possessions *She**'s got** a new mobile phone.*
• our pets *We**'ve got** a dog.*
• our looks *He**'s got** brown hair and blue eyes.*

Positive sentences

I/You/We/They	've/have got	a small flat.
He/She/It	's/has got	

Using *have* is also possible.
*She **has** a new job.   They **have** a lovely cat.*
*I **have** an old computer.*

Negative sentences

I/You/We/They	haven't got	a car.
He/She/It	hasn't got	

Questions

Yes/No question				Short answer
Have	I/you/we/they	got	a big house? a cat? a camera? any pets?	Yes, I/you/we/they have. No, I/you/we/they haven't.
Has	he/she/it			Yes, he/she/it has. No, he/she/it hasn't.

In negative sentences and questions, use *any* with plural nouns.
*I **haven't got any** sunglasses.*
***Have** you **got any** good books?*

Wh- questions			
What car What pet	have	I/you/we/they	got?
What phone Which book	has	he/she/it	

2A

A Correct the mistakes in eight of the sentences.

1 That's I pen.
That's my pen.
2 Look at they're new car!
3 Shona is her niece.
4 That's my uncle. Her name is Nigel.
5 Is that you bag?
6 This is my dog. It name is Lucky.
7 Our parents are nice.
8 What's he's mother's name?
9 Me new bag is great.
10 What is you name?

B Add the possessive 's in the correct place in the conversations.

1 **A:** Is that Alice bike?
   Alice's
   B: No, it's John.
2 **A:** Hi Kevin, this is Kelly. She's Mike sister.
   B: Nice to meet you.
3 **A:** Is Janice Michael mother?
   B: No, she's Tom mother.
4 **A:** Who's Brian?
   B: Brian is Georgia cousin.
5 **A:** What's your brother name?
   B: Alex. My sister name is Jean.
6 **A:** Whose is this bag?
   B: It's my sister.

2B

A Rewrite the sentences using a possessive pronoun.

1 It's Catherine's bike.
It's *hers*.
2 They're John and Margaret's keys.
They're _____ .
3 That bag belongs to you.
It's _____ .
4 It's my jacket.
It's _____ .
5 Those are Mark's sunglasses.
They're _____ .
6 Is this my sandwich?
Is this _____ ?

B Complete the conversation with the words in the box.

hers	his	ours	mine	theirs
Whose (x2)		yours		

A: ¹_____ car is that? Is it ²_____ ?
B: No, it isn't ³_____ . Maybe it's Jack's.
A: No, it isn't ⁴_____ . Jack's car is blue.
B: What about your neighbours, Phil and Sue?
A: No, it isn't ⁵_____ .
B: Very strange. It isn't ⁶_____ , it isn't theirs. ⁷_____ is it?
A: Oh, look at that woman – it's ⁸_____ !

2C

A Complete the sentences with the positive (+) or negative (-) form of *have got*.

1 I _____ a tablet. (+)
2 Jon _____ any cousins. (-)
3 They _____ a son called Mikey. (+)
4 She _____ any pets. (-)
5 We _____ a fantastic new TV. (+)
6 The shops _____ any bottles of water. (-)
7 My car _____ a satnav. (-)
8 My parents _____ a lovely new sofa. (+)
9 My friends _____ a really nice house in London. (+)
10 He's got time today, but they _____ any. (-)
11 Your children _____ very interesting names, Lola. (+)
12 My dog _____ a black body and a white head. (+)

B Complete the conversations with the correct form of *have (got)*.

1 **A:** _____ you _____ a £5 note?
   B: No, I _____ . Sorry. I _____ a £10 note. Is that OK?
2 **A:** _____ Marian _____ a sister?
   B: Yes, she _____ . She _____ a brother, too.
3 **A:** _____ your flat _____ a garden?
   B: No, it _____ . It _____ a balcony.
4 **A:** _____ we _____ any eggs?
   B: Yes, we _____ . I think we _____ six or seven.
5 **A:** _____ your brothers _____ jobs?
   B: Steve _____ . He's a police officer. Alex _____ a job. He's at school.
6 **A:** _____ you _____ a minute?
   B: No, I _____ . Sorry. I _____ a class now.
7 **A:** _____ he _____ blue eyes?
   B: No, he _____ grey eyes.
8 **A:** _____ your house _____ a garden?
   B: Yes, it _____ . Why?

Want more practice? Go to your Workbook or app.

3A Present simple with *I, you, we* and *they*

Use the present simple to talk about ...

• regular activities, habits and routines.
*We **go** to the cinema every Friday.*

• things which are true.
*We **live** in Berlin.   I **work** in an office.*

Use the infinitive to form the present simple with *I/you/we/they*. (The infinitive form is the verb in the dictionary.) Use *don't* + infinitive to make the negative form (*don't = do not*).

+	I/You/We/They	play	football.
-	I/You/We/They	don't play	tennis.

Use time expressions to say when we do regular activities.

• *at* + time, e.g. *at the weekend, at six o'clock, at night*
• *on* + days, e.g. *on Mondays, on Friday mornings*
• *in* + months, time of day and years, e.g. *in June, in the evening, in 2020*

These time expressions usually go at the end of the sentence, but they can come at the beginning, too.

*I go to the gym **on Tuesdays and Thursdays**.*
***In the mornings**, I walk to work.*

Use time expressions to say how often we do activities.
every hour/day/week/month
once/twice/three times a day/week/month/year
These expressions go at the end of a sentence.
*They cook dinner **every day**.*
Use adverbs of frequency to say how often we do activities.

never   rarely   sometimes   often   usually   always

0%   50%   100%

Adverbs of frequency go before the main verb but after the verb *be*. They go after *not* in negative sentences.

*I **usually eat** at my parents' house on Sundays.*
*He**'s sometimes** late for work.*
*We **don't often eat** pizza.   They **aren't always** right.*

Often and *sometimes* can come at the beginning of a sentence.

***Sometimes**, my mum cooks for me.*

Don't use *sometimes, rarely* or *never* with negative verbs.
*I ~~don't~~ **sometimes** go out for dinner.   We ~~don't~~ **rarely** play games online.   He ~~doesn't~~ **never** visits me.*

3B Present simple with *he, she* and *it*

Positive	
He She	likes films. cooks dinner in the evening. studies hard. has breakfast with his family.
It	starts at 4 p.m.

Negative		
He She	doesn't	get up early at the weekend. watch TV in the morning.
It	doesn't	start at 4 p.m.

With most verbs, add *-s* to the end of the verb, e.g.
*Tina **gets up** late at the weekend.*
For verbs which end in *-ch, -sh, -s, -z, -o* or *-x*, add *-es*, e.g.
*My brother **watches** TV in the evening.*
For verbs which end in a consonant + *-y*, delete the *-y* and add *-ies*, e.g. *Mark **studies** economics at school.*
Have changes to *has*, e.g. *John **has** a shower every day.*
To make negative sentences, use *doesn't* (= does not) + infinitive, e.g. *He **doesn't like** his job.*
In negative sentences, don't add *-s* to the main verb, e.g.
*She **doesn't start** work early.* NOT ~~She doesn't starts work early.~~

3C Present simple questions

Use the present simple to ask questions about regular activities, habits, routines and things that are true.
Use *do/does* to form present simple questions.

Question word/phrase	*do/ does*	subject	verb + other information
	Do	I/you/we/they	do sport?
	Does	he/she/it	live here?
Where	do	I/you/we/they	work?
What music	does	he/she/it	listen to?

Short answers
To answer *yes/no* questions, use short answers.

Yes,	I/you/we/they do. he/she/it does.
No,	I/you/we/they don't. he/she/it doesn't.

*A: Do you like this song? B: **Yes, I do**.*

*A: Does she have a brother? B: **No, she doesn't**.*
Use *How often* to ask about the frequency of an activity.
***How often** do you do sport?*

3A

A Put the words in the correct order to make sentences.

1 every week / we / pizza / have
   We have pizza every week.
2 don't / sports / you / do / often
3 go / my friends and I / every Saturday / for coffee
4 once / to the park / go / they / a week
5 films / enjoy / usually / I / don't
6 pictures / paint / I / of people / sometimes
7 go / they / to the gym / every day / don't
8 at six / dinner / have / we / o'clock / usually
9 always / the weekend / I / relax at
10 never / I / coffee / drink / before bed

B Complete the sentences with the correct form of the verbs in the box.

go (x2)	live	play	see	swim	watch	work

1 I _don't see_ my best friend every week. (-)
2 We usually _____ for a walk on Sundays. (+)
3 My parents _____ TV. (-)
4 We _____ for a small company. (+)
5 Mike and Ali _____ in a big house with a lovely garden. (+)
6 I _____ basketball every week. (-)
7 We _____ in the sea once a year. (+)
8 I _____ online in the evening. (-)

3B

A Choose the correct alternatives.

My boss ¹*work/works* really hard. He gets up early every day at 5 a.m. He ²*haves/has* a quick shower, but he doesn't ³*have/has* breakfast. He ⁴*get/gets* to the office before anyone else and when we ⁵*arrive/arrives* he talks to us about our work for the day. During the day, he ⁶*don't/doesn't* relax. When he hasn't got any work, he ⁷*helps/help* us with ours. We all have lunch together and talk about what we do in our free time. At the end of the day, he doesn't ⁸*leave/leaves* work until we all go home. In the evening, he ⁹*have/has* dinner with his family, then I think he ¹⁰*go/goes* to bed because he's tired.

B Complete the sentences with the correct form of the verbs in brackets.

1 My sister _____ (not leave) work late.
2 My dad _____ (go) to work with my mother every day.
3 Lucas _____ (not have) breakfast in the morning.
4 I _____ (have) a shower every morning.
5 Carla _____ (do) her hair before she goes out.
6 My friend _____ (start) work at 2 p.m.
7 Mark _____ (not get) dressed before he has breakfast.
8 We _____ (not work) on Tuesdays.

3C

A Complete the conversations with the correct form of *do*.

1 **A:** _____ you get up early?
   B: No, I _____ .
2 **A:** _____ he know Jenny?
   B: Yes, he _____ . They're good friends.
3 **A:** _____ she drink coffee?
   B: No, she _____ . She drinks tea.
4 **A:** _____ they work at the hospital?
   B: Yes, they _____ . They're doctors there.
5 **A:** _____ he go to bed early?
   B: Yes, he _____ . He goes to bed at about nine.
6 **A:** _____ they have children?
   B: No, they _____ .
7 **A:** My brother _____ like coffee, but I love it.
   B: I'm the same as your brother. I _____ drink coffee.
8 **A:** _____ Ron and Jan live here?
   B: Yes, they _____ .

B Write a question for each answer. Use the underlined words to help you.

1 I live in Madrid.
   Where do you live?
2 She lives with her parents.
3 I listen to music two or three times a week.
4 He works in Melbourne.
5 I get up at six o'clock.
6 She watches TV in the living room.
7 We go for coffee at the café near our house.
8 The painting costs £2000.
9 We go to bed at ten o'clock.
10 Heather only eats meat on Mondays.

Want more practice? Go to your Workbook or app.

4A *There is/are* with *a, an, some, any* and *a lot of*

Singular	+	There	's	a	park in my city.
	-		isn't	an	office building near the park.
	?	Is there a hospital in your town?		+	Yes, there is.
				-	No, there isn't.
Plural	+	There	are	some	train stations.
				a lot of	little shops in the centre.
	-		aren't	any	restaurants in my area.
	?	Are there any museums?		+	Yes, there are.
				-	No, there aren't.

Use *There is/are* to say things and places exist.
There's a post office in the street.
There are four pens in my bag.
Use *There isn't/aren't* to say things and places don't exist.
There isn't a train station in my town.
There aren't any books on my desk.
Use *a/an* with singular nouns.
There's **a** garage.   There's **an** office.
Use *some* with plural nouns.
There are **some** shops at the end of the street.

Use *any* with plural things and places which don't exist.
There aren't **any** taxis around at night.
There aren't **any** restaurants in this street.
Use *a lot of* for a large quantity.
There are **a lot of** people in the station at this time.
Use *not a lot of* for a small quantity.
There are**n't a lot of** museums here.
Use *There is + some/a lot of + uncountable nouns*, and *There isn't + any + uncountable nouns*.
There**'s some** empty space in the centre.
There **isn't any** milk in your coffee.

4B Articles

The articles *a, an* and *the* come before nouns.
Use *a/an* ...
• before a singular noun to mean 'one' or 'one of many'.
Is that **a** new bag?   Have you got **a** pen?
• before jobs.
He's **a** doctor.   She's **an** engineer.
• in some phrases, e.g. *once a week, twice a month, a lot of*.
We go to the beach **once a month**.   There are **a lot of** people here.
Use *a* before nouns that start with a consonant sound (e.g. *doctor*). Use *an* before nouns that start with a vowel sound (e.g. *engineer*).
Use *the* ...
• before a noun when there is only one.
The sun feels hot today.   I want to go to **the** cinema.
He's at **the** dentist's.

• before a few countries, e.g. *the UK, the USA, the UAE*.
She's from **the USA**.   They live in **the UAE** these days.
• in some phrases, e.g. *all the time, in the afternoon, on the right, in the summer*.
The supermarket's **on the left**.
It's cold here **in the evenings**.
Use *a/an* to mention something for the first time and *the* after that.
I've got **a lovely coat** and **hat** for the winter. **The coat** is black and **the hat** is red.
Use no article ...
• before plural nouns to speak generally.
Young people don't wear watches these days.
• before most countries, cities and towns.
We live in **Washington DC**.   He's from **Argentina**.
• in some phrases, e.g. *at work, at home, at university, at school, on holiday*.
He's **on holiday** in Spain.   Cara goes **to school** at 7a.m.

4C *need + noun, need + infinitive*

Use *need + noun* to say which objects are necessary.
You **need an umbrella** - it's raining.
We **need a blanket**.
Put adjectives between *need* and the noun.
We need some **warm** clothes.   They need a **big** bowl.
Use *need + infinitive* with *to* to say what it is necessary to do in a situation.
I **need to go** to bed early tonight.   You **need to stay** safe.

Form the negative with *don't/doesn't*.
We **don't** need a blanket.
She **doesn't** need to leave early.
Form questions with *Do/Does*.
Do you need to stay at home?
Do they need some warm clothes?

4A

A Choose the correct alternatives.

1 There's *a/an* big train station in the centre.
2 There aren't *some/any* offices in this building.
3 Is there *a lot of/a* zoo in your city?
4 There *is/are* a lot of cinemas.
5 There *isn't/aren't* a police station in this town.
6 *Is/Are* there any parks where you live?
7 There are *some/a* museums in the old part of the city.
8 There are *a lot of/any* buses in the city.
9 There are *any/some* nice cafés here.
10 There *are/aren't* any buses today.
11 There's *lot of/a lot of* traffic today.
12 *Is there/There is* a train station here?

B Complete the text.

I live in a very small town in the countryside. There's ¹_____ small shop in the centre where you can buy basic things but there ²_____ a lot of things in the shop. There ³_____ a lot of very old houses. I think they're beautiful. There aren't ⁴_____ buses and there isn't ⁵_____ train station, so you need a car to go anywhere. There ⁶_____ a really nice restaurant and a lot of visitors come to the town and eat there. In the area around the town, there ⁷_____ some nice places to walk and take photographs, so a lot ⁸_____ people come here. Sometimes there isn't ⁹_____ space to park your car.

4B

A Correct the mistake in ten sentences.

1 We swim in a sea every day in August.
2 Can you open the door for me, please?
3 Richard's got a new job. He's the nurse.
4 I travel to the work by bus.
5 We live in US.
6 Kate studies at an school.
7 I go to the sports centre for dance lessons twice a week.
8 I don't like the small towns. I prefer big cities.
9 They are a very nice people.
10 They live in the Barcelona.
11 There's an TV in the kitchen.
12 I usually study in afternoon.

B Complete the text with *a/an, the* or no article (-).

One-bedroom flat for sale

This is ¹_____ beautiful flat in ²_____ Brighton. It's got four rooms. ³_____ living room and ⁴_____ bedroom are large. ⁵_____ kitchen and ⁶_____ bathroom are modern. In the bedroom, there's ⁷_____ large window with ⁸_____ fantastic view of the sea. ⁹_____ beach is just a five-minute walk away. It's ¹⁰_____ popular beach with a lot of ¹¹_____ visitors in ¹²_____ summer.

4C

A Put the words in the correct order to make sentences.

1 some / need / bread / We
   We need some bread.
2 to / water / Do / need / you / some / take ?
3 new / I / need / laptop / a
4 to / early / They / need / don't / leave
5 leave / She / to / soon / needs
6 more / Do / need / any / drinks / we ?
7 you / Do / need / help / some ?
8 need / doesn't / He / to / drive
9 don't / I / a shower / need
10 What / need / I / do / do / to ?

B Make sentences using the prompts.

1 He / need / hot water.
   He needs hot water.
2 I / not / need / go / early.
3 They / need / study / more.
4 you / need / food?
5 We / not / need / blanket.
6 we / need / tell / them?
7 I / need / go home.
8 you / need / sit down ?
9 She / not / need / your help.
10 We / need / some food.

Want more practice? Go to your Workbook or app.

5A Position of adjectives

Put adjectives before nouns.
*She's a **pretty** woman.   He's a **tall** man.*
Use modifiers to say how strong or weak the adjective is.
*She's a **very pretty** woman.   He's a **fairly tall** man.*
To use two adjectives before a noun, put the opinion adjective first, then the fact adjective. Use a comma between the two adjectives.
*She's a **nice, old** lady.   He's a **good-looking, young** man.*

Use adjectives after some verbs, e.g. *be, look* and *feel.*
*Susan **is** young.   Ben **looks** thin.   I **feel** tired.*
Adjectives don't have plural forms.
These new cars NOT *These news cars*
The young women NOT *The youngs women*

5B *was/were*

The past simple of *be* is *was/were* (positive) and *wasn't/weren't* (negative).

+	I/He/She/It	was	at home last night.
-		wasn't	tired.
+	You/We/They	were	fun.
-		weren't	happy.

In a question, the subject and verb change position.
We were late.
Were you late?

?	Was	I/he/she/it	happy? quiet? outside?	Yes,	I/he/she/it	was.
				No,		wasn't.
	Were	you/we/they		Yes,	you/we/they	were.
				No,		weren't.

To make a *wh-* question, add a question word to the beginning of the question.
Where *were you at ten o'clock?*
What *was your favourite toy?*

5C *can/can't* for ability

Use *can/can't* + infinitive to talk about an ability we have/don't have.

+	I/You/He/She/It/We/They	can	speak French. play the drums. ride a motorbike.
-	I/You/He/She/It/We/They	can't	bake lovely cakes.

Add *can* + infinitive + (*very*) *well* to talk about strong abilities.

*Tom **can sing very well**.   They **can cook well**.*
Use *can't* + infinitive + (*very*) *well* to talk about weak abilities.
*I **can't play** the piano **well**.   Robbie **can't ride** a bike **very well**.*

To make a question, the subject and object change places.

?	Can	I/you/he/she/it/we/they	cook? swim? ride a bike? drive?	Yes,	I/you/he/she/it/we/they	can.
				No,		can't.

To make a *wh-* question, add a *wh-* question to the beginning of the question.

Where *can I sit?*
What *can you play?*
Who *can we call?*

5A

A Correct the mistakes in ten of the sentences.

1 My uncle's a man good-looking.
2 James has got eyes blue.
3 She looks attractive.
4 He's a short.
5 My brother looks good-looking.
6 You look are nice.
7 Renata's a very tall girl.
8 John's a middle-aged, good-looking man.
9 Is young Susan?
10 He's a nice very man.
11 Wow! Your brother tall!
12 I've got quite smalls hands.

B Put the adjectives in brackets in the correct place in each sentence.

1 Sandra's got long hair. (dark)
   Sandra's got long, dark hair.
2 He's a young man. (tall)
3 He looks. (attractive)
4 I have three children. (beautiful)
5 My grandfather's very but he looks young. (old)
6 I think he's a man. (good-looking)
7 Tom's got brown eyes. (nice)
8 She's got a face. (thin)
9 I feel today. (tired)
10 Selena has got three horses. (beautiful)

5B

A Choose the correct verb in each sentence.

Hey, Paul! How are you?
I ¹*was/were* in Paris last week with a friend. The city ²*was/were* beautiful and the weather ³*was/were* lovely. It ⁴*was/were* a holiday so the streets ⁵*was/were* full of people. One of the streets ⁶*was/were* really busy. A lot of artists ⁷*was/were* there with their paintings. Some of the paintings ⁸*was/were* fantastic. It ⁹*was/were* a good day. My friend and I ¹⁰*was/were* happy. By the way, how ¹¹*was/were* your holiday? ¹²*Was/Were* you in New York, or did you travel?

B Make questions using the prompts. Add *was* or *were*.

1 where / you / yesterday?
   Where were you yesterday?
2 they / at work / this morning?
3 who / that woman in your garden yesterday?
4 why / you / late to class?
5 he / a good child / at school?
6 when / they / on holiday?
7 where / she / born?
8 your hair / long / when you were young?
9 what time / the show?
10 How many people / at the party?

5C

A Complete the sentences and questions with *can* or *can't*.

1 I _____ speak French very well. I don't know many words.
2 What musical instruments _____ Mike play?
3 Antony _____ sing very well. He has a lovely voice.
4 Sammy has a flat tyre. _____ you help her to fix it?
5 Where are you? I _____ see you.
6 Tessa _____ help you learn English. She speaks it well.
7 _____ you drive? I can't.
8 Nihal _____ play chess. He doesn't know how.
9 I can swim but I _____ surf.
10 _____ he speak Portuguese? I know he speaks Spanish.
11 I _____ meet you today. I'm really busy.
12 When _____ I see you again?

B Make sentences about Oliver and Lily using *can/can't* and a verb.

Oliver can play a musical instrument.

		Oliver	Lily
1	a musical instrument/play	√	X
2	a meal/cook	√	X
3	Spanish/speak	X	√
4	a horse/ride	X	√
5	chess/play	√	X
6	a car/drive	X	√
7	swim	√	X
8	sing	X	√

Want more practice? Go to your Workbook or app.

6A Past simple (regular verbs)

Use the past simple to talk about finished actions in the past.

*I **played** the guitar when I was a child.*
*Last weekend I **stayed** at home.*

Use time expressions with the past simple, e.g. *last night, yesterday, when I was a child.*

*I talked to Barbara **last night.***
*I didn't like vegetables **when I was a child.***

I	+	watched a film last night.	
you		arrived early.	
he/she/it		didn't	study for the exam.
we	-		like the food.
they			

For most regular verbs, form the past simple with verb + -ed

*I call**ed** Helen today.*
*We finish**ed** the class early yesterday.*

If the verb ends in -e, add -d.

*We arrive**d** at the party early.*
*When I was a child, I live**d** in a small town.*

If the verb ends in consonant + y, delete the -y and add -ied.

*I stud**ied** a lot for my exam.*
*I cr**ied** a lot when my team lost the game.*

Form the negative with *didn't* + infinitive.

*Judith **didn't stay** at the party last night for very long.*
*We **didn't like** the music.*

6B Past simple (irregular verbs)

I	+	had dinner late last night.	
you		went home after a long day at work.	
he/she/it		didn't	buy anything at the supermarket.
we	-		do the homework last night.
they			

Many verbs have an irregular past form. This is usually different for each verb.

*I **bought** some new shoes last weekend.*
*They **came** over to our house last night.*

Because there aren't any rules for forming irregular verbs, learn the past simple forms as new vocabulary.

Form the negative in the same way as with regular verbs, with *didn't* + infinitive.

*I **didn't know** he was a teacher.*
*You **didn't do** your homework last night.*

6C Past simple (questions)

Use *did* + infinitive to make past simple questions.

***Did** you **have** breakfast this morning?*
*What **did** you **do** yesterday?*

Don't use the past simple verb in the question form.

What school did you ~~went~~ go to?
Did you ~~arrived~~ arrive on time?

Yes/No questions

Did	subject	infinitive + other information
Did	I/you/he/she/it/we/they	go out last night? see a film last week? do your homework? work today?

Short answers

Yes,	I/you/he/she/it/we/they	did.
No,	I/you/he/she/it/we/they	didn't.

Don't use the full verb in the answer.

Did you go out last night? Yes, I ~~went out~~ did.

Wh- questions

Question word	did	subject	infinitive + other information
What			do yesterday?
Where			go last night?
When	did	I/you/he/she/it/we/they	arrive?
Who			talk to yesterday?
How			come to class?

We often ask follow-up questions when someone gives us information. We use a mix of questions for those.

A: I went out for a meal last night.
B: Oh, where did you go?
A: The French restaurant on George Street.
B: Oh right. Did you enjoy it?
A: Yeah, the food was great.
B: What did you have?
A: I can't remember the name of it but it was a kind of pizza.

6A

A Complete the text with the past simple form of the verbs in brackets.

Last weekend was my mum's birthday. We wanted to do something nice for her, so we ¹_____ (invite) her round to our house. On her way round she ²_____ (miss) the bus so she arrived very late. It was too late to eat, so we ³_____ (not cook) dinner but we all sat down round the table and ⁴_____ (talk) to each other. She was so happy that she ⁵_____ (cry)! Then she ⁶_____ (start) to tell us some funny stories about when she was young. Well, to be honest, they weren't very funny and we ⁷_____ (not laugh) but it was nice anyway. It was a lovely evening and we were all sad when it ⁸_____ (end).

B Complete the sentences with the past simple form of the verbs in the box.

call   laugh   like   love   miss   ~~play~~
study   work

1 I _didn't play_ (-) a musical instrument when I was a child.
2 James _____ (+) me yesterday to ask about the meeting.
3 It was a very funny film. We _____ (+) all the way through.
4 I _____ (-) cheese when I was younger.
5 Sorry I'm late. I _____ (+) the bus.
6 Last week, I was ill so I _____ (-).
7 Fiona _____ (+) all weekend for her exam.
8 I _____ (+) the food at the festival, it was delicious!

6B

A Correct the mistakes in six of the sentences.

1 He didn't went to work yesterday.
2 You goed home early.
3 I knew Mike when he was a small child.
4 I haved a big dinner last night.
5 She sayed she was hungry.
6 They didn't came to my party.
7 I didn't saw you at work yesterday – were you here?
8 I did the exercise quickly.

B Rewrite the sentences to make them positive.

1 We didn't know you were here.
   We knew you were here.
2 Graham didn't go to school yesterday.
3 I didn't think it was important.
4 She didn't have dinner at home.
5 I didn't buy a new car.
6 They didn't wake up early.
7 He didn't get the email you sent.
8 Julia and Steve didn't come to the meeting.

6C

A Complete the conversation.

A: What ¹_____ you do last night?
B: Nothing special. I had a bath and then went to bed. How about you?
A: I went to the cinema to see a film.
B: Oh, right. What did you ²_____ ?
A: That new action film.
B: ³_____ you enjoy it?
A: Yes, I ⁴_____ . It was funny. I liked it.
B: Who did you ⁵_____ with?
A: My dad.
B: Ah, right. ⁶_____ he like it?
A: No, he ⁷_____ . He said it was boring.
B: Why did he ⁸_____ that?
A: I'm not sure. He fell asleep in the middle of the film!

B Write a question for each answer.

1 We got here at nine o'clock.
   What time _did you get here_ ?
2 I had a pizza for dinner last night.
   What _____ ?
3 Joe went to Rome last summer.
   Where _____ ?
4 I watched a film and went shopping yesterday.
   What _____ ?
5 I talked to Jane on Monday.
   Who _____ ?
6 Emma went to university in Glasgow.
   Where _____ ?
7 Max started his job in 2016.
   When _____ ?
8 I got up at five o'clock this morning.
   What time _____ ?

Want more practice? Go to your Workbook or app.

7A Countable and uncountable nouns; *some, any, lots of* and *a lot of*

Some nouns in English are countable because we can say how many there are, e.g. *banana, tomato, bean*. Countable nouns have a singular and a plural form. Use a singular verb form with singular nouns and a plural verb form with plural nouns.

*Can I have **an apple** please?*
*There **are** some **tomatoes** in the fridge.*

Some nouns in English are uncountable because it's not easy to count them, e.g. *pasta, rice, meat*. Uncountable nouns don't have a plural form. Always use a singular verb with them.

*There **isn't** any **coffee** in the house.*
*The **butter's** in the fridge.*

Use numbers with countable nouns but not with uncountable nouns.

*We've got **four tomatoes**.*
*~~We've got **five pastas**.~~*

To count uncountable nouns, use containers, measurements or units.

*There's **a bottle of lemonade** in the fridge.*

Some nouns are always plural, e.g. *trousers, glasses, scissors*. Use a plural verb with these.

***Are** these **trousers** big?   Where **are** my **glasses**?*

Use *some* with both countable and uncountable nouns in positive sentences.

*There's **some tea** in the cupboard.*
*I've got **some money** in my purse.*

Use *any* with both countable and uncountable nouns in negative sentences and questions.

*There aren't **any tea bags** in the cupboard.*
*There isn't **any milk** in the fridge.*

Use *lots of/a lot of* when you want to talk about a large amount.

*There's **lots of** cake left.*
*We haven't got **a lot of** eggs.*

7B *How much/how many?* + quantifiers

Use *How much* + uncountable noun to ask about quantities of uncountable nouns.

***How much milk** would you like?*
***How much fruit** do we have?*

Use *How many* + countable noun to ask about quantities of countable nouns.

***How many apples** do we need?*
***How many potatoes** are there?*

Use quantifiers to answer *How much/many* questions.

*A: How many apples do we need?   B: **A few**, maybe four.*
*A: How much rice is there?   B: **A lot**.*

Use quantifiers to say how much or how many things there are. We can use some quantifiers with both countable and uncountable nouns. We can use some quantifiers only with countable or uncountable nouns.

	Nothing	Small number	Medium number	Large number
With countable nouns	none/not any	a few	some	a lot of/ lots of
With uncountable nouns	none/not any	a little	some	a lot of/ lots of

*We don't have **any milk**.*
*A: How many apples have we got? B: **None**.*
*There are **a few onions** in the cupboard.   I've got **some money** in my bag.   There are **some empty chairs** in the next room.   I drink **a lot of tea**.   I eat **lots of vegetables** every day.*

7C Comparative adjectives

Use comparative adjectives (+ *than*) to compare people, places and things.

*Maddie**'s taller than** her brother.*
*This hotel **is nicer than** the other one.*
*My old laptop **was more expensive than** my new one.*
Form comparative adjectives like this:

One-syllable adjectives	adjective -r/-er	nice - nicer tall - taller long - longer
Two-syllable adjectives ending with -y	change -y to -ier	busy - busier noisy - noisier healthy - healthier
Two or more syllable adjectives (not ending in -y)	more + adjective	more expensive more beautiful more exciting

When a one-syllable adjective ends in an -e, only -r is added.

*My car's really small. I need a **larger** one.*
*This book is **stranger** than the last book I read.*

When a one-syllable adjective ends in a single vowel and consonant, the consonant doubles, e.g. *big - bigger, fat - fatter, hot - hotter, sad - sadder, thin - thinner.*
*Why is your sandwich **bigger** than mine?*
*It's **hotter** today than yesterday.*

A few two-syllable adjectives have two forms, e.g. *polite - politer/more polite, common - commoner/more common.*
*Toby is **more polite** than his sister.*
*Thank you very much' is **politer** than 'Thanks'.*

A small number of comparative adjectives are irregular, e.g. *good - better, bad - worse, far - further.*
*Your house is **further** from here than my house.*
*Your singing is **better** than mine.*

7A

A Are the nouns in the box countable (C) or uncountable (U)?

> bean   carrot   jam   juice   lemonade
> milk   nut   pasta   red pepper   salad
> sweet   yoghurt

B Which sentences can be completed with a countable noun (C), an uncountable noun (U) or both (B)?

1 There are lots of …
2 I've got some …
3 There isn't any …
4 We've only got ten …
5 We don't have any …

C Complete the sentences with *is*, *are*, *some* or *any*.

1 There are _____ eggs in that bowl over there.
2 There _____ some homemade lemonade in the fridge.
3 I haven't got _____ coins for the coffee machine. Have you?
4 _____ there any batteries in the cupboard?
5 I don't take _____ fruit to work but I have _____ fruit on my cereal in the morning.
6 Is there _____ sugar in this tea?
7 I don't put _____ salt in my food. It's not good for you.
8 _____ there any coffee left?

7B

A Choose the correct alternatives.

1 **A:** How *much/many* milk do we have?
  B: We don't have *any/some* milk, sorry.
2 **A:** How *much/many* peppers do we need?
  B: Just a *few/little*.
3 **A:** How *much/many* pasta did you buy?
  B: *A lot/A lot of*!
4 **A:** How *much/many* salad would you like?
  B: Just a *few/little*, please.
5 **A:** How *much/many* biscuits do you want with your tea?
  B: I'd like *two/any*, please.
6 **A:** Do you have *any/little* sugar?
  B: Sorry, I don't have *little/any*.
7 **A:** How *much/many* pasta do you want?
  B: *None/No*.

B Write a question with *How much?* or *How many?* for each picture.

1 *How many* lemons do we have?

2 _____ rice do we have?

3 _____ eggs did you buy?

4 _____ nuts do we need?

5 _____ bread do we have?

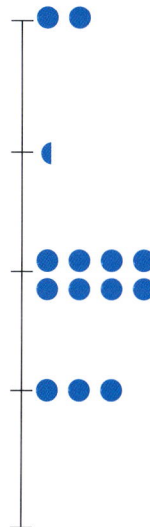

C Write the answers to the questions in Exercise B with the quantifiers in the box.

> a lot   just a few   just a little   none   ~~two~~

1 Two.

7C

A Correct the mistakes in six of the sentences.

1 My cooking is more bad than yours.
2 This magazine feels thiner than usual.
3 The sea is more beautiful in summer than winter.
4 This shop is expensiver than the shop next door.
5 The sun today is hotter yesterday.
6 The shops are more crowded on Saturdays than Sundays.
7 The last Stars Wars film was gooder than the one before.
8 My new neighbour's friendly than my last neighbour.

B Make comparative sentences using the prompts.

1 bikes / cars / fast
  Cars are faster than bikes.
2 apples / chocolate / good for you
3 walking / driving / slow
4 walking / driving / healthy
5 Brazil / Greece / big
6 football / tennis / popular
7 summer / winter / warm
8 Tokyo / Rome / busy

Want more practice? Go to your Workbook or app.

8A Present continuous

+	I'm He's/She's We're/They're/You're	relaxing on the beach.	
-	I'm not He/She isn't We/They/You aren't		
?	Am I Is he/she Are we/they/you	relaxing on the beach?	
+	Yes, I am. Yes, he/she is. Yes, we/they/you are.		
-	No, I'm not. No, he/she isn't. No, we/they/you aren't.		

Use the present continuous to describe something which is happening at the time of speaking.

I'm standing on a famous bridge.
Some people are shouting in the street.

Use the contracted form of the verb *be* when speaking.

We're having a great time. (= We are having ...)
Lucy's not working at the moment. (= Lucy is not working ...)

Add *-ing* to most verbs.

look = looking   listen = listening

With verbs that end with *-e*, delete the *-e.*

give = giving   drive = driving

With verbs that end consonant + vowel + consonant, double the final consonant.

swim = swimming   run = running

8B Present simple and present continuous

Use the present simple for things which are generally true.

The view is beautiful.
Shona doesn't like oranges.

Use the present simple for things we often do.

I walk to work every morning.
You work hard.

Use adverbs of frequency and time expressions with the present simple.

We usually watch TV in the evenings.
I never travel by taxi.

Use the present continuous for things which are happening now.

I'm not walking to work at the moment. It's Sunday!
He's having dinner. Can you call back later?

Use the phrases *right now* and *at the moment* with the present continuous.

I'm not working right now.
They're relaxing on the beach at the moment.

8C Superlative adjectives

Use *the* + superlative adjectives to compare three or more people, places and things.

My grandad's the oldest person in my family.
My bedroom is the biggest room in my house.
I want to drive the most expensive car in the world!

Form superlative adjectives like this:

One-syllable adjectives	the + adjective + -st/-est	nice – the nicest kind – the kindest long – the longest
Two-syllable adjectives ending with -y	change -y to -iest	busy – the busiest noisy – the noisiest healthy – the healthiest
Two or more syllable adjectives (not ending in -y)	the most + adjective	the most expensive the most beautiful the most exciting

When a one-syllable adjective ends in *-e*, only *-st* is added.

This is the strangest show on TV.
Your house is the largest on the street.

When a one-syllable adjective ends in a single vowel and consonant, the consonant doubles, e.g. *big – biggest, fat – fattest, hot – hottest, sad – saddest, thin – thinnest.*

Today is the hottest day of the year.
This is the biggest piece of chocolate cake I could find!

A few two-syllable adjectives have two forms, e.g. *polite – the politest/the most polite, common – the commonest/the most common.*

The most common morning drink is coffee.
He's the politest young man I know.

A small number of superlative adjectives are irregular, e.g. *good – the best, bad – the worst, far – the furthest.*

My house is the one furthest from us.
I'm the worst at sports in my family.

8A

A Correct the mistake in each sentence.

1 Jack's haveing breakfast.
2 We're aren't enjoying this movie.
3 The children is playing in the park.
4 I'm have a nice time.
5 Are you cook?
6 She's play a video game.
7 I waiting for you outside.
8 My mum and dad is walking in the mountains.
9 You are watching the news?
10 He doesn't watching the game.

B Put the words in the correct order to make sentences.

1 are / we / sitting / outside
We are sitting outside.
2 doing / not / any work / Joanna / is
3 what / doing / Yuki and / are / Katsu / ?
4 I'm / and my dad / relaxing / is playing golf
5 Jonas / because he doesn't / isn't / dancing / like the music
6 you / me / are / listening to / ?
7 now / I'm / doing anything right / not
8 isn't / it / the moment / raining at
9 where / is / Pedro / going / ?
10 we're / in the park right / sitting / now

8B

A Match sentences 1–5 with endings a–e.

1 I work hard in the week,
2 They usually watch TV in the evening,
3 Kate usually walks to work,
4 We hardly ever go to restaurants,
5 I usually work from home,

a but they're playing cards at the moment.
b but I'm having a meeting at the office at the moment.
c but we're celebrating my birthday with a nice meal at the moment.
d but it's raining so she's driving.
e but right now I'm doing nothing!

B Choose the correct alternatives.

A: Hi, Linda. What [1]*are you doing/do you do?*
B: I [2]*cook/I'm cooking* a stew.
A: What? But [3]*you never cook/you're never cooking!*
B: [4]*I/I'm* sometimes try. I'm just not very good at it so [5]*I don't usually enjoy/I'm not usually enjoying* it.
A: Well, that smells fantastic!
B: Thanks! Would you like some?
A: Sorry, [6]*I'm going/I go* out right now.

8C

A Complete the family description with the superlative form of the adjectives in the box. Don't forget *the*.

| attractive | clever | happy | heavy | lazy |
| noisy | old | rich | tall | young |

My dad is [1]_____ person in the family. He's about 185 cm. He's also [2]_____ . He weighs about 95 kg. My mum is [3]_____ . She's very pretty. My brothers are 13 and 15, but I'm 16 so I'm [4]_____ child. My middle brother plays the electric guitar so he's [5]_____ . He's so loud sometimes! I think I'm [6]_____ child because I work hard at school. My [7]_____ brother doesn't work hard at all. He's the baby of the family and he's probably [8]_____ ! I know we're not [9]_____ family in the world, we don't have much money, but we're [10]_____ one. We have fun and smile every day of the week.

B Make sentences using the prompts and superlative adjectives.

1 The Burj Khalifa in Dubai / tall / building in the world
2 The Amazon / long / river in the world
3 Russia / big / country in the world
4 Singapore / expensive / country in the world
5 Bangkok / popular / city for visitors in the world
6 Guangzhou / noisy / place in the world
7 The Pacific / large / ocean / world
8 Everest / high / mountain / world
9 The cheetah / fast / land animal
10 The Mariana Trench / deep / place / world
11 heavy / onion / world / weighed 8.5 kg
12 Antarctica / cold / place / on Earth

Want more practice? Go to your Workbook or app.

9A should/shouldn't

Use *should* to say that something is a good idea.
*We **should leave** now.*
*I **should text** Jack.*

Use *shouldn't* to say that something is a bad idea.
*He **shouldn't talk** to his parents like that.*
*I **shouldn't call** my mum when she's at work.*

Use *should/shouldn't* to give someone advice.
*You **should go** and see a doctor.*
*You **shouldn't eat** all that chocolate. It's not good for you.*

After *should/shouldn't*, use an infinitive without *to*.
*You **should wear** that new dress you bought.*

To make advice softer and more polite, use *I think/I don't think*.
***I think** you **should** get more sleep.*
***I don't think** you **should** go out tonight.*

To make the question form, don't use an auxiliary verb – *should* and the subject change places.
***We should** take an umbrella.* ⟶ ***Should we** take an umbrella?*
***We should** play some games.* ⟶ *What **should we** do?*

Use short answers to *yes/no* questions with *should*:
***A:** Should I wear a hat?*
***B:** Yes, you should.*
***A:** Should I have another piece of cake?*
***B:** No, you shouldn't.*

9B be going to

+	I'm He's/She's You're/We're/They're	going to	get married next year. start a new job next month. eat less chocolate.		
-	I'm not He/She isn't You/We/They aren't				
?	Am I Is he/she Are you/we/they		get married next year? start a new job next month?	Yes,	I am. he/she/it is. you/we/they are.
			eat less chocolate?	No,	I'm not. he/she/it isn't. you/we/they aren't.

Use *be going to* + infinitive to talk about plans and intentions for the future.
*We**'re going to move** to another country next month.*
*I**'m going to finish** university this year.*
*They **aren't going to have** a holiday this year.*

Use future time phrases with *be going to* + infinitive, e.g. *next week/month/year, this week/month/year/summer, later*.
*He's going to look for a job **this summer.***
*You aren't going to buy a house **next year.***

When the main verb is *go*, use the present continuous.
*She**'s going to Mexico** this summer.*
*I**'m not going** to the party tonight.*

9C would like/want

Use *would like* and *want* to talk about future wishes.
*I**'d like** to have a holiday.*
*Jenny **wants** to go out with us tonight.*

After *would like/want*, use a noun or an infinitive.
*Sam **would like to be** a policeman one day.*
*I **want to study** business at university next year.*

Note that *like* + noun and *would like* + noun are different. *Like* + noun talks about things we like now. *Would like* + noun talks about future wishes.

Use *wouldn't like to* and *don't/doesn't want to* to make the negative form. These are future wishes we hope don't come true.
*I **don't want to go** to school tomorrow.*
*I **wouldn't like to live** in a big city.*

Use *would like to/want to* to ask about future wishes.

To make the question form with *would like to*, *would* and the subject change places.
*He**'d** like a new car.* ⟶ ***A: Would he** like a new car?*
***B:** Yes, he would./No, he wouldn't.*
*I**'d** like to eat something.* ⟶ ***A: Would you** like to eat something? B:** Yes, I would./No, I wouldn't.*

To make the question form with *want to*, use the auxiliary verb *do*.
***A: Do** you **want to** go shopping tomorrow? B:** Yes, I do.*

Use *would like/want to* make requests.
*I**'d like** a hot chocolate, please.*
*We **want to** speak to the manager.*

To make a request, *would like* is more polite than *want*.
I'd like a cheese sandwich.
What kind of tea would you like?

9A

A Complete the advice with *should/shouldn't* and a verb in the box.

ask   be   dress   forget   ~~get~~   say   take   work

> **Top tips for being successful at work**
>
> 1 You *shouldn't get* to work late. Arrive on time!
> 2 You _____ well. Wear smart clothes.
> 3 You _____ friendly and polite to everyone.
> 4 You _____ too many breaks.
> 5 You _____ hard.
> 6 You _____ questions so you can learn more.
> 7 You _____ to do things. Make a list to help you remember.
> 8 You _____ bad things about your boss online! He or she might see them.

B Correct the mistakes in four of the sentences.

1 I should to go to bed early tonight.
   I should go to bed early tonight.
2 Do we should take the bus to the theatre?
3 You shouldn't drink coffee before you go to bed.
4 She shouldn't going out without a coat.
5 I should wash my hair tonight.
6 Should Tom to come to the meeting?

9B

A Choose the correct alternatives.

A: What [1]*are/do* you going to do this weekend? Any plans?
B: Yes! We're [2]*going/going to* away for the weekend.
A: Nice! Where are you [3]*going/to go*?
B: Normandy, in France. We're going [4]*drive/to drive* there.
A: Really? How long does that take?
B: Oh, not long, really. We [5]*'re going leave/'re going to leave* after work tonight, then take the ferry across. We're [6]*going to arrive/going arriving* at our hotel around midnight tonight.
A: Lovely. Think of me – I'm just going [7]*to stay/staying* at home with the housework!

B Make sentences using the prompts and *be going to*.

1 She / buy / car
   She's going to buy a car.
2 You / learn / drive
3 they / get married?
4 I / not get / new job.
5 you / get home / early / tonight?
6 He / not do / the course.

9C

A Choose the correct alternatives.

1 **A:** Do you have any holiday plans?
   B: We *would/are* like to have a holiday in Türkiye.
2 **A:** Jon wants to *play/playing* football later.
   B: Where does he play?
3 **A:** I wouldn't *to like/like to* work in an office.
   B: I would!
4 **A:** *Do/Would* you like to have some coffee with me?
   B: Sorry, I don't have time today.
5 **A:** Becky doesn't *like/want* to go to work tomorrow.
   B: Why not? Is she ill?
6 **A:** What *would/do* you want to do later?
   B: I'd like to have dinner.
7 **A:** Ed *don't/doesn't* want dinner. He's not hungry.
   B: Would he like a cup of tea?
8 **A:** Do you want some dessert?
   B: Yes, but I don't *would like/like* ice cream. Do they have cake?

B Make conversations using the prompts.

1 **A:** *Marie / not / want / come out with us tomorrow.*
   Marie doesn't want to come out with us tomorrow.
   B: Oh, why not?
   A: *She / want / see Fran.*
2 **A:** *What time / you / want / go shopping?*
   B: In an hour.
   A: OK. *you / want / get the bus or walk?*
3 **A:** *I / wouldn't like / live abroad.*
   B: Why not?
   A: *I / not want / live away from my family.*
4 **A:** *you / would like / come to a party at my house tomorrow night?*
   B: Yes! *I / would like / bring someone.* Is that all right?
   A: Sure, no problem.
5 **A:** *Max / want / join a gym.*
   B: Oh right. *he / want / somewhere close to work?*
   A: No. *He / would like / find / somewhere close to his house.*
6 **A:** *What kind of coffee / would like / you?*
   B: *I / would like / a latte, please.*

Want more practice? Go to your Workbook or app.

GRAMMAR

10A Verb patterns

Use these verbs to talk about our likes, dislikes and preferences:

- ←——————————————————→ +

hate   don't like   don't mind   like   love

After these verbs, use a noun.
*I **love apples**.   She **doesn't like housework**.*

We can also use a verb + *–ing* after these verbs.
*We **like going out** with friends at the weekend.*
*I **don't like doing** the laundry.*
This is different from *would like* + infinitive.
*I **like watching** TV after work.*
(= a general like)
*I'**d like to watch** TV after work.*
(= a specific wish, probably for today)

10B *have to* and *don't have to*

+	I/You/We/They	have to	wear a uniform at work.
	He/She/It	has to	
-	I/You/We/They	don't have to	
	He/She/It	doesn't have to	
?	Do	I/you/we/they	have to	wear a uniform at work?
	Does	he/she/it		

Use *have to* + infinitive to describe something which is necessary.
*You **have to be** here at 8.30 a.m.*
*I **have to tidy** my room every morning.*

Use *don't have to* + infinitive to describe something which is not necessary.
*We **don't have to wear** a suit to work (but we can if we want to).*
*They **don't have to bring** a present to the party (but they can if they want to).*

Use (*What*) *do* (*you*) *have to* + infinitive to ask about what's necessary.
*Do you **have to wear** a uniform?*
*What do you **have to do** in the morning?*

10C Present perfect simple

Use the present perfect simple to talk about a past experience in our lives. Don't say when it happened.
*I'**ve been** to Japan.   He'**s seen** this film.*

	subject	has/have	past participle
+	I/You/We/They	have	used a DVD player.
-		haven't	cooked Thai food.
+	He/She/It	has	studied German.
-		hasn't	been to Florida.

Use *never* with a positive verb to make a sentence negative.
*We'**ve never eaten** Greek food.*
*She'**s never danced** the tango.*

Use *ever* in questions. It means 'in your life'.

Have	I/you/we/they	(ever) used a DVD player? (ever) been to Florida?
Has	he/she/it	(ever) seen *Star Wars*? (ever) downloaded a film on your phone?
Yes,	I/you/we/they he/she/it	have. has.
No,	I/you/we/they he/she/it	haven't. hasn't.

Form the present perfect using the past participle. To make regular past participle verbs, add *-ed* to the infinitive.
watch – watched   play – played   walked – walked
When an infinitive ends in *-e*, just add *-d*. When an infinitive ends in consonant + *-y*, add *-ied*.
bake – baked   like - liked   study – studied
Irregular verbs have an irregular past participle.
eat – eaten   see – seen   write - written
Turn to page 159 for a list of irregular verbs.

10A

A Choose the correct alternatives.

I think I'm an easy person to live with. I don't mind ¹*share/sharing* bills and I have a good job so I can always pay the rent on time. I love ²*cleaning/to cleaning* the house – it's really good exercise. I hate ³*live/living* somewhere dirty so I clean every day. I like ⁴*cooking/cook* meals for other people and I don't mind ⁵*washing up/wash upping* afterwards. I love ⁶*going out/go out* with friends at the weekend but I don't come home late and make a lot of noise. I hate ⁷*fixing/to fix* things though, because I'm not very good at it. But overall, I'm a good housemate, I think!

B Make sentences using the prompts.

1 I / hate / get up / early.
2 I / love / travel / train.
3 Karen / like / shop.
4 you / like / share / house?
5 We / not mind / share / bills.
6 He / hate / cook / meals.
7 I / not mind / drive.
8 She / would like / stay at home / tonight.
9 We / not like / go to bed / late.
10 Terry / not like / Jane.

10B

A Correct the mistake in each sentence.

1 She have to work at the weekend.
2 They don't has to arrive early.
3 You don't have wear a suit to work.
4 We have to doing homework every day.
5 He don't have to bring his passport.
6 I has to buy my ticket today.
7 I not have to work tomorrow.
8 I haven't to go to the meeting.

B Complete the sentences with *(don't) have to* and the verbs in the box.

arrive	buy (x2)	finish	get up	show
take	wait	walk	wear	

1 You _____ smart clothes for the party, just wear what you want.
2 What time do we _____ there?
3 Do we _____ a ticket or is it free?
4 We _____ , we can take a taxi.
5 I _____ really early tomorrow for work.
6 She _____ her ID at reception when she arrives.
7 We _____ a ticket. They're free.
8 You _____ the bus. You can walk.
9 I _____ this work by 5 p.m.
10 Our table isn't ready. We _____ for 30 minutes.

10C

A Complete the conversations with the present perfect form of the verbs in brackets.

1 **A:** Lucy, _____ (you/ever/go) skiing?
   B: Yes, I have but I _____ (never/go) snowboarding.
2 **A:** _____ (Gary/watch) this film?
   B: Yes, I think so but he _____ (not/see) that one.
3 **A:** I _____ (never/swim) in the sea.
   B: Really? I _____ (swim) in three different oceans.
4 **A:** _____ you _____ (ever/eat) Thai food?
   B: No, I haven't. I _____ (try) a lot of Asian food but not Thai.
5 **A:** _____ Jane _____ (ever/travel) in Asia?
   B: Yes, she _____ (visit) Vietnam and Cambodia.
6 **A:** _____ you _____ (ever/see) *Back to the Future?*
   B: No, I _____ . Is it good?

B Make sentences and questions in the present perfect using the prompts.

1 We / not / travel much.
2 Jon / start / a company.
3 Kay / not learn to cook.
4 They / drive / to Scotland a few times.
5 I / never / bake a cake.
6 She / not ride / a horse.
7 you / ever / go / up a mountain?
8 I / run some races but I / never / win.
9 We / not study / British History.
10 Brian / meet / a king.
11 Tanya / never / win / a prize.
12 They / visit / New York.

Want more practice? Go to your Workbook or app.

Vocabulary bank

1A Countries, nationalities and continents

1 a Complete the nationalities with *ish, -ian, an* or *-ese*.

Germany	Germ_____
Argentina	Argentin_____
Italy	Ital_____
Portugal	Portugu_____
Sweden	Swed_____
Nigeria	Niger_____
India	Ind_____
Ireland	Ir_____
Colombia	Colomb_____
Vietnam	Vietnam_____

b Can you think of a person or thing that comes from these countries?
Lionel Messi is Argentinian.

2 a Label the continents A–D with the words in the box.

Africa   Asia   Europe
North and South America

b Match the countries in Exercise 1a to the continents A–D.

A _____

B _____

C _____

D _____

1 _____

2 _____
3 _____
4 _____
5 _____
6 _____

7 _____
8 _____

9 _____
10 _____

2B Everyday objects 2

1 **a** Match objects 1–8 with photos A–H.

1 battery	**5** ID card
2 calendar	**6** poster
3 envelope	**7** textbook
4 folder	**8** scissors

b Work in pairs. Look around your classroom. Which objects in Exercise 1a can you see?

2C Describing objects

1 **a** Match the adjectives in the box with A–H.

clean   dirty   fat   hard   high   low   soft   thin

b Work in pairs. Describe objects in the room or the building using the adjectives in Exercise 1a.

3B Jobs

1 Label the pictures 1–12 with the jobs in the box.

> actor   cleaner   doctor   driver   farmer
> journalist   musician   nurse   photographer
> police officer   shop assistant   tennis player

1 _____ 2 _____ 3 _____ 4 _____

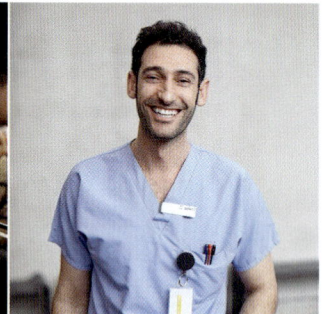

5 _____ 6 _____ 7 _____ 8 _____

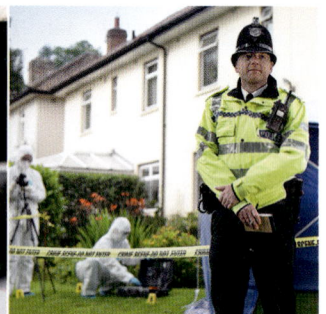

9 _____ 10 _____ 11 _____ 12 _____

2 Work in pairs and discuss the questions. Ask follow-up questions for more information.

1 What do you do?
2 Where do you work?
3 What time do you usually get up?
4 What do you do next?
5 What time do you leave the house?

A: What do you do?
B: I'm a doctor.
A: Where do you work?
B: I work in a hospital in Tokyo.

4A Describing places

1 a Match adjectives 1–10 with photos A–J.

1 crowded
2 dangerous
3 modern
4 dirty
5 quiet
6 noisy
7 pretty
8 rainy
9 safe
10 polluted

b Work in pairs. Use adjectives in Exercise 1a to describe your town or city.

My town is very safe – it's not dangerous.

4B Things in a home

1 a Match the things in the box with photos A–G.

> bin light mirror plate sheet
> shelf towel

b In what room(s) do you usually find the things in Exercise 1a?

c Work in pairs. Where can you find the things in Exercise 1a in your home?

There's a bin in every room.
There are some towels in the cupboard in the bathroom.

5B Feelings

1 Look at the photos and choose the correct alternatives.

1 *happy/bored* **2** *surprised/upset* **3** *angry/bored* **4** *angry/worried*

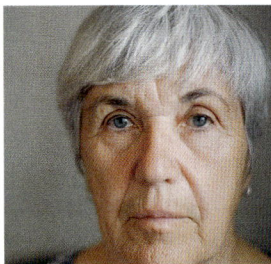

5 *surprised/unhappy* **6** *angry/afraid* **7** *bored/upset* **8** *surprised/happy*

2 Complete the sentences with the adjectives in Exercise 1.

1 I'm _____ . There's nothing to do round here.

2 I'm sorry about your test result, but don't be _____ . You can try again.

3 My dad always gets _____ with other drivers in traffic.

4 Turn the light on – I'm _____ of the dark.

5 I'm _____ about you, you seem sad.

6 TV and chocolate – that's all I need to be _____ !

3 Work in pairs. Describe situations when you have the feelings in Exercise 1. Why do you have these feelings?

I'm always happy on my birthday. I'm rarely angry.

6C Verbs + prepositions

1 a **Match phrases 1–14 with pictures A–N.**

1 agree with someone
2 ask for something
3 belong to someone
4 think about something/someone
5 give something to someone
6 know about something
7 smile at someone
8 lend something to someone
9 send something to someone
10 stay with someone
11 fill in a form
12 share something with someone
13 point to something
14 look at something

b **Complete the sentences so they are true for you.**

1 I know a lot about ____*cars*____ .

2 Last week, I asked my teacher for _____ .

3 Last month, I posted _____ to _____ .

4 That _____ doesn't belong to me but I want it!

5 I don't always agree with _____ .

6 Last week, I lent _____ to _____ .

7 It helps me when the teacher points to _____ .

8 I sometimes stay with _____ .

9 When I'm on the internet, I usually look at _____ .

10 I often think about _____ .

11 I often give _____ to _____ .

12 I filled in _____ last month.

13 I always smile at _____ .

14 I often share _____ with _____ .

c **Work in pairs and compare your sentences. Give more information.**

I know a lot about cars but I don't have one. I cycle

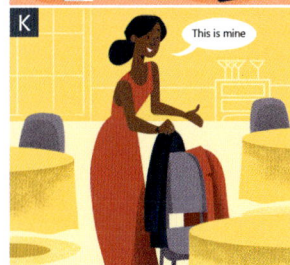

7A Food

1 Match foods 1–8 with photos A–H.

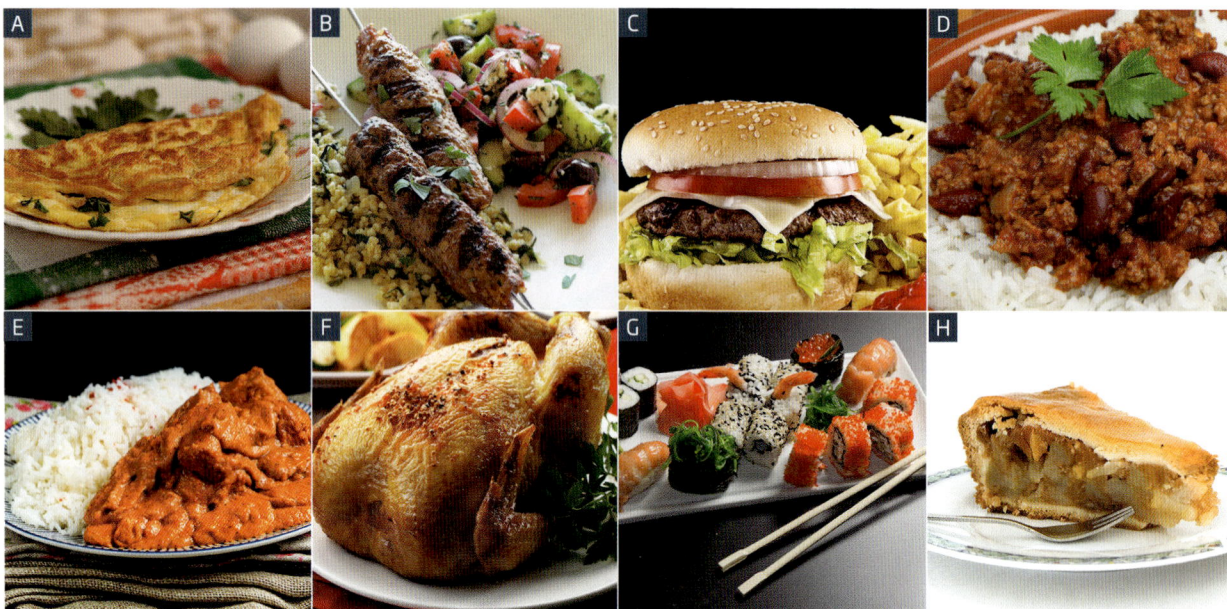

1 roast chicken	**5** curry
2 sushi	**6** an omelette
3 kebabs	**7** a burger
4 apple pie	**8** chilli

2 Work in pairs and discuss the questions.
   1 Which of the food in Exercise 1 do/don't you like? Why?
   2 How often do you eat each one?
   3 Which meals do you make at home?

7B Cooking verbs

1 Match the verbs in the box with pictures A–I.

add	bake	boil	cut	fry
grill	mix	roast	stir	

2 a Choose the correct alternatives.
   1 *Boil/Fry* the water, then *cut/add* the rice.
   2 *Mix/Cut* the banana into small pieces.
   3 *Mix/Grill* the butter and the eggs together.
   4 *Bake/Grill* the chicken for five minutes on each side.
   5 *Add/Fry* the onions and the garlic for about two minutes.
   6 *Cook/Mix* the chicken in the oven. *Bake/Roast* it for one and a half hours.
   7 *Stir/Grill* the soup often.

b Work in pairs. How do you usually cook these things?

burgers	cheese	chicken	eggs	fish
pasta	potatoes			

8C Travel

1 a Match forms of transport 1–14 with photos A–N.

1. aeroplane (UK) / airplane (US) / plane
2. boat
3. bicycle/bike
4. bus
5. coach
6. helicopter
7. lorry (UK) / truck (US)
8. metro/subway/underground
9. motorbike
10. scooter
11. ship
12. taxi
13. train
14. tram

b Complete phrases 1–13 with the forms of transport in Exercise 1a. One form of transport is not used.

drive

1. _a bus_
2. _____
3. _____
4. _____
5. _____
6. _____

ride

7. _____
8. _____
9. _____

fly

10. _____
11. _____

sail

12. _____
13. _____

c Work in pairs and discuss the questions.

1. Which transport in Exercise 1a can you find in your town/city?
2. What transport do you usually use? Why?
3. What transport do you never use? Why?
4. How did you travel to class today?
5. When was the last time you travelled by aeroplane? Boat or ship? Train?

9A Health problems

1 Match words and phrases 1–14 with pictures A–N.

1. break your arm/leg
2. have an accident
3. have toothache
4. have a headache
5. have a stomach ache
6. have a temperature
7. catch a cold
8. cut your finger
9. make an appointment (to see the doctor/dentist)
10. chemist's
11. doctor
12. dentist
13. take medicine
14. ambulance

2 Work in pairs and discuss the questions.

1. When was the last time you were ill? What was wrong?
2. What advice would you give to people with the problems in phrases 1–8 in Exercise 1?

10C Technology

1 a **Match verbs 1–6 with pictures A–F.**

1 record		**4** play	
2 turn on		**5** turn off	
3 delete		**6** save	

A

B

C

D

E

F

b **Match items 7–14 with photos G–N.**

7 a (phone) battery	**11** a keyboard
8 a (tablet) computer	**12** a digital camera
9 a PC	**13** a blog
10 a games console	**14** a web page

G

H

I

J

K

L

M

N

2 **Work in pairs and discuss the questions.**

1 Which of the actions in Exercise 1a do you often do? When?
2 Which of the things in Exercise 1b do you own?

Communication review

Three in a line (Units 1–2 review)

Work in pairs or two teams. Choose a square and start the game. If you get the answer correct, you win the square. Try to get a line in a row.

Game 1

1 My sister _____ name is Sam. Fill the gap.

2 What jewellery do people wear on their fingers?

3 Women keep their money in a _____ . Fill the gap.

4 _____ notebook is this? Fill the gap.

5 That's not our car. That one over there is _____ . Fill the gap.

6 *A:* Excuse me, how _____ is this? *B:* It's £4.99. Fill the gap.

7 Describe an object in the classroom using three different adjectives.

8 What do you put on your hands in cold weather?

9 My father's brother is my _____ . Fill the gap.

Game 2

1 *A:* That's £3. *B:* Here's £10. *A:* Thanks. That's £7 _____ . Fill the gap.

2 Describe an object in your bag or pocket using three different adjectives.

3 What object do people use to put electricity in their phone?

4 My parent's parents are Sue and Martin. They're my _____ . Fill the gap.

5 Make a true sentence about you with *haven't got.*

6 That's £7.17, please. _____ you like a bag? Fill the gap.

7 His brother is called Ben and _____ daughter is called Lily. Fill the gap.

8 Is this umbrella _____ ? I know you have a blue one. Fill the gap.

9 These boots are not light. They're really _____ . Fill the gap.

Game 3

1 What jewellery do people wear in their ears?

2 *A:* Is that Rick and David's car? *B:* No, _____ car is blue. Fill the gap.

3 *A:* _____ you got a red pen? *B:* No, I _____ , sorry. Fill the gaps.

4 My watch isn't round, it's s_____ . Fill the gap.

5 *A:* Excuse me, where's the milk? *B:* It's _____ there next to the bread. Fill the gap.

6 This object says you can drive a car and has a photo of you on it. What is it?

7 Ask a student in the other team three questions with *Have you got ...?*

8 *A:* Here's your jacket. *B:* It's not _____ . It's Belinda's. Fill the gap.

9 The opposite of old is new or m_____ . Fill the gap.

Reach the end (Units 3–4 review)

Work in groups. Roll the dice and move your counter to the correct square. Follow the instructions in the square. The first person to reach *Finish* wins.

FINISH

28 Where can you buy stamps?

27 Which verb do we use with *video games* and *the piano*?

23 Complete the question: *What time _____ the film start?*

24 Say two things you *rarely* do.

25 Say three things in your city you like.

26 Say two things you need when you travel.

22 Make a question: *often / she / go out / Saturday / night?*

21 Complete the phrase: *_____ ready*

20 What's the opposite of *upstairs?*

19 Complete the statement: *Sorry, the 7.15 film is sold _____ .*

18 Say two things you always do at the weekend.

17 What are these?

13 Make a question: *you / ever / go / cinema / alone?*

14 Complete the question: *How _____ is a ticket?*

15 Complete the phrase: *_____ sport on TV*

16 Complete the statement: *There aren't _____ castles in my city.*

12 What are these?

11 Complete the statement: *There's a sofa in _____ living room.*

10 Make the sentence negative: *She goes to bed late.*

9 Complete the statement: *It's _____ interesting house.*

8 Say a question an assistant might ask at a cinema box office.

7 Complete the phrase: *_____ for a coffee*

3 Change the subject to *she: I worry about my job.*

4 Complete the sentence: *There are a _____ of parks in my city.*

5 Say two things you need to do to learn English.

6 Say two things in your home you don't like.

2 Say two things you listen to in the morning.

1 Complete the phrase: *_____ my hair*

START

Cross the board (Units 5-6 review)

Work in pairs or two teams. Choose a number. Answer the question correctly and win the hexagon. Make a line of hexagons from left to right and you win!

1 What is the past tense of these verbs: *go, take, speak?*

2 You're late for class. What do you say to the teacher?

3 Describe what you did last night. Speak for 30 seconds.

4 What does one of your friends look like? Use at least three different adjectives to describe him/her.

5 Complete the sentence about you: *I usually meet up with ... at the weekends.*

6 What kind of person were you when you were a child? Use at least three different adjectives.

7 Ask your partner/ the other team two questions about yesterday.

8 Say three things in the classroom and where they are. Use correct prepositions.

9 Someone stands on your foot and says sorry. What do you reply?

10 A friend asks you *Can I use your mobile phone? I need to call a friend.* What do you reply?

11 This is the answer: *I grew up in Dubai.* What's the question?

12 Describe last weekend. Speak for 30 seconds.

13 Complete the sentence about you: *I usually listen to _____ in the car.*

14 What adjective describes someone with yellow hair?

15 Where were you at these times yesterday? 10 a.m., 2 p.m., 6 p.m., 9 p.m.

16 You break your mum's favourite glass. What do you say to her?

17 Correct the sentence. *He look is tired.*

18 Ask your partner/ the other team three questions about last weekend.

19 Say three things you can't do. Think about your skills/abilities.

20 Say three things you didn't do yesterday with correct past verbs.

21 There's a bag on your chair. You want the owner to move it. What do you say?

22 Is the word order in this sentence correct? *My brother is a man good-looking.*

23 What is the past tense of these verbs: *bring, talk, feel?*

24 This is the answer: *My parents met twenty years ago.* Complete the question: *When ...?*

25 Say three things you can do. Think of your skills/ abilities.

Keep talking (Units 7–8 review)

Work in two teams, A and B.

- Each team, choose a topic in the table below.
- You have two minutes to plan what to say. Decide which team member will speak.
- Team A member, speak about your topic for 30 seconds. Team B, listen and decide how many points they get.
- Team B member, speak about your topic for 30 seconds. Team A, listen and decide how many points they get.
- Repeat the activity four more times. You cannot repeat a topic. Choose a different speaker each time.
- The team with the most points at the end wins.

Describe the ingredients needed to make a dish you know (1 point)

Use at least two quantifiers (2 points)

Describe any unusual weather at the moment (1 point)

Use at least one present simple sentence and one present continuous sentence (2 points)

Describe the last time you went to a café (1 point)

Use at least one phrase for a customer and one phrase for an assistant (2 points)

Compare two places in your city (1 point)

Use at least three comparative forms (2 points)

Describe your favourite supermarket (1 point)

Use at least four kinds of food and drink (2 points)

Describe what people you know are doing at the moment (1 point)

Use at least three present continuous sentences (2 points)

Describe your favourite season (1 point)

Use at least two weather words (2 points)

Describe what you bought the last time you went food shopping (1 point)

Use at least two countable nouns and two uncountable nouns (2 points)

Describe your journey to work/school (1 point)

Use at least two verbs phrases for travel (2 points)

Describe the last time you made travel plans on the phone (1 point)

Use at least two phrases for making travel plans on the phone (2 points)

Describe a nice meal you had recently (1 point)

Use at least two adjectives to describe food (2 points)

Describe your favourite way to travel (1 point)

Use at least two superlative forms (2 points)

Describe what's in your kitchen at home (1 point)

Use at least three containers (2 points)

Describe your last holiday (1 point)

Use at least two geographical features (2 points)

Snakes and ladders (Units 9–10 review)

Throw the dice, move your counter forward the correct number of squares and answer the question. If correct, stay on the square. If incorrect, move back to the square you were on before. If you land on a square with a ladder, move up it. If you land on a square with a snake, go down it. The first person to reach *Finish* wins.

FINISH

34 Complete the sentence with one word. *Jonny doesn't mind _____ the bills with his housemates.*

30 Say two activities that you love doing.

31 Say three things you have to do tomorrow.

32 Complete the sentence: *Did you _____ Tara a message about dinner tonight?*

33 Answer the question: *What food do you like?* Make a full sentence.

29 Say three things you're going to do next weekend.

28 *Rings* and *earrings* are examples of what?

27 Complete the sentence with one word. *I want to _____ a gym but I don't know which one.*

26 What do you use to print something?

25 Your friend asks *Do you want to come to a party tomorrow?* You want to say yes. How do you reply?

24 Say three things you have to do in your job/studies.

20 Complete the sentence. *I try and _____ fit. I go running and do yoga every day.*

21 Say three things you haven't done in your life.

22 Say what you want to eat for dinner tonight. Make a full sentence.

23 What are two ways to save money?

19 Complete the sentence: *I downloaded a fun health _____ onto my phone yesterday.*

18 Say three things you don't have to do today.

17 You're meeting your friend for coffee tomorrow. Ask him for a time to meet.

16 What do you wear on your head when you go cycling?

15 Say three activities that you hate doing.

14 Complete the sentence. *I need to do the _____ so I have some clean clothes.*

10 Jon wants to sleep better. Tell him three things he shouldn't do.

11 Say what job you wouldn't like to do. Make a full sentence.

12 Complete the sentence. *Marie and Mike are going to _____ married on Saturday.*

13 Invite your partner to a party tomorrow night.

9 Say three things you're not going to do tomorrow.

8 Say three sports that start with *go _____ing.*

7 Say three activities you've done in your life. *I've …*

6 What do runners wear on their feet when they run?

5 Where did you last go on holiday?

4 Jon wants to live a healthier life. Give him three pieces of advice with *He should …*

START

1 Complete the sentence. *After you cook, you have to wash _____ .*

2 Say three things you'd like to do in your life.

3 Complete the sentence. *A pilot and a fire officer have to wear a _____ to work.*

Communication bank

Lesson 1C

Exercise 10

Student A

Look at the items for sale. You are a customer. Think of questions to ask the seller about the items. Plan what to say.

Lesson 2D

Exercise 5

Student A

Part 1

You're a shop assistant in a supermarket. A customer wants batteries. Decide where they are and how much they cost. Serve the customer.

Part 2

You're a customer in a chemist's. You want some medicine for a stomach ache. Decide what questions to ask. Buy the medicine.

Lesson 8C

Exercise 8a

Student A

VANCOUVER, Canada

WHEN TO GO
December to March for snow sports
Spring and autumn for sightseeing

WHERE TO GO
Take a bus to Grouse Mountain – wonderful views of the city. Ski there in winter.
Walk or cycle along the beach for a view of the mountains.

WHERE TO EAT
Visit the popular Gastown area of the city – great restaurants, amazing food.
Go to Chinatown for fantastic Asian food.

THINGS TO DO
Ski at one of the three mountains in the area.
Swim in the sea or try surfing.
Take a boat tour and look for sea life.

GETTING AROUND
Take a bus tour and get on and off where you want.
Use the Translink system (electric bus, sea bus) – cheap and safe. You only need one ticket.

Lesson 8D

Exercise 6

Student B
Read about four situations. Plan what to say.
1 You need to see a dentist. Call the Crocus Dentist's Surgery and make an appointment.
2 You work for a taxi company. A customer wants to book a taxi. A taxi to the city centre costs £12. A taxi to the airport costs £24. Check which street the hotel is on.
3 You want to book a table for two at a restaurant for next Friday at 8 p.m. (Friday 16th). Call The Sun Restaurant and make your booking.
4 You're at the shops with your friend but you lost him/her. You're in a clothes shop on Green Street. Answer your phone and give this information to your friend. Decide where to meet and when.

Lesson 2B

Exercise 11

Student A
You had a party last night. There are some things in your house after the party.
You're going to ask Student B questions to find out who the things in the box belong to.
Plan what to ask.

| books | camera | gloves | hairbrush | make-up | notebook | sweater |

Whose camera is this?
Student B had a party last weekend. There are some things in their flat after the party.
Use the information below to answer Student B's questions.

- cap – Chris
- earrings – Alice
- handbag – Fiona
- laptop – Sarah and Tom
- phone charger – Andy and Becky
- ring – you!
- sunglasses – Kyle

Lesson 4A

Exercise 10

Student B
Look at the information about Town B.
Plan what to say about how many of each place there are.
There are some shops

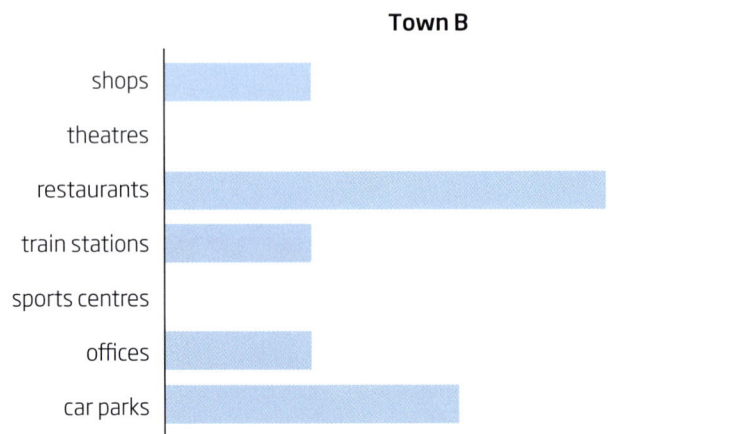
Town B

shops
theatres
restaurants
train stations
sports centres
offices
car parks

Lesson 3C

Exercise 2d

Stay in or go out?

Mostly **a:** Wow, you go out a lot! You like meeting new people. Be careful you don't become too tired. Life isn't always one big party – or is it?

Mostly **b:** You enjoy going out with friends but you're also happy to stay in. You like the best of both worlds!

Mostly **c:** Your home is your favourite place – a place to get comfortable and enjoy life on your own or with friends and family. You're a true home lover.

Lesson 4D

Exercise 5

Student B

Conversation 1
You work in a tourist information centre. A visitor asks you about the science museum. Use the information to plan what to say.
- Science museum? – Yes. It's very good.
- Where? – John Street
- How much? - £5 for adults, £2 for children
- Where to pay? – Reception in entrance
- Take photos? – Yes.

Conversation 2
You visit an information office in a new place. You want to know the following:
- a shopping centre?
- where the shopping centre is
- what time the shopping centre opens and closes
- what kind of cafés and restaurants are there
- where the cafés and restaurants are

Plan what to say.

Lesson 6C

Exercise 8

Student A

Read your information about the 1990s in the UK and compare your ideas in Exercise 7. Then, write questions to ask Student B about the 1980s.

What did people wear in the 1980s?

- Clothes
  - Jeans, T-shirts, trainers for men and women
  - Sportswear for everyday use
- Entertainment
  - Films – DVDs at home
  - TV – over 200 channels
  - Music – electronic dance music, rock music
- Family life
  - Children had TVs in their bedrooms
  - More holidays every year
- Free time
  - The gym, music concerts, TV, video games
- Food
  - Popular – different fruit and vegetables from around the world, snack food
  - New – microwave meals
- Technology
  - New – the internet, CD players, DVD players, mobile phones

Lesson 2D

Exercise 5

Student B

Part 1
You're a customer in a supermarket. You want some batteries. Decide your questions. Buy the batteries.

Part 2
You're a shop assistant in a chemist's. A customer wants some medicine for a stomach ache. Decide where it is and how much it costs. Serve the customer.

Lesson 1C

Exercise 10

Student B

Look at the items for sale on your stall. Decide how much each item costs. Think about extra information you can give about each item. Plan what to say.

Lesson 2B

Exercise 11

Student B
You had a party last weekend. There are some things in your flat after the party. You're going to ask Student A questions to find out who the things in the box belong to. Plan what to ask.

cap   earrings   handbag   laptop   phone charger   ring   sunglasses

Whose cap is this?

Student A had a party last night. There are some things in their house after the party. Use the information below to answer Student A's questions.

- books – Lidia and Alex
- camera – Harry and Johanna
- gloves – you!
- hairbrush – Claire
- make-up – Maria
- notebook – Richard
- sweater – Peter

Lesson 4A

Exercise 10

Student A

Look at the information about Town A. Plan what to say about how many of each place there are.

There are some shops.

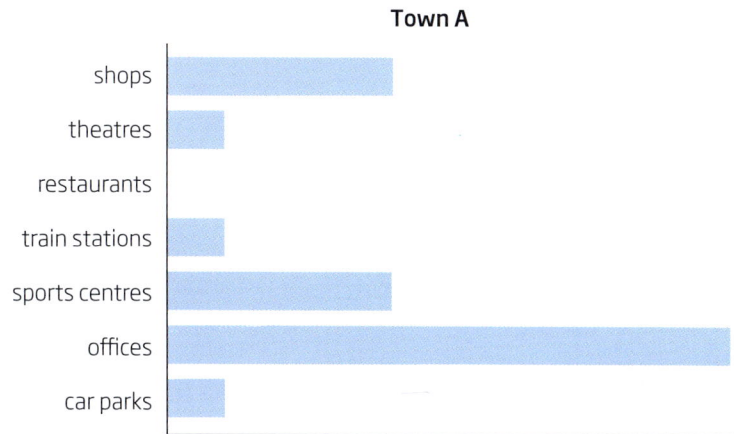

Lesson 5A

Exercise 8

Student A

Student B

Lesson 6D

Exercise 6

Student A

1 You're in a supermarket with your young nephew. He's crying a lot. Student B is another customer in the supermarket. Say sorry and explain what the problem is.

2 You're in a restaurant. Student B drinks your drink by mistake. Tell him/her. Then, accept his/her apology.

3 Student B is your teacher. You didn't bring your coursebook to class. Say sorry.

4 You'd like to practise your English with Student B at a café. Ask him/her. Then, accept his/her apology.

5 You're at the theatre. Student B's phone rings. You're not happy. Tell him/her to turn it off. Then, accept his/her apology.

6 You forgot one of your parent's (Student B) birthdays. Say sorry.

Lesson 7A

Exercise 10b

Student A

Read the information about you. What's in your shopping basket? Make a list of at least eight things.

You're a student so you don't have a lot of money. You share a flat with another student. You're a vegetarian. You try to be healthy but you love anything with sugar in it. Every week, your friends come to your house and you have a party.

Lesson 4B

Exercise 9

Student A
You're an estate agent. Student B is interested in one of your flats. Think about possible answers to Student B's questions about:

- furniture
- outside spaces – garden/garage?
- rooms
- what's in the bathroom

Lesson 10D

Exercise 5

Student B
You have invited an employee to your house for dinner. The employee works hard for you. You want to say thank you. Show the employee your house and then take him/her to the dining room for dinner. Give a compliment about the following:
- The employee is always kind and polite.
- The employee did a good job with a work project.
- The employee always works hard.

Lesson 4D

Exercise 5

Student A

Conversation 1

You're in a new city. You want to know the following:
- a science museum in the city?
- where it is
- how much it is
- where you pay
- can you take photos

Plan what to say.

Conversation 2

You work in a tourist information centre. A visitor asks you about the shopping centre. Use the information to plan what to say
- Shopping centre? – Yes, Grand Shopping Centre
- Where – Green Street
- Times – opens 9 a.m., closes 9 p.m.
- Cafés and restaurants – Italian, Indian, fast food
- Cafés and restaurants – third floor

Lesson 8D

Exercise 6

Student A
Read about four situations. Plan what to say.
1 You work at the Crocus Dentist's Surgery. Help a customer book an appointment.
2 You want to book a taxi from the Crown Hotel to the airport. Call and book one for two o'clock this afternoon. The Crown Hotel is on Mill Road.
3 You work at The Sun Restaurant. Help a customer to book a table. Check the date and time.
4 You're at the shops with your friend but you lost him/her. Call him/her and find out where he/she is. You don't hear the street name – ask your friend to repeat it. Decide where to meet and when.

Lesson 8C

Exercise 8a

Student B

Prague

WHEN TO GO
Spring and early autumn – the weather is beautiful but not very hot.

WHERE TO GO
Walk across the Charles Bridge for views of the city.
Visit the old town and look at the pretty, old buildings.
Go to Prague Castle. It's the largest old castle in the world.
The park near the castle is pretty and quiet.

WHERE TO EAT
Walk to restaurants outside the old town – fantastic Czech and international food.

THINGS TO DO
Go to a concert in one of the beautiful theatres.
Take a Czech food tour.
Book a boat trip along the river. Look at the fantastic view.

GETTING AROUND
Go on foot – you can see the lovely buildings. It's free!
Or take a tram – quick, easy and cheap.
Use the metro for longer trips outside the city centre.

Lesson 6D

Exercise 6

Student B

1 You're in a supermarket. Student A is with a child. The child is crying a lot and making a lot of noise. Accept Student A's apology.
2 You're at a restaurant. You drink Student A's drink by mistake. Say sorry.
3 You're a teacher. Student A is your student. He/she didn't bring a coursebook to class. Accept his/her apology.
4 Student A would like you to invite you somewhere. Say sorry. Say why.
5 You're at the theatre. Your phone rings in the middle of an important part of the play. Student A's not happy. Say sorry.
6 You're one of Student A's parents. Student A forgot your birthday. Accept his/her apology.

Lesson 7A

Exercise 10b

Student B
Read the information about you. What's in your shopping basket? Make a list of at least eight things.
You're an animal lover. You live with your partner and one rabbit, one cat and three dogs. You try to give your animals the best food. You and your partner spend all your time looking after the animals. You don't have time to cook for yourself.

Lesson 8B

Exercise 11

Place	Weather
Kamchatka, Russia	very cold, -16ºC, snowing
Perth, Australia	hot, 30ºC, sunny
Beijing, China	cold, -8ºC sunny
San Francisco, the US	cool, very foggy

Lesson 10A

Exercise 2b

Mostly **a:** You don't like living with other people. You like having your own space and doing things for yourself.

Mostly **b:** You don't mind sharing a house with other people. You don't mind working hard to do this, but you expect others to do the same.

Mostly **c:** You love living with other people! You're a very good housemate to have around, and you like doing things for other people.

Lesson 6C

Exercise 8

Student B

Read your information about the 1980s and compare your ideas in Exercise 7. Then, write questions to ask Student A about the 1990s.

What did people wear in the 1990s?

- Clothes
  - Bright colours
  - Big hair
- Entertainment
  - Films – videos at home
  - TV – four channels
  - Music – dance pop, soft rock
- Family life
  - Meals in front of the TV together
  - Holidays outside of Europe
- Free time
  - Sports, books, radio, TV
  - Children play outside in the street
- Food
  - Popular - fast food, curry, pizza
  - New - vegetarian food
- Technology
  - New - first home computers and games

Lesson 10D

Exercise 5

Student A

Your boss has invited you to his/her house for dinner. When you arrive at the house, give compliments about the following:
- the house and garden
- the painting in the dining room
- the food on the table

Lesson 4B

Exercise 9

Student B

You want to rent a flat. Student A is an estate agent with a flat for rent. Prepare questions to ask Student A about the flat. Think about:
- rooms
- furniture
- outside spaces - garden/garage?
- what's in the bathroom

How many rooms are there?

Irregular verbs

Verb	Past simple	Past participle
be	was	been
become	became	become
begin	began	begun
bite	bit	bitten
blow	blew	blown
break	broke	broken
bring	brought	brought
build	built	built
buy	bought	bought
catch	caught	caught
choose	chose	chosen
come	came	come
cost	cost	cost
cut	cut	cut
do	did	done
draw	drew	drawn
drink	drank	drunk
drive	drove	driven
eat	ate	eaten
fall	fell	fallen
feel	felt	felt
find	found	found
fly	flew	flown
forget	forgot	forgotten
freeze	froze	frozen
get	got	got
give	gave	given
go	went	gone
grow	grew	grown
have	had	had
hear	heard	heard
hide	hid	hidden
hit	hit	hit
hold	held	held
hurt	hurt	hurt
keep	kept	kept
know	knew	known
learn	learned/learnt	learned/learnt
leave	left	left

Verb	Past simple	Past participle
lend	lent	lent
let	let	let
lie	lay	lain
lose	lost	lost
make	made	made
mean	meant	meant
meet	met	met
pay	paid	paid
put	put	put
read	read	read
ride	rode	ridden
ring	rang	rung
run	ran	run
say	said	said
see	saw	seen
sell	sold	sold
send	sent	sent
shine	shone	shone
show	showed	shown
shut	shut	shut
sing	sang	sung
sit	sat	sat
sleep	slept	slept
smell	smelled/smelt	smelled/smelt
speak	spoke	spoken
spend	spent	spent
spill	spilled/spilt	spilled/spilt
stand	stood	stood
swim	swam	swum
take	took	taken
teach	taught	taught
tell	told	told
think	thought	thought
throw	threw	thrown
understand	understood	understood
wake	woke	woken
wear	wore	worn
win	won	won
write	wrote	written

Pearson Education Limited
KAO TWO
KAO Park
Hockham Way
Harlow, Essex
CM17 9SR
England
and Associated Companies throughout the world.

english.com/roadmap

First published 2020
Fourth impression 2024

ISBN: 978-1-292-39306-3

Set in Soho Gothic Pro

Printed in Slovakia by Neografia

Acknowledgements

The Publishers would like to thank the following people for their feedback and comments during the development of the material:

Mary-Ann Bell, David Byrne, María Lidia Camporro, Inigo Casis, Konrad Dejko, Sally Fryer, Inga Konuhova, Anuka Rico Manteca, Peter Mason, Mike Mooney, Gordon Andrew Semple, Jasper Luke Stein

Dedicated to Claire Sparkes.

Illustration acknowledgements

Ash Jin p. 16, 26, 60, 63, 84; Daniel Limon (Beehive) p. 30, 32, 78, 102, 137, 141, 144; Lauren Radley p.10, 11, 38, 44, 52, 151; Tony Richardson p 12, 14, 24, 74, 145, 147

Image Credit(s):

123RF.com: Aaron Amat 140, Alexander Smirnov 16, Andrey Armyagov 142, Anton Starikov 57, Auttapon Moonsawad 18, Burnel1 16, Donato Fiorentino 137, Eightstock 34, Grazvydas 10, Ifong 57, J Vd 65, Jacek Chabraszewski 75, Jan Novak 74, Karnizz 143, Kasto 46, Konstanttin 143, Lynne Carpenter 110, Magone 142, Nan728 143, NejroN 81, Rjycnfynby 66, Scanrail 90, Sean Pavone 3, 31, Serjio74 143, Siraphol 16, Thisislover 140, Vitalii Tiahunov 16, Wavebreakmediamicro 54; **Alamy Stock Photo:** A. Astes 10, Adrian Buck 50, Archive Image 50, Chris Rout 100, ClassicStock 114, Cultura Creative (RF) 24, Ewing Galloway 50, Frankie Angel 54, George Oze 59, Ian Allenden 113, Image Source 39, ImageBROKER 66, JULTUD 105, Lamb 88, Marc Zakian 67, Martyn Evans 10, MBI 18, 49, Novastock 14, Olha Rohulya 65, Pablo Paul 16, Patcharapa Limpongstorn 115, PhotoAlto 12, Photosil 90, Redsnapper 64, Robertharding 7, SeventyFour Images 6, Slawek Staszczuk 95, Tetra Images, LLC 107, Thierry GRUN - Aero 63, Trinity Mirror / Mirrorpix 50; **Getty Images:** Agafapaperiapunta 101, AlessandraRC 57, Alexander Spatari 55, Alvis Upitis 25, Anchiy 72, André Rocha / EyeEm 5, 59, andreswd 54, Andrew Rublev 140, Annabelle Breakey 142, Ariel Skelley 27, Ascent / PKS Media Inc. 18, 73, AzmanL 94, B&M Noskowski 104, Barry Thomas / EyeEm 5, 75, Betsie Van Der Meer 86, Bim 139, Bobex-73 71, Caiaimage / Paul Bradbury 40, Caiaimage / Sam Edwards 12, Caiaimage / Trevor Adeline 74, Carlosalvarez 10, Caroline Sale 57, Catherine Falls Commercial 70, Cavan Images 56, Chain45154 111, Chris Ware / Stringer 103, Christian Petersen-Clausen 104, Christopher Hope-Fitch 140, Colin Hawkins 22, Creativ Studio Heinemann 57, D3sign 3, 40, David Patrick Valera 46, Deepak Sethi 5, 63, Delpixart 140, DenisTangneyJr 139, Dorling Kindersley 91, Dougal Waters 138, DuKai photographer 139, Easyturn 139, Emilija Manevska 140, Erik Witsoe / EyeEm 89, Ezra Bailey 140, FG Trade 8, Flashpop 48, 140, Fotog 139, Francesco Perre / EyeEm 16, George Pachantouris 101, Gravity Images 12, Grogl 62, H3k27 109, Hemera Technologies 57, Hero Images 5, 22, 38, 40, 49, 73, 114, 138, 138, 139, Hinterhaus Productions 142, Hispanolistic 99, Hoxton/Sam Edwards 78, Ian Ross Pettigrew 38, Image Source 16, 24, 32, Jacobs Stock Photography Ltd 8, Jeffrey Coolidge 145, Jeremie Gerhardt / EyeEm 91, JGI/ Tom Grill 72, Jiraroj Praditcharoenkul 106, John Fedele 12, John Rensten 22, Johner Images 139, JohnnyGreig 93, Jonpic 34, Juan Jimenez 34, Judith Haeusler 110, Karl Tapales 8, Kesh West 7, Kirsty Lee / EyeEm 3, 25, Kvkirillov 34, Laurent Fievet / Staff 109, Linda Raymond 94, Lumina Images 18, MarcusPhoto1 47, Mario Gutiérrez 143, Masahiro Noguchi 107, Maskot 8, 48, 138, Massimofusaro 74, Michael Blann 46, Mirko Vitali / EyeEm 28, Monty Rakusen 138, Morsa Images 155, 155, MrPliskin 54, Nick Dolding 82, Nigel Allison / EyeEm 54, Oliver Rossi 94, Paul Mansfield Photography 139, PeopleImages 46, 71, Peter Cade 108, 142, Phongthorn Hiranlikhit / EyeEm 140, PhotoAlto / Frederic Cirou 87, PhotoObjects.net 34, Photos by R A Kearton 62, Pictafolio 145, Pinghung Chen / EyeEm 142, Plume Creative 49, 64, PNC 99, Portra 86, Puneet Vikram Singh, Nature and Concept photographer 64, Rawpixel 49, Renate Frost / EyeEm 57, Richard Drury 64, Roland Magnusson / EyeEm 34, Rolf Bruderer 86, Russ Rohde 20, Sam Edwards 86, 98, Scanrail 57, Science Photo Library 91, Sean Murphy 76, Silvia P / EyeEm 89, Simon Ritzmann 81, 112, 155, Six_Characters 140, Slobo 34, 139, Solskin 70, Stanislaw Pytel 71, Stígur Már Karlsson /Heimsmyndir 108, StockstudioX 62, Sturti 68, Subman 19, Taketan 139, Tempura 65, Tim Robberts 86, 92, 113, Tim Robberts / The Image Bank 82, Tom Merton 62, Tommaso Tuzj 140, Tooga 18, 22, Tumteerasak 59, Tuul & Bruno Morandi 107, Ugur Karakoc 59, Vgajic 5, 81, Victoriabee 80, Vm 24, We Are 81, Westend61 43, 54, 82, 140, 145, Wundervisuals 145, Xavier Arnau 12; **Pearson Education Ltd:** 137, Debbie Rowe 143, Gareth Boden 16; **Shutterstock:** 1tomm 97, 2p2play 138, 43619 137, Aerogondo2 28, Africa Studio 90, 142, AJR_photo 38, 155, AleksWolff 142, Alena Ozerova 22, Alexander Ryabintsev 143, Altrendo Images 98, AM-Studio 91, AmaPhoto 88, Anatolir 16, Andrew S 88, Andrey_Kuzmin 72, Anton Kudelin 142, Anton Starikov 34, Anton_Ivanov 7, Antoniodiaz 87, arek_malang 18, Artazum 32, 32, 32, B747 143, Bardocz Peter 136, Belenos 30, Bodiaphvideo 43, Bonezboyz 137, Cat Act Art 9, Catalin Petolea 142, Celeste Duffy 16, Christophe Testi 34, Csaba Peterdi 28, Danzky 136, Darren Baker 7, Denis Belitsky 143, Dmytro Vietrov 75, Dragon Images 38, Dulce Rubia 16, Eric Isselee 140, Eugenio Marongiu 42, Evgeniy Dzyuba 136, Evgeniya68 142, Ewa Studio 57, FabrikaSimf 17, Fernando Pedrotti 48, Filipe Frazao 35, Fotosv 143, FrameAngel 10, Franck Boston 39, Frotos 57, G-stockstudio 43, 80, Gaf_Lila 32, Gajus 38, Georgejmclittle 145, grekoff 88, Hong Vo 73, Hurricanehank 82, Igor Kardasov 74, Ilona Ignatova 66, Incredible Arctic 34, Ivbar 107, Jacob Lund 48, 75, Jin young-in 34, 91, Jo Ann Snover 30, jocic 145, Joe Gough 142, Jose L Vilchez 107, Juice Dash 42, K. Miri Photography 34, 140, Kanjanee Chaisin 138, KieferPix 138, Kirill Vorobyev 10, Kokulina 3, 14, Korvit 72, Koya979 108, Lifestyle Travel Photo 34, Lina Balciunaite 143, Lisovskaya Natalia 7, Look Studio 39, 155, Lyly 7, Lyudmila2509 99, 99, Maksim Shmeljov 48, Maksud 108, Maridav 40, Marie Maerz 142, Mark Nazh 39, 155, Martin Prochazkacz 48, MBI 15, 39, 68, 78, 142, Melica 88, Mile Atanasov 10, Milkovasa 88, Mimagephotography 9, Mipstudio 142, Monticello 10, 91, Natali_ Mis 138, Nataliia Orletska 43, NYS 16, Odin M. Eidskrem 18, Oleksiy Mark 83, 91, Ollirg 7, Oneinchpunch 7, Phatthanun.R 58, Philip Lange 66, Phomphan 16, Preto Perola 137, Racorn 86, Rafal Kulik 143, Rapeephun Pannim 142, Rawpixel.com 15, 83, REDPIXEL.PL 83, Renata Sedmakova 66, Restyler 34, Robert Vincelli 97, Roberto Caucino 75, S Curtis 65, S-F 143, Saikorn 145, Sarsmis 110, Shamaan 11, Siamionau Pavel 73, Skreidzeleu 34, Skumer 74, Slavoljub Pantelic 10, Sofiaworld 7, Spaxiax 10, stocker1970 92, Stokkete 138, Stuart Monk 54, Studio_G 10, STUDIO492 10, Supertrooper 143, Syda Productions 6, 28, Taina Sohlman 115, Tarzhanova 88, Tatiana Popova 90, Tatuin 137, Terekhov Igor 88, TerraceStudio 16, The Polovinkin 137, Thomas Bethge 10, TinasDreamworld 34, Tom Tom 79, Ton Blackmarine 145, Tonkaa 136, Trekandshoot 31, Treter 10, TunedIn by Westend61 88, Valeriy Lebedev 88, Vangelis Aragiannis 96, Veeraphun Puttakan 115, VictorH11 34, Viktor1 140, Vitaliy Netiaga 110, Vrjoyner 137, Warren Price Photography 90, Wasu Watcharadachaphong 138, Wavebreakmedia 142, welcomia 138, Ysbrand Cosijn 39, Yury Gulakov 91

Cover image: *Front:* **123RF.com:** Igor Plotnikov